Documents in Contemporary History

General editor
Kevin Jefferys
Faculty of Arts and Education, University of Plymouth

British trade unions, 1945–1995

British trade unions, 1945–1995 examines one of the most contentious areas of post-1945 British political and economic history. Chris Wrigley provides an analysis of trade union development, trade union relations with government, and trade union impact on industrial relations and the economy generally.

In setting trade union history in a broad context, Professor Wrigley offers a fresh and succinct reassessment. He draws on a wide range of primary sources, providing material from unfamiliar sources as well as from key documents such as the Donovan Report. Among other things, this material highlights the changing attitudes within the Conservative Party towards the trade unions.

This is a very welcome guide to many controversial issues as well as an important new selection of primary source material. An important book for all those interested in trade union history and an invaluable textbook for all those studying modern British history, politics and industrial relations.

Chris Wrigley is Professor of Modern British History at the University of Nottingham

D1384006

Documents in Contemporary History is a series designed for sixth-formers and undergraduates in higher education. It aims to provide both an overview of specialist research on topics in post-1939 British history and a wide-ranging selection of primary source material.

Already published in the series

Alan Booth *British economic development since 1945*

Stephen Brooke *Reform and reconstruction: Britain after the war, 1945–51*

Kevin Jefferys *War and reform: British politics during the Second World War*

Ritchie Ovendale *British defence policy since 1945*

Scott Lucas *Britain and Suez: the lion's last roar*

Harold L. Smith *Britain in the Second World War: a social history*

Sean Greenwood *Britain and European integration since the Second World War*

John Baylis *Anglo-American relations: the rise and fall of the special relationship*

Steven Fielding *The Labour Party since 1951*

Forthcoming

Stuart Ball *The Conservative Party, 1940–1992*

Ralph Negrine *The British media since 1945*

Richard Aldrich *Security, intelligence and assessment in Britain, 1945–1968*

Documents in Contemporary History

British trade unions, 1945–1995

Edited by

Chris Wrigley

Professor of Modern British History,
University of Nottingham

Manchester University Press
Manchester and New York
Distributed exclusively in the USA by St. Martin's Press

Published by Manchester University Press
Oxford Road, Manchester M13 9NR, UK
and Room 400, 175 Fifth Avenue, New York, NY 10010, USA

Distributed exclusively in the USA
by St Martin's Press, Inc., 175 Fifth Avenue, New York, NY 10010,
USA

British Library Cataloguing-in-Publication Data
A catalogue record for this book is available from the British Library

Library of Congress Cataloging-in-Publication Data
Wrigley, Chris.
    British trade unions, 1945–95 / Chris Wrigley.
    p. cm. – (Documents in contemporary history)
    Includes bibliographical references and index
    ISBN 0-7190-4146-5 (cl). – ISBN 0-7190-4147-3 (pb)
    1. Trade unions–Great Britain–History –20th century. 2. Industrial
relations–Great Britain–History–20th century. I. Title. II. Series.
    HD6664.W75 1997
    331.88'0941'09045–dc21   97–11589

ISBN   0 7190 4146 5   hardback
       0 7190 4147 3   paperback

First published 1997

01 00 99 98 97   10 9 8 7 6 5 4 3 2 1

Printed in Great Britain by
Bell & Bain Limited, Glasgow

Contents

Tables

Preface

Trade union activities enter a wide range of areas. It would be possible to present collections of documents dealing with trade unions in the workplace (using oral history and local material), in the local community (using similar sources plus trades council records and the local press), in education, internationally and in other roles (using various sources). This collection, in line with many volumes in its series, focuses mostly on the trade unions and national public policy. For many people this is their initial interest in the subject and is the type of documents they require.

Since the Second World War the Trades Union Congress (TUC) has played a major role nationally for the trade union movement. Hence many documents in this volume stem from the TUC. Its annual reports are publicly available and are open to critical comment from both the media and the annual Congress if they are deemed unfair accounts. The views expressed in the annual reports reflect the dominant views among TUC officials and 'the big battalions' of the trade union movement. Dissident voices can be heard in the reports of the debates at the TUC and at individual unions' conferences, as well as in shop stewards' and others' pamphlets. This collection (notably Chapter 9) also draws on trade union journals and other records.

Key extracts of trade union legislation and some major reports (notably the Donovan and Bullock Reports) are included here. There are also extracts from the official reports of House of Commons debates. In these debates the government speakers emphasise the reasonableness of the legislation and how it fulfils the national (not the party political) interest, whereas Opposition speakers stress the opposite. There are also extracts from party general election manifestos.

I am grateful to all copyright holders. In particular I wish to acknowledge my gratitude to Doris Heffer and Gollancz, Jack Jones and Harper Collins, Alistair Cooke and the Conservative Research Department, Noreen Branson and the Labour Research Department, Mel Read MEP, Hilary Benn and the Management, Science and Finance Union, Mike Smith and the TUC, and general Crown copyright for the reproduction of government printed records. I also wish to acknowledge the value of the Modern Records Centre at Warwick University. Thanks also to Peter Graham and Jane Raistrick for their help.

For preparing the typescript of the book I am indebted again to Su Spencer, and for advice in preparing the book generally to Dr Kevin Jefferys, the editor of the series, and to Vanessa Graham and Carolyn Hand of Manchester University Press.

I am also grateful to those who listened to, and commented on, earlier versions of the chapter on strikes at research seminars in the Economic History Departments of Leicester University (December 1992) and Queen's University, Belfast (October 1996), the chapter on the Macmillan era incomes policies at the Institute of Contemporary History's 'Britain 1945–1995' Conference held in London (July 1995), and the chapter on workers' participation in industry at the Social History Society Conference held at Strathclyde University (January 1996).

Abbreviations

ACAS	Advisory, Conciliation and Arbitration Service
AEU	Amalgamated Engineering Union (later AUEW)
AUEW	Amalgamated Union of Engineering Workers
CBI	Confederation of British Industries
CIR	Commission for Industrial Relations
CPC	Conservative Political Centre
CSEU	Confederation of Shipbuilding and Engineering Unions
DATA	Draughtsmen's and Allied Technicians' Association
EDC	economic development committee
EEC	European Economic Community
FBI	Federation of British Industries
FTAT	Furniture, Timber and Allied Trades' Union
GCHQ	Government Communications Headquarters
GMWU	General and Municipal Workers' Union
ILO	International Labour Organisation
JPC	joint production committee
NBPI	National Board for Prices and Incomes
NCB	National Coal Board
NEDC	National Economic Development Council
NFBTE	National Federation of Building Trade Employers
NFTBO	National Federation of Building Trade Operatives
NIRC	National Industrial Relations Court
NJIC	National Joint Industrial Council of the Hosiery Trade
NUAAW	National Union of Agricultural and Allied Workers
NUM	National Union of Mineworkers
NUVB	National Union of Vehicle Builders
TGWU	Transport and General Workers' Union
TUC	Trades Union Congress
WEA	Workers' Educational Association
WRA	Working Rule Agreement

Introduction

British trade unionism attained its greatest membership in 1979. Since then, the numbers of trade unionists have fallen. In terms of influence the trade unions were notably strong during the Second World War and the period of post-war readjustment, and then again in the later 1970s. After 1979 Margaret Thatcher's governments went out of their way to lessen trade union power in the economy and trade union influence in politics.

Yet the decline of trade union strength in Britain was matched in other Western industrial economies. Changes in international competition, first from Japan, then from other Pacific rim nations and later from China and former communist East European states, had a bigger impact on British trade unions and their memberships than the activities of the British government.

This book provides an introduction to the main trade union developments since 1945, developments affected by changes in the labour market, industrial relations and politics.

The trade unions after the Second World War

After the end of the Second World War the trade unions were widely considered to have been major contributors to the successful mobilisation of the domestic economy for war. Then, as after the First World War, there was a period when there was no serious challenge to their positions in the economy and in politics. In 1920, before the post-war boom had ended, Sidney and Beatrice Webb had written:

> We may ... not unfairly say that trade unionism has ... won its recognition by Parliament and the government, by law and by custom, as a separate element in the community, entitled to dis-

1

tinct recognition as part of the social machinery of the state, its members being thus allowed to give – like the clergy in Convocation – not only their votes as citizens, but also their concurrence as an order or estate.[1]

A similar assessment could have been made after 1945, with the Trades Union Congress (TUC) as a major forum of debate about industry and much more.

Unlike the years immediately following the First World War, the period after the Second World War in Britain was not marked by conflict between the trade unions and the government. In 1945 trade union leaders backed what they felt to be *their* government – the first Labour government able to rely on a majority in the House of Commons. In delivering the Welfare State, substantial measures of nationalisation and much else, the Attlee governments were in effect carrying out a 'social contract' with the trade unions a quarter of a century before the more explicit understandings between the unions and the governments of Harold Wilson and James Callaghan in 1974–79. During the Attlee years the trade union movement did exercise considerable wage restraint in a period of virtual full employment, at least until the effects of the devaluation of the pound by 30.5 per cent in September 1949 adversely affected prices. Moreover, the overall level of strikes remained low (see Table 1, p. 24).

Some historians have argued that the politicians of 1940–51 should not have promised and then provided substantial social reconstruction. Instead they should have directed available public expenditure towards 'the root-and-branch rebuilding of the national transport system' and 'the massive modernisation and development of industry'.[2] Correlli Barnett, the foremost exponent of this view, clearly doubts the wisdom of the wartime provision of large sums for 'free milk and vitamins for children' rather than 'new buildings for trade and industry', and generally deplores the effect of state welfare, writing of 'New Jerusalem ... a dream turned to a dank reality of a segregated, subliterate, unskilled, unhealthy and institutionalised proletariat hanging on the nipple of state maternalism'.[3] Such a view constitutes a

---

[1]   S. and B. Webb, *The History of Trade Unionism* (revised and extended edition), London, 1920, p. 635.
[2]   C. Barnett, *The Audit of War*, London, 1986, p. 264.
[3]   Ibid., pp. 263 and 304. These arguments are amplified in C. Barnett, *The Lost Victory*, London, 1995. The main thrust of such arguments were made at the time, and their denial was the main theme of the presidential address at the 1949 TUC.

further case against the unions for pressing for what was later called 'the social wage' – the benefits working people gain from social welfare provision.[4] That is a case in addition to more widely expressed arguments that the unions (and the working class generally) were indifferent or hostile to increasing industrial productivity.[5]

However, other historians have doubted whether the Attlee government's provision of social welfare was so lavish as to undercut Britain's economic performance. José Harris has commented on Barnett's 'curiously insular assumption that the welfare state stops at the English Channel' and pointed out that even as early as 1950 West Germany, Austria and Belgium were spending more than Britain on social security as a percentage of gross domestic product.[6] Moreover, James Hinton has shown the enthusiasm for increasing productivity among engineers during 1942–47 and Alan Booth has written of the continuing TUC advocacy of greater productivity for at least four or five years after the return to office of the Conservatives in 1951.[7] Indeed, in the immediate post-war period resistance to changes which could enhance productivity came primarily from employers, and the state declined to breach voluntaryist principles and intervene in the workings of private industry.[8] As Keith Middlemas has observed of 1947–49:

> The TUC made a considerable effort to increase production, and responded to [Sir Stafford] Cripps' first Export Conference in September 1947 by accepting that industry should benefit from Marshall Aid rather than the social services. It took a fuller part in the Anglo-American Productivity Council and the Joint Council on Productivity (which brought in outside experts and scientists) than the FBI [Federation of British Industries] who

---

[4] For a discussion of this, see N. Whiteside, 'Industrial relations and social welfare, 1945–79', in C. J. Wrigley (ed.), *A History of British Industrial Relations, 1939–1979*, Aldershot, 1996, pp. 107–27.

[5] Barnett, *Audit*, pp. 189–92.

[6] J. Harris, 'Enterprise and the welfare state: a comparative perspective', in T. Gourvish and A. O'Day (eds), *Britain Since 1945*, London, 1991, pp. 39–58.

[7] J. Hinton, *Shop Floor Citizens: Engineering Democracy in 1940s Britain*, Aldershot, 1994. A Booth, 'Corporate politics and the quest for productivity: the British TUC and the politics of industrial productivity, 1947–1960', in J. Melling and A. McKinlay (eds), *Management, Labour and Industrial Politics in Modern Europe: The Quest for Productivity Growth in Britain, Germany and Sweden During the Twentieth Century*, Aldershot, 1996, pp. 45–66.

[8] N. Tiratsoo and J. Tomlinson, *Industrial Efficiency and State Intervention: Labour 1939–51*, London, 1993, pp. 66–152.

3

remained throughout rather defensive, taking the whole US Economic Co-operation Organisation (correctly enough) to be an implied criticism of management rather than unions.[9]

The post-war alternative postulated by Correlli Barnett of an interventionist state which would have 'imposed plans of development' was not politically feasible in Britain after 1945. Not only had the electorate been repeatedly promised better social provision (jam tomorrow for a near empty wartime larder today), but frequent pledges had been given to both sides of industry that intervention was to meet exceptional war needs and that afterwards there would be a return to the traditional voluntaryism in British industry. After the First World War the majority of industrialists had been emphatic as to the need for a quick return to 'Home Rule for Industry' and vested interests had wrecked the government's 1919 plans for controlling an integrated transport system. After the Second World War, in the late 1940s and in the 1950 and 1951 general elections, the Conservative Party, with some success, made much of ending state controls in the economy and 'setting the people free'. To have done anything other than return industry and industrial relations to voluntaryism would have clashed with the Conservatives' main message to the electorate.

The Conservative governments and the trade unions in the 1950s

For a decade after 1945 the Conservative Party leadership was generally disinclined to denounce official trade union leaders or trade unionism in general. In reappraising their policies after the unexpected 1945 general election defeat, the Conservatives issued a series of 'charters'. The choice of word indicated that these were to be seen as being internal equivalents of the Anglo-American Atlantic Charter of 1941 which had outlined the two countries' broad principles for reshaping the post-war world. For the Conservatives, their charters gave the party a new sense of direction. R. A. Butler, who chaired the party's Industrial Policy Committee, later recalled, 'Peel's Tamworth Manifesto [of 1834] made a rallying point for Conservatism in much the same way as our Charters made a rallying point'.[10]

[9] K. Middlemas, *Power, Competition and the State, Vol. 1: Britain in Search of Balance 1940–61*, London, 1986, p. 162.
[10] J. Ramsden, *The Making of Conservative Party Policy: The Conservative Research Department Since 1929*, London, 1980, p. 112.

The Industrial Charter of 1947 accepted much that had developed in industrial and employment policy since 1940 while promising to 'free industry from unnecessary controls and restrictions' and to restore to it 'freedom' and 'fair incentive'. One section of *The Industrial Charter* gave what was called the 'Workers' Charter', which set out a code of good practice for employers to follow if they wished, with the suggestion that public authorities should not accept tenders from firms which, after a reasonable period, failed to meet such standards.[11] 'The Workers' Charter' went into the Conservatives' 1950 general election manifesto. There a Code of Conduct, not legislation, was promised. It was stated, 'We shall ensure that this Code is strictly applied in all undertakings under government control'. 'The Workers' Charter' was a determined attempt to win back working-class votes, including those of trade unionists; especially as it was put in the same manifesto as a pledge, if the economic situation permitted, 'to proceed at an early date with the application in the government service of the principle of equal pay for men and women of equal value' and a declaration that, 'We regard the maintenance of full employment as the first aim of a Conservative government'.[12] *The Industrial Charter* was a very different approach to trade unionism than that of the Conservative policies of the 1980s. Later, in the early 1960s, one of those involved in formulating *The Industrial Charter* was in somewhat repentant mood, commenting that 'in retrospect it appears ... that, like Labour thought at the time, it [the Charter] was too concerned with the problem of the thirties – unemployment – and not sufficiently with the problem of the fifties – inflation'.[13]

Churchill, who may well have been lukewarm about *The Industrial Charter*, took a very emollient approach to the trade unions in his speeches between 1947 and his victory in the 1951 general election. Once back in office, he made it very clear that he was determined to continue in this vein. He did so by appointing a near non-party figure, Walter Monckton, as Minister of Labour, and by instructing him and, when necessary, his Cabinet colleagues to avoid major pub-

---

[11] The Conservative Political Centre, *The Industrial Charter*, London, 1947, pp. 3–4 and 29.
[12] The Conservative Party, *This is the Road: The Conservative and Unionist Party's Policy*, London, 1950. The pledge on employment stemmed from the 1944 White Paper, *Employment Policy* (Cmd 6527).
[13] J. D. Hoffman, *The Conservative Party in Opposition 1945–51*, London, 1964, p. 148.

lic sector confrontations with the trade unions.[14] Churchill also personally cultivated Vincent Tewson, the General Secretary of the TUC, and other senior trade unionists, surprising at least one senior Conservative colleague by inviting trade unionists to a party at 10 Downing Street. During Churchill's post-war government, ministers appointed even more trade unionists to consultative committees than had been the case under Attlee.[15]

Both Churchill's successors as Prime Minister – Sir Anthony Eden (1955–57) and Harold Macmillan (1957–63) – were 'One Nation' Conservatives who were disinclined to confront the trade unions. Nevertheless, both were concerned about the pressure of wage rises on inflation and about industrial disputes, especially unofficial strikes. The problems of maintaining stable prices during a period of near full employment were spelt out in the government's White Paper, *The Economic Implications of Full Employment*, published in March 1956. Between its publication and December 1956, Harold Macmillan, as Chancellor of the Exchequer, had discussions with both sides of industry in an attempt to secure a 'price and wage plateau'. Then Macmillan rejected price controls to deal with inflation, observing

if we do it by controls, it's obvious that we must also fix wages, salaries and profits.

It's a possible system – but it isn't really consistent with freedom and democracy. Its the end of the trade unionist as well as the capitalist.[16]

In this analysis, Macmillan was expressing sentiments shared by some major left-wing trade union leaders.[17]

With concern growing about inflation and its impact on the competitiveness of British exports, the priorities of many Conservatives changed. Increasing numbers of party members wished for trade union legislation and to replace low levels of unemployment with low levels of inflation as the Conservatives' key economic policy objec-

---

[14] P. Addison, *Churchill on the Home Front 1900–1955*, London, 1992, Chapter 12. A. Roberts, *Eminent Churchillians*, London, 1994, Chapter 5.
[15] A. Seldon, *Churchill's Indian Summer: The Conservative Government 1951–55*, London, 1981, pp. 29, 199 and 568–9. V. L. Allen, *Trade Unions and Government*, London, 1960, pp. 34 and 304.
[16] In a speech at Newcastle on Tyne on 25 May 1956; H. Macmillan, *Riding the Storm, 1956–1959*, London, 1971, p. 55.
[17] See, for example, section 5.2 in this volume.

tive. In June 1958 the Inns of Court Conservative and Unionist Society published a study entitled *A Giant's Strength*, which recommended a range of measures to be incorporated into trade union law, many of which were enacted in the 1971 Industrial Relations Act.[18]

Conservative divisions over economic priorities became very apparent in the government during the year that Peter Thorneycroft was Chancellor of the Exchequer, Enoch Powell was Financial Secretary to the Treasury and Nigel Birch was Economic Secretary to the Treasury (January 1957 – January 1958). By the autumn of 1957 the Treasury ministers were convinced of the need to limit inflation even if unemployment rose. Thorneycroft told the Conservative Party Conference on 10 October, 'Honest money is a pre-requisite of full employment and good wages'. Powell condemned Keynesian economics when speaking to an audience in Halifax on 13 December 1957: 'So far from it being true that inflation and a high level of employment hang together, the fact is that, for a nation in Britain's situation, dependent on world trade and commercial dealings with other countries for its livelihood, continued inflation is the greatest threat to full employment'.[19] On 6 January 1958 the three ministers resigned when the rest of Macmillan's Cabinet refused to hold government expenditure in 1958–59 at the same level as that for 1957–58, a policy which entailed deflation and austerity in the period before a general election.

Although Thorneycroft and his Treasury team left office in early 1958, their ideas remained very influential at Tory grass roots. Increasing numbers of newly selected Conservative Party parliamentary candidates subscribed to views which prioritised monetary controls and an emphasis on reducing inflation rather than maintaining low levels of unemployment and improving social welfare provision. Indeed, Thorneycroft and Powell resumed Cabinet office under Macmillan. Their viewpoint (or a development of it) became dominant under Margaret Thatcher's leadership of the Conservative Party (1975–90). It inevitably involved a very different approach to the trade unions than the corporatist approach of the Conservative governments of the early 1960s and 1972–74.

[18] R. Taylor, *The Trade Union Question in British Politics: Government and Unions Since 1945*, London, 1993, pp. 90–108.
[19] A. Roth, *Enoch Powell: Tory Tribune*, London, 1970, p. 180. J. Wood (ed.), *A Nation Not Afraid: The Thinking of Enoch Powell*, London, 1965, p. 115.

The era of prices and incomes policies, 1961–1979

The period 1961–79 was marked by repeated attempts to create effective prices and incomes policies. Such policies heavily involved the trade unions. Incomes policies affected trade union negotiators' freedom to bargain. Tighter controls of incomes than prices – as happened in 1972–73 and 1975–76 – resulted in drops in working-class real incomes (i.e. though money wages went up, prices went up faster so wage earners could buy less with that money). Yet most trade union leaders realised that when inflation was soaring, as in 1973–75, it was in their members' interests, as well as the general interest, to control it. In supporting counter-inflation policies, the trade union leaders wished to see tight price controls and broad packages of social welfare measures accompany wage restraint. So Edward Heath's packages of measures in 1973 in Stages Two and Three of his prices and incomes policy were more sophisticated than those of 1965–70, and, in turn, the Social Contract of 1974–79 was broader still in its scope.

Substantial government measures on prices and incomes resumed (after the Attlee period) with Selwyn Lloyd's July 1961 'pause' in increases in wages and salaries. The Chancellor of the Exchequer informed the House of Commons, at the time of the final report of the Council on Prices, Productivity and Incomes (set up in 1957), that as 'at present we are heavily overdrawing on our productivity account' he required 'a pause until productivity has caught up'. He commented:

> A pause must mark the beginning of a new long-term policy. That policy is that increases in incomes must follow and not precede or outstrip increases in national productivity. During the pause we must work out methods of securing a sensible long-term relationship between increases in incomes of all sorts and increases in productivity.

His 'pay pause' was applied to 'those areas for which the government have direct responsibility', with the hope that 'the same lines should be followed elsewhere both in the private sector and in those parts of the public sector outside the immediate control of the government'.[20]

In this action the public sector employees felt the full force of the pay curb. This had also been the case earlier. In 1957 the government

---

[20] *House of Commons Debates*, 5th Series, 645, cc. 222–3; 25 July 1961.

had vetoed part of a pay increase agreed by the Whitley Council for the National Health Service. The part blocked was 3 per cent for the lower paid (earning under £1,200), but a 5 per cent rise was allowed to go ahead for those earning more. Also in 1957, the government rejected part of an agreed award to probation officers and, in the next year, one to firewomen. In addition the government applied firm fixed cash limits to the civil service and the BBC, making clear that pay increases would have to be offset by fewer staff.[21] Similarly, in the nine months of Selwyn Lloyd's 'pay pause' those working in the public sector had their standards of living squeezed, while most of those in the private sector were unaffected. Such treatment for public sector employees during 1961–79 contributed to them becoming more politicised and militant as well as more unionised. Those public sector workers with 'industrial muscle' – such as miners, electricity and railway workers – often gained wage increases by strikes or threats of strikes, their only recourse when the established collective bargaining procedures were in abeyance.

Selwyn Lloyd's 'pay pause' was followed by the government setting up a tripartite forum (government, employers and trade unions) – the National Economic Development Council (NEDC, nicknamed 'Neddy' from its acronym) – to advise the government in its efforts in long-term economic planning. Both the trade unions and the employers' organisations were eager to influence policy-making and both had been critical of the damage inflicted to economic growth in the long run by the short-term considerations of the government's stop—go economic measures. Some employers, in particular, had been impressed by the French planning system and the *Commissariat du Plan*. The TUC and its General Secretary, George Woodcock, hoped that 'Neddy' would be a bargaining forum on economic issues, a complement to national collective bargaining on industrial relations matters.[22] The National Economic Development Council met for the first time on 7 March 1962 and began discussing ways 'to increase the rate of sound growth'.[23]

However, before 'Neddy' had met, the government issued in February 1962 a statement, *Incomes Policy, The Next Step*, outlining its

---

[21] Allen, *Trade Unions and Government*, pp. 108–10.
[22] S. Blank, *Industry and Government in Britain: The Federation of British Industries in Politics 1945–65*, Farnborough, 1973, pp. 167–74.
[23] National Economic Development Council, *Growth of the United Kingdom Economy 1961–1966*, London, 1963, p. viii.

pay policy after the end of the 'pause'. This stated that where there was justification for increases, such rises should be kept to about 2 to 2.5 per cent a year. It deemed arguments derived from the cost of living or from trends in profits or productivity would not be sufficient in themselves. Arguments on productivity would have to be linked to direct contributions by the workers concerned; arguments of comparability should be given secondary weight to general national economic considerations; and arguments as to shortage of labour should only be effective where it was having general and severe effects.[24] In late July 1962 Harold Macmillan announced that another body, the National Incomes Commission (nicknamed 'Nicky'), would be set up 'to provide impartial and authoritative advice'. This body, which began its work in October 1962, was chaired by a barrister and composed of others deemed 'independent', and had powers under Royal Warrant to require information to be provided or people to appear before it.[25]

However, the TUC, which was unwilling to discuss incomes policies on the National Economic Development Council (thereby lessening the government's interest in that forum), boycotted it. The trade unions were hostile to a body which was empowered to investigate incomes but not prices or profits. In particular they were vigorously opposed to a group of allegedly independent people who would intervene in specific wage agreements, undermining free collective bargaining. Even before 'Nicky' had begun its activities, the TUC's Economic Committee issued a statement in October 1962 in which it deplored 'the government's refusal to implement wage increases to which certain groups of workers in the public services had become entitled as a result of negotiation and of arbitration and to approve certain agreements which had been reached in wages councils' and expressed 'grave concern at the continued interference by the government with collective bargaining and arbitration machinery'.[26] While some groups of public sector employees were affected by the second phase of this incomes policy, generally it had little impact outside the public sector.

Under Harold Wilson's governments of 1964–70 there was first a voluntary prices and incomes policy (1964–66) and then a statutory

---

[24] *Incomes Policy, The Next Step* (Cmnd 1626), 1962.
[25] *National Incomes Commission* (Cmnd 1844), 1962.
[26] TUC General Council's Report, *Report of 94th Annual Trades Union Congress*, London, 1962, pp. 246 and 468–71.

policy (1966–70). The voluntary policy was agreed within the context of the National Plan, which represented a development of the Labour movement's concerns during and after the Attlee governments of 1945–51. The need for some form of political solution to the powerful pressure for wages to rise in conditions of near full employment was widely recognised among leading Labour politicians as well as by 'One Nation' Conservatives and Keynsian economists.[27] In April 1965 a pay norm of 3.5 per cent was set, based on an optimistic assessment of likely national economic growth. Special cases (for example, where there had been increases in productivity directly brought about by the workforce) were examined by the National Board for Prices and Incomes (which, unlike 'Nicky', also scrutinised proposed price increases referred to it by the government).

Before its abolition by Edward Heath, the National Board for Prices and Incomes (NBPI) made an influential contribution towards better practices in industrial relations. This it did in particular through the reports and guidelines it prepared. It drew on recent successful productivity agreements – such as those negotiated by Esso at its refinery at Fawley in 1959–63 – to encourage others. It prepared reports on broad issues such as payment by results, job evaluation and shiftworking as well as on specific pay or price increases.[28]

The July 1966 sterling crisis provided the occasion for the government to introduce a six months pay freeze and a statutory prices and incomes policy. The freeze was followed by a period with a nil norm, with only 'a severely limited' number of exceptional cases on grounds such as increased productivity. Subsequently this was eased, with a 3.5 per cent ceiling on wage, salary and dividend increases from August 1968, and a further relaxation of the policy a year later. The statutory policy ended in January 1970.

While Edward Heath entered office in 1970 determined not to introduce a statutory incomes policy, his government nevertheless had an incomes policy. As under the previous Conservative governments, this was one that was applied to the public sector workers with the hope that the private sector would follow suit. The policy was to try

---

[27] M. J. Artis, 'Incomes policies: some rationales', in J. L. Fallick and R. F. Elliott (eds), *Incomes Policies, Inflation and Relative Pay*, London, 1981, pp. 7–8.
[28] S. Kessler and F. Bayliss, *Contemporary British Industrial Relations*, 2nd edn, London, 1995, pp. 9–11. On the Fawley agreements, see A. Flanders, *The Fawley Productivity Agreement*, London, 1964 and B. Ahlstrand, *The Quest for Productivity: A Study of Fawley After Flanders*, Cambridge, 1991.

to ensure that each public sector pay award was 1 per cent less than the previous (known as the 'N minus one' policy). This was shattered by the national coal-mining dispute of 1972.

In the second half of 1972 Heath tried to win TUC support for an incomes policy by offering much greater consultation on economic policy through the National Economic Development Council. Politically, especially given the trade unions' implacable hostility to the 1971 Industrial Relations Act, it was not possible for the General Council of the TUC to agree to assist a Conservative government in operating an incomes policy. So the Heath government went ahead with a statutory prices and incomes policy. As with all such policies it was hoped that the policy would have an impact in educating people to have lower expectations, and to do so by giving them confidence that inflation would not be permitted to accelerate unchecked. The Heath government's policy went further in that it tried to remove wage bargainers' guesses as to future higher rates of inflation by providing threshold indexing (i.e. an automatic wage increase each time prices passed certain levels). In doing this it put relatively too much emphasis on internal wage agreements and too little on external world market commodity prices as the cause of the accelerating inflation. As a result the threshold agreements became a serious liability.

Stage One of Heath's policy was a freeze on pay, prices, dividends and rents between November 1972 and April 1973. Stage Two, which ran from April to November 1973, allowed maximum pay increases of £1 a week (a flat rate sum to help the lower paid) plus 4 per cent up to a maximum of £250 per annum. Stage Three, which ran from November 1973, allowed for increases in pay up to 7 per cent on total pay for a group of employees (so allowing bargainers to determine its distribution) or for each person £2.25 per week or 7 per cent up to a maximum of £350 per annum. On top of this there was a 1 per cent margin allowable for productivity improvements, sick pay schemes or holiday entitlement and threshold agreements which gave wage increases of 40 pence per week for each percentage point that the Retail Price Index rose above 7 per cent. However, this policy broke down when the coal-miners united to insist on a higher pay award than the terms of Stage Three permitted, in order to recover in real terms what they had gained in 1972, and the government refused to allow them to be treated as an exceptional case (even with TUC pledges that other unions would not use a concession to the miners as an argument in their negotiations). When Edward Heath called an early general election for February 1974, his party lost its majority.

The Labour governments of Harold Wilson (1974–76) and James Callaghan (1976–79) tried to work with the trade unions on a broad economic and social front, under the Social Contract (an agreement between the TUC and the Labour Party). The Wilson government repealed the 1971 Industrial Relations Act and successfully carried a wide range of social legislation important to the trade union movement. In the face of accelerating inflation the TUC took up a proposal from Jack Jones, General Secretary of the Transport and General Workers' Union (TGWU), to curb inflation within the context of wider measures. Phase One of this Social Contract, covering July 1975 to July 1976, set a pay increase limit of £6 per week (a flat rate increase to help the lower paid) with no increases for those earning over £8,500. Phase Two for July 1976 to July 1977 also agreed with the TUC, set pay increases of 5 per cent, with a £2.50 per week minimum and a £4.00 per week maximum. Thereafter, James Callaghan's government unilaterally set the targets: at 10 per cent per annum (with self-financing productivity agreements permitted in addition) for 1977–78 and 5 per cent per annum (plus self-financing productivity agreements) for 1978–79. As Denis Healey, the Chancellor of the Exchequer, later reflected, the 5 per cent figure was too low – and the policy collapsed in the so-called 'winter of discontent'.[29]

A notable feature of the Social Contract was Denis Healey's use of the budget as an incentive to secure wage restraint. In part this reflected the view that union bargainers seek not just pay rises but rises in real wages after tax. Indeed tax levels have been seen by some economists as one trigger for larger pay demands.[30] In his 1976 and 1977 budgets Healey made certain cuts in taxation – £900 of £1,200 million in 1976 and £900 of £1,300 million in 1977 – conditional on there being lower wage settlements. Wage earners received something in the region of an average of 4.5 per cent higher take-home pay without directly adding to British industry's costs.[31] Another important feature of Healey's approach to wage restraint was to take up the ideas of neo-classical economics concerning the relationship between wage levels and jobs. He reduced the rate of increase of the money

[29] D. Healey, *The Time of My Life*, London, 1989, pp. 398 and 462.
[30] D. Jackson, H. A. Turner and F. Wilkinson, *Do Trade Unions Cause Inflation?*, Cambridge, 1973.
[31] W. Fishbein, *Wage Restraint by Consensus: Britain's Search for an Incomes Policy Agreement, 1965–79*, London, 1984, p. 186.

supply after the October 1974 general election, introduced a notably deflationary budget in April 1975 and introduced firm cash limits on spending by government departments. Several years before the advent of Margaret Thatcher to power, trade unionists were faced with monetary and fiscal policies which threatened substantial job losses if there was insufficient wage restraint.

In recent years many economists have condemned incomes policies as ineffective or harmful. As the editors of a substantial 1981 collection of essays on the subject put it, 'incomes policies can reduce the rate of wage inflation in the short run but no more', adding that after the policy 'catch-up increases occur with the result that incomes policies affect the *path* but not the level of wage inflation over time'.[32] However, others have estimated that pay increases were lower than they otherwise would have been, especially under Attlee's government in 1948–50 (where 2 per cent lower is often suggested) and under the first two years of the Social Contract. Both periods were times of economic crisis when not only trade union leaders, but trade union members and the general public appear to have supported the incomes policies. In 1975–77 increases in average earnings were reduced from 26 per cent per annum to 9 per cent, though the cost of living only fell from 26 per cent per annum to 17.6 per cent (thereby undermining TUC support for a continuation of the policy). The incomes policy played the major role in this reduction of levels of earnings, but other developments contributed: more stable international commodity prices, a rising exchange rate, monetary and fiscal policies and a rise in unemployment being the most mentioned by analysts.

The impact of the other incomes policies was more marked in their earlier, strong (or 'harder') phases than the later ('softer') phases. Hence there were marked reductions in the rate of increase of wage rates in 1961–62, 1966–67 and 1972–73. However, there were catching-up periods, with large pay claims, especially from public sector unions, in 1969–70, 1974–75 and 1978–79. Even so, the incomes policies of the late 1960s and the 1970s did achieve the return to pay negotiations being annual, not more frequent, events.[33]

---

[32] R. F. Elliott and J. L. Fallick, 'Incomes policies, inflation and relative pay: an overview', in Elliott and Fallick (eds), *Incomes Policies*, p. 260. For a vigorous denunciation of incomes policies, see S. Brittan and P. Lilley, *The Delusion of Incomes Policy*, London, 1977.
[33] R. J. Flanagan, D. W. Soskice and L. Ulman, *Unionism, Economic Stability and Incomes Policies*, Washington DC, 1983, pp. 415–16.

Trade union law: the 1960s and 1970s

From the standpoint of the trade unions, the history of trade union legislation has frequently been a story of gains apparently made in Acts of Parliament being undermined by subsequent court cases. This had been so after 1825 and 1875.

In the post-1945 period, the House of Lords judgement in 1964 in the *Rookes* v. *Barnard* case undermined trade union immunity from legal action arising from industrial disputes. In the words of the Queen's Counsel acting on behalf of the affected union, the Draughtsmen's and Allied Technicians' Association (DATA), in the Court of Appeal, the judgement drove a 'coach and four' through the Trades Disputes Act 1906. The case involved Douglas Rookes, who worked in the British Overseas Airways Corporation's design offices at London airport. He had been a trade union activist, even being involved in the securing of a closed shop agreement in 1954, but had resigned from the union in late 1955 in disgust at his union's failure to take 'more direct action' in a dispute over working conditions. As a result of the union's threat to take strike action over his non-membership, Rookes eventually lost his job. After he sued union officials for damages, his case went through the courts to an appeal to the House of Lords. There the award of £7,500 in damages to Rookes was upheld.[34]

Rookes v. *Barnard* was soon followed by the House of Lords judgement in 1965 in the case of *Stratford* v. *Lindley*. This also undercut the immunities the trade unions felt they had from legal actions under the 1906 Act. *Stratford* v. *Lindley* related to secondary boycotting.[35]

These decisions were very welcome to many in the Conservative Party. Indeed, the views of the Law Lords were similar to those of many Conservative lawyers, as expressed in the Inns of Court Conservative and Unionist Society's pamphlet, *A Giant's Strength*. This argued for legal restrictions on trade union power, especially condemning the closed shop, restrictive practices, secondary strike ac-

---

[34] P. Davies and M. Freedland, *Labour Legislation and Public Policy: A Contemporary History*, Oxford, 1993, pp. 243–6. DATA, *Keep the Unions Free: A Statement on the Rookes v. Barnard Case*, Richmond, 1964, pp. 4–8. D. Rookes, *Conspiracy*, London, 1966. (In 1955 the union was named the Association of Engineering and Shipbuilding Draughtsmen.)
[35] Davies and Freedland, *Labour Legislation*, p. 245.

tion and demarcation disputes.[36]

The Labour Party responded to *Rookes* v. *Barnard* by pledging to introduce legislation to restore what was thought to be the intention of the Trade Disputes Act 1906 and to set up a Royal Commission to report on trade unions and employers' organisations. It carried out both pledges in 1965, with the Trade Disputes Act 1965 and the Royal Commission chaired by Lord Donovan. The resulting Donovan Report (1968) proved to be influential in its commitment to voluntaryism in industrial relations, but both Labour and Conservative governments made efforts to go further in legislation than it advised. The Donovan Report urged the reform of industrial relations by voluntary, not legal, means.

Harold Wilson, however, felt there were both economic and political needs for state intervention in critical areas of British industrial relations. The White Paper *In Place of Strife* (1969) was based on the Donovan findings but did include proposals for powers to require compulsory ballots before certain major strikes; to call conciliation pauses before unofficial strikes or where it was deemed that inadequate negotiations had taken place; and to deal with inter-union disputes. Wilson failed to carry these proposals in the face of strong opposition within the Parliamentary Labour Party as well as from the trade union movement.

The Heath government's Industrial Relations Act 1971 owed more to *A Giant's Step*, the broad spirit of the *Rookes* v. *Barnard* decision and the Conservative Party's 1968 document *Fair Deal at Work* than to the Donovan Report. It represented a break with the system underpinned by the Trades Disputes Acts of 1906 and 1965, which gave the trade unions very wide immunities from legal action. It rejected reliance on voluntary approaches to industrial relations in favour of attempting to create a comprehensive legal framework.[37] The trade union movement saw the Industrial Relations Bill (and then the subsequent Act) as a massive attack on itself and more generally on the industrial relations conditions under which it had operated for most of the period since 1906 (the main variation being the Trade Disputes and

---

[36] Inns of Court Conservative and Unionist Society, *A Giant's Strength: Some Thoughts on the Constitutional and Legal Position of Trade Unions in England*, London, 1958.
[37] Davies and Freedland, *Labour Legislation*, Chapter 7. B. Weeks, M. Mellish, L. Dickens and J. Lloyd, *Industrial Relations and the Limits of Law: The Industrial Effects of the Industrial Relations Act, 1971*, Oxford, 1975.

Trade Unions Act 1927, which followed the General Strike, but was repealed in 1946). As the Industrial Relations Act 1971 did so much in one measure, it proved relatively easy to unite most of the trade union movement behind a policy of boycotting registering under it. As action in defiance of it could – and did – result in individual trade unionists ending up in prison, it had the capacity for creating martyrs. The expectation that many employers would use the provisions of the Act proved mistaken. Moreover, in some instances the actual operation of aspects of the Act – such as compulsory ballots before major strikes – did not assist in resolving the disputes but lessened the flexibility of negotiators (as the Donovan Commission had warned).

The Wilson government (1974–76) repealed the Industrial Relations Act 1971 and passed legislation to restore the trade unions' position in the law to what it had been after the Trade Disputes Acts of 1906 and 1965. The Trade Union and Labour Relations Act 1974 and the Employment Protection Act 1975 gave legislative effect to many of the positive proposals for improving the voluntary system of industrial relations and providing broader employment rights that had been proposed by the Donovan Commission and the TUC. The Wilson and Callaghan governments, however, did not act on another long-discussed matter: workers' participation. This had been advocated both as a means of enthusing workers and drawing on their abilities to improve productivity and as an extension of democracy. A Committee of Inquiry under Lord Bullock reported on industrial democracy in February 1977 but the government did little about it (apart from in the Post Office, which had been a front-runner in this area).

Overall, the impact of the 1974–79 Labour government's legislation was, as Lord Scarman described it in a 1979 judgement, to return both to the pre-1971 situation concerning industrial disputes and to clarify the law:

> [The] policy of the statutes is to exclude 'trade disputes' from judicial review by the courts ... Briefly put, the law is now back to what Parliament had intended when it enacted the Act of 1906 – but stronger and clearer than it was then.[38]

---

[38] *NWL Ltd.* v. *Woods* (1979). Quoted in J. Elgar and R. Simpson, 'The impact of the law on industrial disputes in the 1980s', in D. Metcalf and S. Milner (eds), *New Perspectives on Industrial Disputes*, London, 1993, p. 72.

The Thatcher and Major governments and the trade unions

The Conservative governments of Margaret Thatcher and John Major took a very different attitude to the trade unions than had the earlier Conservative governments of Churchill, Eden, Macmillan and Douglas-Home (1951–64). In the earlier period the governments had consulted the trade unions and latterly had brought them into tripartite (government, employers and unions) forums to discuss the management of the economy, notably the National Economic Development Council. After 1979 the trade unions were kept at a distance. The NEDC was increasingly marginalised, its monthly meetings being reduced to quarterly ones in 1984 and it was axed after the 1992 general election (with effect from 1 January 1993). Government legislation between 1980 and 1993 steadily weakened the trade unions, both in industrial relations and politics.

The attack on the trade unions was a fundamental part of the government's economic policy. This was highlighted in 1984 and 1985 when government plans in this area were included in the economic overview parts of the budget statements. The Thatcher and Major governments rejected the Keynsian consensus of full employment and comprehensive state welfare. High levels of unemployment weakened trade union bargaining strength in the labour market. These governments also firmly rejected incomes policies as another distortion of the free market, thereby removing a further reason for national consultations with the unions. They also rejected the 'safety net' provisions that gave safeguards to lower paid workers. In 1988 young workers (aged 16–21) were removed from the protection of wages councils and in 1993 the councils themselves were abolished. Drawing from the right-wing economist Friedrich von Hayek, the Thatcher government developed a version of free market and monetarist economics which was hostile to trade unions. In this view trade union bargaining power distorted the working of free labour markets, adding to labour costs and, as goods and services became uncompetitive, to unemployment. Added to this economic rationale, Margaret Thatcher, Norman Tebbitt and others of the Tory Right made it very clear that they disliked, even detested, trade unionism and trade union leaders collectively.

Under Margaret Thatcher and John Major industrial relations legislation was passed piecemeal (unlike the one big 1971 Industrial Relations Act of the Heath government). Though there was no long-term plan, the legislation was intended to reduce trade union power and to make the labour market more flexible (a phrase which is often a euphemism for a situation in which workers are induced to take jobs with lower pay and less good working conditions). The earlier legislation of the Thatcher governments stemmed from Conservative policy-making in Opposition. There was a determination to undo major aspects of the Employment Protection Act 1975. The upsurge of industrial unrest in late 1978 and early 1979 (the 'winter of discontent') emboldened the Tory leadership to feel that legislation curbing trade unions was again likely to be an electoral asset, not a liability as in 1971–74.

In its 1979 general election manifesto the Conservative Party had specified three areas of trade union reform. These were to weaken the closed shop (an issue made much of by the Tory Right at the 1977 Conservative Party Conference), to confine picketing to those directly involved in disputes, and to provide funding to encourage unions to hold secret ballots for union elections, before strikes and for other important issues.

Once in power both James Prior, Secretary of State for Employment, and Margaret Thatcher wished to move forward, learning from the mistakes of 1970–74. However, for Prior this was to move forward by means of a 'cautious, step-by-step approach' which would 'make it virtually impossible for them [the unions] to whip up an effective campaign of opposition, since the measures being introduced could scarcely be portrayed as draconian'. Indeed, he later recalled, 'My main purpose in all this was to put the onus on the trade unions'.[39] This cautious approach was in line with the views of the Confederation of British Industry (CBI) and the Engineering Employers' Federation. Indeed the latter gave out the opinion that the government's proposals to curb closed shops could do more harm than good: 'Most existing closed shop agreements cause few practical problems either to employees or employers who are within their scope'.[40]

Margaret Thatcher had learned from 1971–74 not to criminalise individual trade unionists and so create martyrs. As she noted in her memoirs, 'the changes we made ... including that of picketing, were changes in the civil, not the criminal, law ... The civil law could only change the way in which unions behaved if employers or, in some

---

[39] Jim Prior, *A Balance of Power*, London, 1986, p. 158.
[40] *The Times*, 17 October 1980, p. 2.

cases, workers, were prepared to use it.'[41] Otherwise, events pushed her in the direction of her own inclinations, which were that the lesson of 1971–74, and of the 1970s generally, was that the trade unions needed to be firmly controlled by legislation. The main event during the passage of Prior's Bill that affected her view and that of other right-wing ministers was secondary picketing in the steel strike of January–April 1980. While Prior succeeded in getting his limited Bill through the House of Commons, Margaret Thatcher disregarded Cabinet collective responsibility by making clear on the BBC's *Panorama* programme that if the 1980 Bill was not successful she wished for further trade union legislation which would deal with the immunity of trade union funds from claims for damages.[42] In an ITN interview she explicitly said of her government's Bill that it was 'not going as far as some of us wish, but it was going further than the existing law does'.[43]

Margaret Thatcher went on to replace Prior with the right-wing Norman Tebbit. Prior's emollient approach did, however, have some success in 'putting the onus' on the unions. The TUC's rejection of public funds for strike ballots was a public relations mistake. Labour's Shadow Employment spokesperson, Eric Varley, observed in May 1980, 'I cannot see any great objection to accepting money to finance ballots' and went on to comment, 'I am in favour of facing the trade unions with their great responsibility. They have had it too easy under Labour governments in the past.'[44] Jim Prior's measure also divided the major trade unions in their resolve to undermine it. Terry Duffy, the President of the Amalgamated Union of Engineering Workers, made it clear that his union was not willing to support all-out opposition to the 1980 legislation similar to that shown to the 1971 Industrial Relations Act. In August 1980 he commented, 'We have told the TUC that we would oppose the Bill, but if it became law we would not be advising our members to break the law'.[45] Norman Tebbit later felt that Prior's Act, along with the Employment Act 1982 and the Trade Union Act 1984, while not perfect, cumulatively had 'a very significant effect', including on the outcome of the 1984–85 coal-mining dispute.[46]

[41] Margaret Thatcher, *The Downing Street Years*, London, 1993, p. 100.
[42] Hugh Stephenson, *Mrs Thatcher's First Year*, London, 1980, pp. 75–6.
[43] *The Times*, 24 July 1980, p. 2.
[44] *The Times*, 8 May 1980, p. 2.
[45] *The Times*, 13 August 1980.
[46] Hugo Young and Anne Sloman, *The Thatcher Phenomenon*, London 1986, p. 74.

Norman Tebbit, in his memoirs, commented on the Employment Act 1982, 'I have no doubt that Act was my greatest achievement in government and I believe it has been one of the principal pillars on which the Thatcher economic reforms have been built'. For him the key to undermining trade unions' power was to remove their legal immunity from civil actions for damages, immunities enjoyed by the unions since the Trade Disputes Act 1906. He was also determined to curtail the closed shop. As he felt it was not feasible to ban it, he 'set out to undermine it' by various restrictions on its operation.[47]

The next round of trade union reform was based on the premise that there would be substantial changes in trade union policy if the ordinary members could control the unions by secret postal ballots. The government's arguments were outlined in a Green Paper (these being consultative documents), *Democracy in Trade Unions*, in January 1983. The ensuing legislation, the Trade Union Act 1984, followed the government's victory in the 1983 general election, and required secret ballots before strikes were called, ballots every five years for all voting members of trade unions' principal executive committees, and ballots every ten years to establish or to continue having political funds. The ballots before strikes may have made union leaders think longer before holding a ballot, but generally such ballots have supported the holding of strikes.[48] In the case of political funds, ballots supported the continuation of the funds in 52 of 53 unions which had such funds, and a further 20 unions held ballots and established political funds for the first time.[49]

After the Conservative victory in the 1987 general election there was a further series of measures which were designed to limit or undermine the trade unions' ability to take collective action. Before the 1987 general election the government had issued a further Green Paper, *Trade Unions and Their Members* (1987), which referred to the 1984–85 miners' strike and argued that trade union members needed the right not 'to be intimidated by threats from union leaders'. Of the Employment Act 1988 Simon Auerbach, in a major study of the 1979–90 legislation, observed:

Whilst the claims to be handing rights to trade union members, and strengthening the internal democracy of trade unions, still

---

[47] Norman Tebbit, *Upwardly Mobile*, London, 1988, pp. 233–4.
[48] *ACAS Annual Report*, 1989, p. 6; cited in Taylor, *Trade Union Question*, p. 300.
[49] Taylor, *Trade Union Question*, p. 301.

not surprisingly formed a central part of the broad 'selling' to union members and public opinion of the measures introduced in 1988, any more than cursory examination of the documents and debates reveals a striking candidness of the government's commitment to the individual rather than the internal member-ship dimension, but above all to the external goal of inhibiting industrial action itself.[50]

There were further restrictions on trade unions in the Employment Acts of 1989 and 1990. The latter Act in effect outlawed the closed shop and secondary strike action. Following its general election vic-tory in 1992, the Major government brought in another batch of re-strictions on trade unions with the Trade Union Reform and Employment Rights Act 1993. The measures after the 1987 general election went further than many employers wished. For instance, the Institute of Personnel Management criticised the proposals in the 1990 Employment Bill, commenting of the Green Paper which preceded it that it was biased against the trade unions and that its proposed end-ing of the closed shop failed to take into account the stability associ-ated with controlled collective bargaining. With regard to the 1992 Bill, Norman Willis, the General Secretary of the TUC, observed that 'the moves were not even supported by employers and would create rather than solve problems'.[51]

There was even less enthusiasm from employers' organisations when the Major government brought forward another Green Paper, *Indus-trial Action and Trade Unions*, in November 1996. Its proposals in-cluded removing unions' immunity from being sued, with courts deciding whether any particular strike action was 'disproportionate or excessive' in its effects on the community or the economy. The Institute of Directors responded that the proposals were 'impractical, unworkable and liable to create a field day for lawyers', while the CBI observed that they were unlikely to resolve disputes and could 'lead to more uncertainty in the workplace'.[52]

Historians and economists have disagreed as to the part played by the Thatcher and Major governments' legislation in changing the cli-mate of British industrial relations. Trade unions were similarly 'tamed' in other countries, often without such legislation. Legislation in itself

---

[50] S. Auerbach, *Legislating for Conflict*, Oxford, 1990, pp. 186–7.
[51] *The Times*, 21 June 1989, p. 2; 7 May 1992, p. 7.
[52] *Guardian*, 30 January 1997, p. 20

did not lessen industrial conflict; the attempts of 1969 and the Industrial Relations Act 1971 appear to have added to the causes of industrial tension and strife.

Strikes

Levels of strike activity have tended to rise and fall according to international economic circumstances. This generalisation is broadly true for the main industrial economies. Contrary to notions of strikes being a (or even the) 'British disease', the British pattern has been little different from that of other countries, though in Britain matters appear to have become notably worse in the early 1970s when trade union and strike issues were markedly politicised.

The issue of whether Britain was more strike-prone than others was taken up by the Donovan Commission (1965–68). Table 1 provides the basic UK strike figures for 1945–95. The Donovan Commission drew on International Labour Organisation (ILO) statistics which provided information on major sectors (mining, manufacturing, construction and transport) of industrialised countries' economies. These statistics have drawbacks: like all international statistics the basis on which they were compiled may vary from one country to another; and the sectors covered in the earlier figures may distort the overall picture for some countries. Nevertheless, such figures – especially of working days lost in relation to numbers of people employed – do give a reasonably good pattern of change over several years. The figures for the United Kingdom and other major industrial countries are presented in Table 2 (with the rank order given in brackets). The fourth column does provide figures for all industries, information which is not available for the 1970s or earlier. Table 3 presents the figures in five-year averages from 1946 to 1991.[53]

From Table 3 it can be seen that in the 1960s Britain was not among the most strike-prone countries, but rather in an intermediate group between those with a very high number of days lost through stoppages and a group with relatively few days lost through stoppages. The Donovan Report noted, 'While this country has a comparatively

---

[53] Table 2 is drawn from my essay, 'Trade unions, strikes and the government', in R. Coopey and N. Woodward (eds), *Britain in the 1970s: The Troubled Economy*, London, 1996, p. 280. Table 3 is drawn from D. Gilbert, 'Strikes in post-war Britain', in Wrigley (ed.), *A History of British Industrial Relations*, p. 132.

Table 1 Industrial disputes in the UK, 1945–1995

Year	No. of disputes	No. of workers involved (000s)	Total working days lost (000s)	Workers involved per dispute	Working days lost per involved worker	% of stoppages involving pay
1945	2293	531	2835	231.6	5.3	43.2
1946	2205	526	2158	238.5	4.1	43.6
1947	1721	620	2433	360.3	3.9	46.9
1948	1759	424	1944	241.0	4.6	41.5
1949	1426	433	1807	303.6	4.2	42.8
1950	1339	302	1389	225.5	4.6	43.8
1951	1719	379	1694	220.5	4.5	48.5
1952	1714	415	1792	242.1	4.3	42.4
1953	1746	1370	2184	784.7	1.6	45.3
1954	1989	448	2457	225.2	5.5	46.6
1955	2419	659	3781	272.4	5.7	50.9
1956	2648	507	2083	191.5	4.1	45.6
1957	2859	1356	8412	474.3	6.2	44.7
1958	2629	523	3462	198.9	6.6	45.9
1959	2093	645	5270	308.2	8.2	46.2
1960	2832	814	3024	287.4	3.7	48.9
1961	2686	771	3046	287.0	4.0	48.6
1962	2449	4420	5798	1804.8	1.3	45.9
1963	2068	590	1755	285.3	3.0	46.2
1964	2524	872	2277	345.5	2.6	47.9
1965	2354	868	2925	368.7	3.4	50.1
1966	1937	530	2398	273.6	4.5	46.5
1967	2116	731	2787	345.5	3.8	46.9
1968	2378	2255	4690	948.3	2.1	54.0
1969	3116	1654	6846	530.8	4.1	59.4
1970	3906	1793	10980	459.0	6.1	64.3
1971	2228	1171	13551	525.6	11.6	52.8
1972	2497	1722	23909	689.6	13.9	59.3
1973	2873	1513	7197	526.6	4.8	50.9
1974	2922	1622	14750	555.1	9.1	65.8
1975	2282	789	6012	345.7	7.6	57.8
1976	2016	666	3284	330.4	4.9	43.4
1977	2703	1155	10142	427.3	8.8	57.6
1978	2471	1003	9405	405.9	9.4	61.1
1979	2080	4583	29474	2203.4	6.4	59.1
1980	1330	842	11964	633.1	14.2	47.7
1981	1338	1513	4266	1130.8	2.8	48.9
1982	1528	2103	5313	1376.3	2.5	40.2
1983	1352	574	3754	424.6	6.5	39.7
1984	1206	1391	27135	1153.4	19.5	42.5
1985	903	791	6402	876.0	8.1	37.3
1986	1074	720	1920	670.4	2.7	34.3
1987	1016	887	3546	873.0	4.0	31.7
1988	781	790	3702	1011.5	4.7	36.0
1989	701	727	4128	1037.1	5.7	37.1
1990	630	298	1903	473.0	6.4	31.9
1991	369	176	761	477.0	4.3	34.7
1992	253	148	528	585.0	3.6	36.0
1993	211	385	649	1824.6	1.7	33.7
1994	205	107	278	522.0	2.6	43.9
1995	235	174	415	740.4	2.4	40.2

Sources: *Ministry of Labour Gazette, Employment and Productivity Gazette, Department of Employment Gazette* and *Labour Market Trends.*

Table 2 Working days lost through strikes per 1,000 workers in mining, manufacturing, construction, and transport and communication (rank order in brackets; fourth column gives all industries and services)

	Annual averages			
	1961–1969	1970–1979	1980–1989	All industries 1980–1989
Australia	424 (5)	1298 (3)	770 (2)	350 (4)
Canada	1026 (3)	1840 (1)	960 (1)	470 (2)
France	321 (6)	312 (7)	150	80
Germany (West)	24	92	50	50
Ireland	1114 (2)	1163 (5)	530 (4)	380 (3)
Italy	1438 (1)	1778 (2)	290 (7)	620 (1)
Japan	239	215	20	10
Sweden	18	42	330 (=5)	180 (6)
United Kingdom	274 (7)	1088 (6)	740 (3)	330 (5)
United States	1001 (4)	1211 (4)	330 (=5)	120 (7)

Source: *Employment Gazette*, December 1971, October 1973, January 1981 and December 1991.

Table 3 Working days lost through strikes per 1,000 workers in mining, manufacturing, construction, and transport and communication

	Annual averages							
	1946–1950	1957–1961	1962–1966	1967–1971	1972–1976	1977–1981	1982–1986	1987–1991
Australia	1292	306	358	796	1490	1250	630	544
Canada	1088	596	768	1682	2198	1562	944	770
France	1537	288	322	313	338	230	148	82
Germany (West)		26	34	80	32	86	100	6
Italy		676	1388	1692	1996	1508	612	414
Netherlands	200	61	16	42	82	80	30	40
Sweden	36	10	26	62	18	470	8	174
United Kingdom	148	352	228	608	968	1120	976	236
United States	2458	1166	790	1644	1054	900	316	206

Sources: *International Labour Office Year Book, Ministry of Labour Gazette, Employment Gazette.*

Note: Figures show five-year average, not weighted for employment. The series for France does not include 1968.

large number of stoppages, they are of fairly short duration and do not usually involve very large numbers of people'. It also pointed to an upward trend in unofficial strikes. The Donovan Report presented figures for official and unofficial stoppages of work for 1964–66, and commented on these that they

> show that the overwhelming majority of stoppages – some 95 per cent – are due to unofficial strikes. Over these three years each unofficial strike involved on average about 300 workers and lasted a little over 2½ days. By contrast each official strike involved on average approximately 1,370 workers, lasted nearly three times as long, and caused the loss of over twelve times as many working days.[54]

However, in terms of strikes, Britain's relative position to other industrialised countries weakened in the late 1960s and early 1970s. Britain's position in the rank order may not have changed much but she moved from the intermediate group of countries into the lower end of the strike-prone group. David Metcalf and Simon Milner have argued of Britain in the 1970s:

> Memories of the 1970s cloud much of the comment about the decline of industrial action in the 1980s, but the data suggest that it was the 1970s that was the peculiar decade, whereas the 1980s simply saw a return to the underlying trend of strike ac-tivity apparent since 1930.[55]

The late 1960s and early 1970s were marked by inflation and by the return of massive mining disputes. In both cases those aggrieved took strike action to pressurise the government to ease incomes poli-cies in the public sector or more generally to affect collective bargain-ing. Alongside this there was substantial politicisation of industrial relations through proposals for legislation (*In Place of Strife*) and ac-tual legislation (the Industrial Relations Act 1971).

Even in this period of higher than usual levels of strikes, many sectors of the economy experienced few stoppages. In contrast, coal-mining, the docks, shipbuilding, car manufacturing and iron and steel were strike-prone. In 1970–75 they accounted for some 6 per cent of

[54] Royal Commission on Trade Unions and Employers' Associations 1965–1968, *Report*, London, 1968 (paras 365 and 368), pp. 96–7.
[55] D. Metcalf and S. Milner, 'A century of UK strike activity: a new perspective', in Metcalf and Milner (eds), *New Perspectives on Industrial Disputes*, p. 238.

employment but for over a quarter of strikes and a third of days lost. A detailed Department of Employment survey of strikes in the three-year period 1971–73 found that 'only five per cent of plants experienced stoppages and of these over two-thirds had only one stoppage'. Of those which had stoppages, 5 per cent 'accounted for a quarter of stoppages and two-thirds of days lost in manufacturing'. Furthermore, the study found:

> In all geographical subdivisions of Great Britain stoppages were concentrated in a minority of plants. In all subdivisions, in an average year, over 90 per cent of manufacturing plant had no stoppages. Even in the more severely affected subdivisions stoppages were concentrated in a minority of plants, demonstrating that the worse record of these areas is due to the worse performance of a minority of plants rather than to a spread of strike activity to a wider range of plants. Thus it is not the case that the poorer record of the plants that have strikes in these areas spreads throughout the area.[56]

The Department of Employment survey also found that there was 'a powerful tendency for the number of days lost in strikes per 1000 employees to increase with plant size'. On average, only 2 per cent of manufacturing plants experienced strikes which were recorded in official statistics and even in 1972, a year with a high loss of days through strikes, less than 11 per cent of manufacturing workers were involved in strikes.[57]

In the motor car industry between the five-year periods 1949–53 and 1969–73 there was a very substantial rise in the number of small strikes. Durcan et al. in their analysis of the motor car industry found that the number of these (defined as strikes involving the loss of less than 5,000 days) went up by 930 per cent, workers involved by 1,440 per cent and days lost by 1,290 per cent.[58] Such disputes could occur frequently in strike-prone parts of plants, rather than in the whole plant.

[56] C. T. B. Smith, R. Clifton, P. Makeham, S. W. Creagh and R. V. Burn, *Strikes in Britain* (Department of Employment Manpower Paper 15), London, 1978, pp. 21–2 and 86–7.
[57] Smith et al., *Strikes in Britain*, pp. 88–9.
[58] W. Durcan, W. E. J. McCarthy and G. P. Redman, *Strikes in Post-War Britain: A Study of Stoppages of Work due to Industrial Disputes, 1946–73*, London, 1983, p. 316. More generally, see also H. A. Turner, G. Clack and G. Roberts, *Labour Relations in the Motor Industry*, London, 1967.

British industry would have benefited from fewer industrial disputes. Yet it is worth seeing strikes in a broad perspective. Strikes occur when procedures for settling disputes fail. In Britain, it has been suggested, 'over 99 per cent of bargains negotiated are settled without a stoppage occurring'.[59] In the early 1990s, one survey of labour in the UK economy observed, 'Despite the publicity which they attract, strikes are quite rare ... even in 1979 – the year of the "winter of discontent" – the average worker lost little more than a single day through industrial stoppage over the whole year'.[60] In terms of days lost against possible working days, the number has been low. Kessler and Bayliss have commented:

> The proportion of all days which could be worked but which were lost through strikes was minute in the 1970s – 0.2 per cent, in the 1980s it became even more minute – less than 0.1 per cent, and by the early 1990s it had virtually disappeared at about 0.001 per cent.[61]

While strikes have an obvious adverse effect on the companies affected, more generally the impact may not have been that great. A 1976 study of differences in efficiency in British and West German industry found that of a 27 per cent differential in favour of the latter, only 3.5 per cent were due to strikes or restrictive practices. Another study of British productivity in 1968 found that even in a strike-prone year there was little or no adverse effect on productivity.[62]

Productive time lost through industrial accidents, ill health, absenteeism and unemployment has been much greater than working time lost through strikes. In 1970, a year with a high level of strikes, some 10 million working days were lost through strikes, whereas some 20 million were lost through industrial accidents and a million unemployed people represented the loss of some 300 million working days.[63]

---

[59] Durcan et al., *Strikes in Post-War Britain*, p. 3.

[60] G. Johnes and J. Taylor, 'Labour', in M. J. Artis, *Prest and Coppock's The UK Economy: A Manual of Applied Economics*, 13th edn, London, 1992, p. 354.

[61] S. Kessler and F. Bayliss, *Contemporary British Industrial Relations*, 2nd edn, London, 1995, p. 227.

[62] C. F. Pratten, *Labour Productivity Differentials within International Companies*, Cambridge, 1976. K. G. Knight, 'Labour productivity and strike activity in British manufacturing industries', *British Journal of Industrial Relations*, 27, 3, 1989, pp. 365–74. P. Edwards, *Industrial Relations: Theory and Practice in Britain*, Oxford, 1995, pp. 455–7.

[63] R. Hyman, *Strikes*, London, 1972, pp. 33–4.

Introduction

A mid-1990s study published by the Health and Safety Executive estimated that the annual costs to employers of personal injury work accidents to be about £900 million and work-related ill health to be about £600 million. Adding to these estimates of the cost of avoidable non-injury accidental events, the study's estimate came to a sum 'equivalent to around 5 to 10 per cent of all UK industrial companies' gross trading profits'. The estimate for the impact of these on the British economy was between £6 and £12 billion, 'equivalent to between 1 and 2 per cent of total Gross Domestic Product [GDP]'. Durcan et al. estimate that in 1972, the most strike-prone year of their survey, 'the impact of stoppages in the UK was to cause an output loss of 0.25 per cent', but that if unemployment had been reduced by a quarter of a million that 'would have permitted additional output equivalent to 2.5 per cent of GDP'.[64]

Trade union recruitment and development

Trade union membership reached a zenith in 1979, and has declined since then. In 1979 male trade union density (the proportion of those in trade unions out of those legally eligible to be in them) was at 63.1 per cent and female trade union density at 39.4 per cent. By 1995 male trade union density had fallen to 34.6 per cent and female to 29.5 per cent (see Table 4).

The trade unions since 1945, as in all other periods, had to adapt to changing employment conditions and to a changing membership. Many major industries which had been growth areas for late nineteenth- and early twentieth-century trade unionism – notably cotton, coal and rail – shed labour. As these had high union densities (all around 80 per cent or higher in 1948) this led to a fall in trade union membership. In the case of manual workers between 1964 and 1979, while their number dropped by 15 per cent, union membership went up within the smaller workforce (the density rising from about 53 to 63 per cent in those years).

A notable feature of the growth of trade unionism between the mid-1960s and 1979 was the growth of white-collar trade unionism.

[64] N. V. Davies and P. Teasdale, *The Costs to the British Economy of Work Accidents and Work-related Ill-Health* (Health and Safety Executive), London, 1994, p. vi. See also section 9.11 of this book.

Table 4 Trade union membership in the UK 1945–1995 (000s)

Year	Total	Males	Females	No. of unions
1945	7875	6237	1638	781
1946	8803	7186	1617	757
1947	9145	7483	1662	734
1948	9362	7677	1685	742
1949	9318	7644	1674	742
1950	9289	7605	1684	732
1951	9535	7745	1790	735
1952	9588	7797	1792	723
1953	9527	7749	1778	720
1954	9566	7756	1810	711
1955	9741	7874	1867	704
1956	9778	7871	1907	685
1957	9829	7935	1894	685
1958	9639	7789	1850	675
1959	9623	7756	1868	668
1960	9835	7884	1951	664
1961	9916	7911	2005	655
1962	10014	7960	2054	649
1963	10067	7963	2104	643
1964	10218	8043	2174	641
1965	10325	8084	2241	630
1966	10259	8003	2256	622
1967	10194	7908	2286	606
1968	10200	7836	2364	586
1969	10479	7972	2507	565
1970	11187	8444	2743	543
1971	11135	8382	2753	525
1972	11359	8452	2907	507
1973	11459	8450	3006	519
1974	11764	8586	3178	507
1975	12193	8729	3464	501
1976	12386	8825	3561	473
1977	12846	9071	3775	481
1978	13112	9238	3874	462
1979	13289	9544	3902	453
1980	12947	9162	3790	438
1981	12106	8406	3776	414
1982	11593	*	*	408
1983	11236	*	*	394
1984	10994	*	*	375
1985	10821	*	*	370
1986	10539	*	*	335
1987	10475	*	*	330
1988	10376	*	*	315
1989	10158	6405	3753	309
1990	9947	6195	3752	287
1991	9585	5813	3772	275
1992	9048	5472	3577	268
1993	8700	5218	3482	254
1994	8278	4762	3516	243
1995	8089	4606	3483	238

Between 1951 and 1966 white-collar trade unionism grew by 29.8 per cent, but as white-collar employment grew even faster, the density of union membership dropped. Between 1964 and 1970 white-collar union membership grew by 33.8 per cent at a time when the white-collar labour force only increased by 4.1 per cent. By 1979 about 44 per cent of all white-collar workers were in trade unions, and of all British trade unionists 40 per cent were white-collar workers.

Another notable feature of trade union membership was the increasing numbers of women. In the past skilled unions had often been keen to keep women out. In the case of the Amalgamated Engineering Union it began recruiting women during the Second World War (from 1 January 1943) (see 9.1). Most unions (even with substantial numbers of women) remained male-dominated and male-orientated until at least the 1980s (see the extracts in 9.1 for some attempts to remedy this, albeit in a maladroit way in the second extract). Between 1970 and 1979 the number of women in trade unions rose from 2,583,000 to 3,822,000, a 47 per cent rise (and in terms of density, from 31.2 to 40.4 per cent). In this decade the proportion of trade unionists who were women went up from 24.2 to 30.2 per cent (a bigger rise than women's share of the labour market, which increased from 37.7 per cent to 41.8 per cent).[65] After 1980 the proportion of women among trade unionists continued to rise. By 1994 42.5 per cent of trade unionists were women. Indeed, a notable feature of that year's statistics was that female membership rose by 1 per cent while male membership fell by 8.7 per cent. Also, in 1994, women outnumbered men in five of the ten largest trade unions.

In response to this change, many unions in the 1980s and 1990s took great pains to ensure greater female representation on their deci-

---

[65] G. S. Bain and R. Price, *Profiles of Union Growth*, Oxford, 1980, pp. 42, 45, 51 and 67.

Sources: Department of Employment, *British Labour Statistics: Historical Abstract 1868–1968*, 1971, p. 395. B. R. Mitchell, *British Historical Statistics*, 1988, p. 137. *Employment Gazette. Labour Market Trends*.

Note* Between 1982 and 1988 the Department of Employment did not publish separate male and female trade union membership statistics. In 1982 the *Employment Gazette* noted that unions covering 87 per cent of trade union members had differentiated between male and female members, and of these 38 per cent were female; and in 1983 unions covering 82.7 per cent had made the more detailed returns, and of these members 28 per cent were female.

sion-making bodies and as officials. A most notable example of change is the case of UNISON, which between 1993 and 1995 increased its percentage of women national executive members from 42 to 65 (while women were 68 and 71 per cent of its members), though the proportion of women as national officers only increased marginally.[66]

Women are not only lower paid workers but also – through preference as well as employment opportunities – more likely than men to be part-time workers. Trade unions, as always, have had to adapt to changes in the way that work has been organised, and such change has been considerable since the 1970s. Between 1971 and 1989 the number of part-time workers grew by over 50 per cent, from 3.4 to 5.2 million; of the latter figure 82.5 per cent were female. In 1989 22.4 per cent of these part-time workers were in unions, against 43.5 per cent of full-time workers. By 1995 the gap between unionisation among part- and full-time workers had narrowed, with 20.6 and 36.0 per cent unionised respectively. In responding to part-time work in 1996, which by then accounted for a fifth of all employment, John Monks, General Secretary of the TUC, called for a 'radical shake-up of unions' "9 to 5" culture' when he launched a campaign for trade union recruitment.[67]

The adverse political climate of the 1980s and 1990s further encouraged the unions to recruit workers from ethnic groups and among young workers. There had been some signs of reticence to push with vigour for Asian workers in textiles in the late 1960s and early 1970s (see 7.6). However, by the mid-1990s there were higher union densities for workers categorised as 'black', both men (39 per cent) and women (42 per cent), than for white workers (35 and 29 per cent respectively), which was due to black employees working disproportionately in heavily unionised jobs and to preference. Also, in 1995, Indian workers were only a little less unionised than white workers (at 30 per cent for men and 27 per cent for women) but Pakistani and Bangladeshi males were less unionised (at 20 per cent, with too few women to provide a reliable estimate). Perhaps more worrying for the

[66] J. Waddington, 'Unemployment and restructuring in trade union membership in Britain 1980–87', *British Journal of Industrial Relations*, 30, 1992, pp. 290–3. Wrigley, 'Trade unions, strikes and the government', pp. 273–91. *Labour Research*, 85, 3, 1996, pp. 5 and 11–13.

[67] C. Wrigley, 'Trade unions, the government and the economy', in Gourvish and O'Day (eds), *Britain Since 1945*, pp. 80–3. *Labour Research*, 85, 6, 1996, pp. 15–6 and 19–21.

trade unions was the low level of unionisation among younger workers. In 1995 union densities were 35 per cent or higher for age groups from 30 upwards, but among men and women in their twenties the densities were 24 per cent for both sexes, while for male and female teenagers they were only 6 per cent each.[68]

In a period of public and private policy based on encouraging free market forces and 'flexible' (or cheap) labour, trade unions remained attractive to large numbers of working people. While many economists have written of the adverse employment effects of 'the trade union mark-up', many workers have been aware that their unions have presented, or delayed, an employers' 'mark-down'. In many sectors already low wages have been pushed further down, thereby making not real efficiency savings but simply cutting the labour cost part of the work. In the public sector this has sometimes been the same people doing the same job in the same way for a substantial cut in hourly wage rates (with the difference being divided between public saving and private profit). Moreover, in a period of escalating managerial salaries and extras, and when, in 1995, there were around 100 company directors who were paid more than £1 million a year, talk of the perils of 'high wages' was less convincing to those on low pay.

Trade unions in achieving a 'mark-up' have had what David Metcalf has dubbed a 'sword of justice' effect. They have boosted the pay of lower paid and minority groups, thus lessening inequality of pay. Metcalf estimated trade union activities narrowed inequalities in the wage structure (in the early 1980s) in favour of female workers by 1 per cent, unskilled males by 2 per cent, black workers by 5 per cent and non-manual workers by 9 per cent. He added that 'union presence in the workforce tends to reduce arbitrary treatment of employees by managers and it ensures proper representation over other important matters like health and safety'.[69]

Trade unions have been a major feature of British life in the nineteenth and twentieth centuries. Throughout their role has been a matter of political and economic controversy. This is likely to remain the case in the twenty-first century also.

---

[68] *Labour Market Trends*, May 1995.
[69] D. Metcalfe, 'Trade unions and economic performance: the British evidence', *LSE Quarterly*, 3, 1, 1989, pp. 21–42.

1

The trade unions as widely respected parts of post-war society: the Attlee and Churchill Years, 1945–1955

The trade unions had been much consulted and much involved in organising the 'home front' during the Second World War. They continued to work in association with 'their government' during 1945–51. Both senior Labour politicians and trade union leaders were eager to strengthen 'official' trade unionism and to discourage 'unofficial' strikes. They were also keen to raise industrial productivity in the national struggle to increase exports and generally to recover from the war. After the Conservatives' defeat in the 1945 general election, Churchill and his senior colleagues tried to appeal to working-class, including trade union, voters and to indicate that the Conservatives were not anti-trade union. Churchill's praise of the trade unions as pillars of society was very different from Mrs Thatcher's views a quarter of a century later.

1.1 The Labour Party's expectations of support from the trade unions, 1945

> Professor Harold Laski, Chairman of the Labour Party, gave the fraternal address on behalf of the party to the Trades Union Congress held at Blackpool on 10 September 1945. Laski urged the trade unions to be active.

But trade union activity involves trade union obligations. It means an informed discipline in the branches. The reckless indulgence in unauthorised strikes, mass wage demands made when a Labour government is in power but never when a Tory government is in power, failure to set the functions of a union in their full civic context, failure to provide a full chance to younger men in the movement – all these in this critical hour will not be easy to forgive. The unions, I hope, will persuade their members fully to realise that the standard of life can only rise as output per man-hour rises. They will, I hope, bend their energies to the need of fitting their members not only to play their full part in the management of socialised industries, but of understanding also, at the highest level, the economic and technical problems of those industries which remain in private hands.

Harold Laski, 10 September 1945, in TUC, *Report of Proceedings at the 77th Annual Trades Union Congress*, 1945, p. 237.

1.2 The TUC and its post-war responsibilities

The President of the 1945 TUC, Ebby Edwards (Secretary of the National Union of Mineworkers), in his address gave an assessment of the 'glorious opportunity' yet 'heavy responsibility' facing the British trade union movement after the successful conclusion of the war. The following extracts include his comments on general issues of industrial co-operation, making nationalisation of coal economically effective and the state intervening to develop industries still in the private sector.

We welcome such a lead as ... the President of the Board of Trade [Sir Stafford Cripps] has given in the case of the cotton textile industry. He has offered government help for the reorganisation of industry; but he has insisted that there must be full consultation between the employers and the unions on reconstruction measures, and that wages must be raised and welfare and other amenities developed. That is a government policy which commands the assent of trade unionists, and I hope that it will be a policy of general application in the reconstruction period. Industry must put its house in order. Co-operation between the trade unions and the employers' organisations is necessary to this end. Unions will have to overhaul and modernise their organisation too, and abandon restrictive practices which impede maximum production and full efficiency in their industry. A concerted effort should be made with government support to raise the standards of employment, and to promote full and free co-operation between employers and unions. Collective bargaining in modern industry has a wider connotation than it had formerly, and we must see to it that the unions in negotiating new agreements insist upon these wider aspects of industrial reorganisation.

... The ownership of the mining industry is important in our national economy; but we must not minimise the fact that it is only as a means of operating the industry with the highest degree of efficiency and economy side by side with correct living standards and working conditions for its employees.

The operating structure of a nationalised coal mining industry involves in experiment vital socialist principles which must of necessity stand the test of industrial efficiency and national welfare....

A general planning of industry and maximum efficiency in production must be obtained in the public interest. The government must ever be on the alert to anticipate the progressive changes in industrial power. Existing essentials now secured by the use of large capital and great toil may be replaced by other means in order to secure abundance with economy. The changing factors in an age of discovery and practical technique must readily be accepted if not anticipated.

Ebby Edwards, in TUC, *Report of Proceedings at the 77th Annual Trades Union Congress*, 1945, pp. 12–13.

1.3 The need for high output in a period of full employment

To match the economics of full employment we need the ethics of full employment. Employers have to realise that those they employ are a national asset that must not be wasted.... On the other side workers must realise that whether they work for the state or for a private employer they are producing the stock of goods and services from which we all derive the necessities and amenities of life. Restrictive practices on either side which often had a justification in the conditions of a past economy are out of place today.

Clement Attlee, Prime Minister, 24 October 1946, in TUC, *Report of Proceedings at the 78th Annual Trades Union Congress*, 1946, p. 414.

1.4 The TUC and the need for productivity in 1947

With a fuel crisis in 1947, the TUC looked to trade union activists to help at factory level, urging its affiliated unions to arrange through their shop stewards 'that fuel watchers should be appointed in all factories in order to enforce the most rigid economy in the use of steam, gas and electricity'. Similarly, the TUC urged that joint production committees (JPCs) be revived to help increase output to meet the economic problems facing Britain.

... the General Council placed before the National Joint Advisory Council to the Minister of Labour and the National Production Advisory Council on industry a memorandum dealing with the difficulties of production under full employment. The document stated that the General Council were convinced that the social service programme of the government, including the raising of the school-leaving age, and the provision of higher social benefits, could only be carried through if the productivity of the country expanded and provided the means to finance these reforms.

The General Council also felt that with the disappearance of any appreciable amount of unemployment the 'whip' which some employers held in order to enforce discipline in their factories had disappeared, probably for all time. The problem was to find a substitute for the lingering fear of unemployment and to create confidence that full employment can be maintained, and there was therefore no necessity for the devices that capitalism had forced upon the trade union movement during the period between the two world wars.

The General Council concluded that there was no alternative except the creation of an atmosphere of mutual confidence throughout the workshops and factories of this country. They felt that there was a limit to the amount of exhortation that could take place from above, whether by the government or the TUC and that the most fruitful place to engender confidence was at the place of production in the factory or workshop.

The General Council also said that they felt that the best possible means of securing this atmosphere of confidence was by a genuine effort to establish Joint Production Committees. They recognised that these had largely fallen into disuse since the end of the war period but felt that in view of the vital necessity for increased production and the elimination of waste of all descriptions (manpower, materials and fuel) there was no alternative but their resuscitation.

TUC General Council's Report, *Report of Proceedings at the 79th Annual Trades Union Congress*, 1947, pp. 231 and 238–9.

1.5 The stabilisation of prices, profits and wages

On 4 February 1948 Clement Attlee made a statement in the House of Commons, which subsequently was issued as a White Paper, *Statement on Personal Incomes, Costs and Prices* (Cmd 7321). In his statement Attlee stated that the government felt that it was 'essential that there should be the strictest adherence to the terms of collective agreements', that at present there was 'no justification for any *general* increase of individual money incomes' and that any wage or salary claim 'must be considered on its national merits and not on the basis of maintaining a former relativity between different occupations and industries'. The TUC's Special Committee on the Economic Situation was very unhappy with this statement, but after seeing the Prime Minister, Chancellor of the Exchequer, Foreign Secretary, Minister of Labour and Lord President of the Council (Attlee, Cripps, Bevin, Isaacs and Morrison), it made the following recommendation, which the General Council endorsed.

In the view of the Committee the principles of the White Paper relating to wage movements are acceptable to the trade union movement to the extent that they:

(a) recognise the necessity of retaining unimpaired the system of collective bargaining and free negotiation;

(b) admit the justification for claims for increased wages where those claims are based upon the facts of increased output;

(c) admit the necessity of adjusting the wages of workers whose incomes are below a reasonable standard of subsistence;

(d) affirm that it is in the national interest to establish standards of wages and conditions in under-manned essential industries in order to attract sufficient manpower; and

(e) recognise the need to safeguard those wage differentials which are an essential element in the wages structure of many important

industries and are required to sustain those standards of craftsman-
ship, training and experience that contribute directly to industrial efficiency and higher productivity.

... General Council should accord

(a) its endorsement of the policy of general stabilisation as set forth
in the White Paper; and

(b) its acceptance of the principles which this statement proposes
should be applied to wage claims at the present time;
on condition that the government pursues vigorously and firmly a
policy designed not only to stabilise but to reduce profits and prices.

[At a Conference of Trade Union Executives held in London on 24
March 1948 this policy was approved by 5,421,000 votes (73 per
cent) to 2,032,000 (37 per cent), a majority of 3,389,000.]

TUC, *Report of Proceedings at the 80th Annual Trades Union Congress*,
1948, pp. 289–91.

1.6 Productivity conferences

> The TUC organised a conference of National Executive Com-
> mittees on 18 November 1948 to discuss ways of improving
> industrial production and efficiency. This was attended by
> 1,350 members of executive committees, representing 144
> trade unions.

Points to which the attention of unions and federations were drawn
included: focusing attention on shortages and bottlenecks; organising
national or local industrial conferences to be addressed by leaders on
both sides of industry, appropriate research scientists and representatives of the Production Efficiency Service of the Board of Trade; and
accelerating the formation of Joint Production Committees [JPCs].
Reviews of the system of shop stewards and other workplace representatives, and methods of raising their efficiency by Training Within
Industry courses and other means, were also suggested.

[By July 1949 eight conferences, seven with different industrial
groups, had been held: with unions in shipbuilding and engineering,
cotton and other textiles, pottery, chemicals, furniture and rubber.]

While discussion at each of the conferences was related to the particular characteristics of individual industries, there were certain as-

pects common to most of them. For instance, though there was in most cases shortages of labour, where sections of an industry, as in wool, were scattered, often in small and isolated localities, and where redundancy might not lead to re-employment except at a distance, there was considerable fear of unemployment and a consequent reluctance to participate in measures to increase productivity.

On production techniques, such as motion study and redeployment and the attitude to industrial consultants, opinions were divided. Again, the fear of redundancy as a result of new methods was an over-riding consideration, although where it was clearly shown that workpeople declared redundant could be reabsorbed, there was little or no union opposition. Some unions had proved willing to examine new proposals, and in some cases were arranging to have their officers trained in such subjects as work-load assessment and time and motion study.

It was also apparent that opinion was divided as to the value of JPCs. All the unions commented on the apathy (in some cases the hostility) of sections of their membership to these committees. Executive Committee members themselves however were generally convinced of the need for good joint consultative machinery in the factories and workshops, although some unions in favouring Works Councils sought a wider and more diverse sphere of consultation than had obtained on JPCs. Unions had however been pressing employers to set up joint consultative committees to include representatives of staff and technicians, and also to improve their scope and responsibility by providing information.

Where employers have refused to set up committees following representation by union members the General Council have advised unions to approach the Industrial Relations Department of the Ministry of Labour who have a special sub-department dealing with joint consultative machinery in industry.

Methods of introducing improved training schemes were discussed and also possibilities of providing courses, for shop stewards and other workshop representatives, on production and management techniques, and industrial relations. There was no consensus of opinion on whether trainees should be trained in model factories, government centres or at their places of work. With regard to the training of shop stewards certain unions were collaborating with technical colleges and the WEA [Workers' Educational Association], in initiating various types of trade union courses.

TUC, *Report of Proceedings at the 81st Annual Trades Union Congress,* 1949, pp. 201–3.

1.7 Devaluation and the collapse of voluntary wage restraint

> On 18 September 1949 the government devalued the pound, from a parity with the dollar of $4.03 to $2.80. Food prices rose rapidly by 7 per cent between September 1949 and June 1950, while male wages rose by 1 per cent. This undermined the General Council of the TUC's post-devaluation policy of urging unions 'to exercise even greater restraint on wage increases', which was succeeded by a policy in June 1950 whereby the General Council recognised 'that there must be greater flexibility of wage movements in the future'. This modified policy proved unsustainable at the September 1950 TUC.

The distasteful but necessary devaluation of the pound sterling has been having the results which we anticipated in promoting our industrial and economic recovery. This action by the government could not have achieved its object without the co-operation of all sections of the community. I should like this morning to pay a special tribute to the wise restraint exercised by the leaders and by the rank and file of the trade union movement. That restraint has made a very great contribution to the improvement of our economic position.

As you know, it has never been the policy of the government to impose rates of wages. It has always been our view that we should maintain the well-tried machinery of collective bargaining. We have, however, felt it our duty to keep both sides of industry fully informed of the broad considerations of the economic position of the country, so that they should bear in mind the effect on the community as a whole of any particular decisions. In pursuance of the same general line of policy the government has not at any time given directions as to the line which they should take to those who have the duty of arbitrating on claims, whether as members of the Industrial Court, the National Arbitration Tribunal or Wages Councils or as single arbitrators. To have done so would clearly have been to destroy the utility of this machinery.

Where we sought the co-operation of everyone to exercise restraint in the matter of personal incomes we did not attempt to impose an arbitrary wage freeze.... As conditions improved we were able to suggest some measure of relaxation, but ... there is still need for restraint. There is still that danger ... of an inflationary spiral. I would reiterate that warning again today, especially as ... this danger is increased by the additional expenditure on armaments which we have been obliged to undertake.

Clement Attlee, Prime Minister, 5 September 1950, in TUC, *Report of Proceedings at the 82nd Annual Trades Union Congress*, 1950, p. 351.

This Congress notes that since the issue of the White Paper on Personal Incomes, Costs and Prices, prices and profits have continued to rise and the living standards of large sections of the working community to fall. Congress protests that no effective steps have been taken to prevent this continued trend of increased profits.

Congress is of the opinion that until such time as there is a reasonable limitation of profits, a positive planning of our British economy, and prices are subject to such control as will maintain the purchasing power of wages at a level affording to every worker a reasonable standard of living, there can be no basis for the restraint on wage applications.

Congress declares that wage increases can be met without resulting in increased prices, for example by reducing profits, and therefore calls on the General Council to abandon any further policy of wage restraint, and at the same time urges the government to introduce statutory control of profits.

[The vote resulted in the first defeat for the General Council by Congress for many years, the motion being passed by 3,949,000 votes (51.4 per cent) to 3,727,000 (48.6 per cent), a majority of 222,000.]

Electrical Trade Union motion during the debate on wages, prices and profits, 7 September 1950, in TUC, *Report of Proceedings at the 82nd Annual Trades Union Congress*, 1950, pp. 467 and 473.

1.8   The Conservatives' Industrial Charter

The Conservative Party's 'Industrial Charter' of May 1947 recognised people's rights to be in trade unions if they wished

42

and promised only to re-enact three aspects of the 1927 Trade Disputes Act repealed by the Attlee government. These three were banning civil servants holding office in organisations with political associations, preventing public or local authorities from requiring employees to be in a specific union and ending the system of workers having to contract out of the political levy if they did not wish to pay it.

We desire to state quite clearly that the official policy of the Conservative Party is in favour of trade unions. Our past record should make this plain. Conservative governments, particularly by the Act of 1875, helped the unions to obtain that privileged position at law without which they could not conduct wage negotiations. Conservative governments as much as any other have recognised collective bargaining in the Civil Service. In the years before the [Second World] war, the National Government gave statutory recognition to collective bargaining, in the road haulage and cotton spinning industries.

Trade unions have in recent years under the National and Coalition governments obtained an important status as members of many advisory committees attached to government departments. We recognise this status and believe that it opens up a wide field of public service in which the unions can make their contribution to the national welfare. In [our economic policy] ... it is clearly shown that the Conservative Party attaches the highest importance to the part to be played by the unions in guiding the national economy. The effective working of this machinery depends upon the participation of union officials at all levels.

Trade unions must depend for their vitality upon a large and active membership and upon a leadership which has the confidence of the members. We condemn unofficial strikes because they undermine the voluntary machinery of collective bargaining and weaken the trade unions.... All members of a union should be encouraged to participate actively in its affairs.

Conservative Political Centre (CPC), *The Industrial Charter*, London, 1947, reprinted in CPC, *Conservatism 1945–1950*, London, 1950, pp. 63–4.

1.9 Churchill on the unions as pillars of society

In his address to the 1947 Conservative Party Conference, Churchill, after referring to Disraeli and his trade union legislation, made the following comments.

The trade unions are a long-established and essential part of our national life. Like other human institutions they have their faults and their weaknesses. At the present time they have much more influence upon the government of the country, and less control over their own members, than ever before. But we take our stand by these pillars of our British Society as it has gradually developed and evolved itself, of the right of individual labouring men and women to adjust their wages and conditions by collective bargaining, including the right to strike; and the right of everyone, with due notice and consideration for others, to choose or change his occupation if he thinks he can better himself and his family.

Conservative Party Conference Report, 1947, 4 October 1947.

1.10 Churchill on the Conservative Party and the trade unions

In his address to the 1950 Conservative Party Conference Churchill said the following.

The salient feature of this conference has been the growing association of Tory democracy with the trade unions. After all it was Lord Beaconsfield and the Tory Party who gave British trade unionism its charter, and collective bargaining coupled with the right to strike. I have urged that every Tory craftsman or wage-earner should of his own free-will be a trade unionist, but I also think he should attend the meetings of the trade union and stand up for his ideas instead of letting only Socialists and Communists get control of what is after all an essentially British institution.

Nationalization of industry is the doom of trade unionism. The trade union leaders in the nationalized industries, for many of whom I have much respect, are increasingly embarrassed by a dual and in some respects divergent loyalty.

Conservative Party Conference Report, 1950, 14 October 1950; *The Times*, 16 October 1950, p. 3.

1.11   Conservative policy for the 1951 general election

Conservatives believe that free and independent trade unions are an essential part of our industrial system. We welcome the public endorsement by the trade union movement of the need for effort to increase production and productivity. We shall consult the leaders of the trade union movement on economic matters and discuss with them fully, and sympathetically, any proposals we or they may have for action on labour problems.

... While we deplore the loss and injury to the community caused by strikes, we have since the days of Disraeli regarded the right to strike as fundamental both to the free working of this system and to personal liberty, subject to the obligation to give notice in the case of certain services essential to the life of the community.

Enterprise must not be frustrated and production limited by unnecessary restrictive practices, either of labour or of employers.... Conservatives will strengthen the Monopolies Commission and speed up its work.

Conservative and Unionist Central Office, *Britain Strong and Free*, London, 1951, pp. 17–18. (This was the policy statement for the general election, a longer version of the manifesto.)

1.12   Churchill on the unions working with a Conservative government

Winston Churchill, in a speech in his constituency during the 1951 general election, responded to Arthur Deakin's enquiries as to Conservative policy towards trade unions with the following comments.

The Conservative Party has no intention of initiating any legislation affecting trade unions, should we become responsible in the new Parliament. We hope to work with the trade unions in a loyal and friendly spirit, and if this is disturbed by party politics the fault will not be on our side.

There is, of course, the question of the political levy being exacted from Conservative and Liberal trade unionists, putting the onus on them to contract out. We do not think that this is fair. But the Conservative and Liberal membership of the trade unions is now so strong, and growing so steadily, that a wider spirit of tolerance has grown up and the question may well be left to common sense and the British way of settling things.

The trade unions will, I am sure, respect the verdict of the people as expressed constitutionally in a general election. If we should be returned we shall consult with them and work with them on a non-party basis in a frank and friendly manner.

Speech at Woodford, 9 October 1951; *The Times*, 10 October 1951, p. 7.

1.13   The Conservatives and consultation

The Conservative 1955 general election manifesto pledged that a re-elected Conservative government would continue to consult with the trade unions and employers.

Team-work is an essential driving force of a dynamic economy. There is really only one side in modern industry, and all of us are on it....

We shall follow up our work for better human relations in industry by discussing with the joint advisory bodies of employers and trade unions, and with the British Productivity Council, how best they can increase their status and the scope of their work. We shall encourage such individual employers as are not already doing so, to keep their workpeople regularly and frankly informed of the fortunes and problems of their firm.

Conservative and Unionist Central Office, *United for Peace and for Progress*, London, 1955.

2

Moving towards consultation: the Conservatives and the trade unions, 1955–1964

By the mid-1950s the government and the trade union movement were diverging very markedly on economic policy. The trade union leadership still aspired to a planned economy, with the government, employers and unions working together for improved productivity, increased investment and higher wages in British industry. The unions had exercised wage restraint during the Attlee years, when they had dealt with Labour in office and there was planning for post-war recovery.

The Conservative governments of Eden (1955–57) and Macmillan (1957–63) were increasingly alarmed at rising inflation and looked for ways to keep wage and salary rises low. The Conservatives were committed to freeing the economy from many subsidies and other remnants of the wartime and post-war government intervention in the economy. Some Conservatives were more willing than others to allow unemployment to rise, thereby weakening the trade unions' bargaining strength in the labour market. Peter Thorneycroft and Enoch Powell were notable advocates of restricting public expenditure and deflating the economy (even at the cost of more people out of work). Thorneycroft was an advocate of getting a carefully selected group of distinguished people, 'the Three Wise Men', to advise on what the country could afford in increased wages, salaries and profits. Macmillan and others were less inclined to deflation. They favoured involving the trade unions and employers in consultations on the running of the economy, and set up the National Economic Development Council in 1962.

2.1 The TUC and the beginnings of the stop–go economic cycle

> In 1955 the TUC was critical of the government's pre-election tax cuts.

The last year has seen a change for the worse in Britain's economic position, marked principally by a sharp deterioration in the balance of payments in the second half of 1954 and a widening deficit in visible trade in the early months of 1955. The General Council had in mind the failure of Britain's exports to rise as much as those of Japan, Germany and other competitors and the continuing need to increase production and investment in industry when they warned the Chancellor of the Exchequer against making tax concessions in his budget....

In their representations to the Chancellor before the Budget, the General Council stated that the overriding objectives must continue to be the need to expand exports, to increase production and investment, and to stabilise costs and prices....

TUC General Council's Report, *Report of Proceedings at the 87th Annual Trade Union Congress*, 1955, pp. 264 and 287.

The fact is that our imports rose by more than 40 per cent at a time when our exports increased only by 4 per cent. In ... the first half of this year, our share of world trade has declined.... The problem and dangers transcend the mere trade union interest, but if the British economy is undermined one of the outstanding risks is the loss that will accrue to the members of the unions we represent.... They will be out of work if there is an economic collapse and it is their children who will suffer if, because of slump conditions, there are cuts in social services or reductions in public expenditure on education.

... How is it all to end? Are we to go on, all of us pushing each other around, while the balance of payments gets worse and worse?...

Now the government must bear its share of the responsibility for this policy of 'freedom for all'.... If you create an atmosphere in which men are encouraged to assert sectional rights and individual claims, if you make it clear that your intention is that every man must be for himself and the devil take the hindmost, naturally everybody will exert himself to see that he is not one of the hindmost. But somebody must be the hindmost, nevertheless and ... the culpability of the government does not absolve us, the trade unions, from facing up to the consequences of our actions and accepting the responsibility which is ours in a situation of this kind. That is why the General Council, year after year, have emphasised in their Annual Reports the precarious nature of our economic position and stressed the importance of higher production and of better and newer production techniques. We realised that unless the situation were kept under control there would be a great effect on the standing and status of our members and a serious fall in employment and living standards.

W. L. Heywood (Dyers, Bleachers and Textile Workers), Chair of the Economic Committee, 7 September 1955, in TUC, *Report of Proceedings at the 87th Annual Trade Union Congress*, 1955, pp. 390–3.

2.2 Full employment and inflation

In 1956 the government issued the White Paper, *The Economic Implications of Full Employment* (Cmd 9725), which stressed that while most parts of the country had experienced full employment since the end of the war no satisfactory solution had been found for the problem of 'continually rising prices'.

26. In order to maintain full employment the government must ensure that the level of demand for goods and services is high and rises steadily as productive capacity grows. This means a strong demand for labour, and good opportunities to sell goods and services profitably. In these conditions it is open to employers to grant them [wage demands] and pass on the cost to the consumer, so maintaining their profit margins. This is the dilemma which faces the country. If the prosperous economic conditions necessary to maintain full employment are exploited by trade unions and businessmen, price stability and full employment become incompatible. The solution lies in self-restraint in making wage claims and fixing profit margins and prices, so that total money income rises no faster than total output.

The Economic Implications of Full Employment (Cmd 9725), 1956.

2.3 The trade unions and free collective bargaining

By the autumn of 1956 the trade union leaders were having to face the fact that the government (now under Sir Anthony Eden) would not intervene in the economy to plan it in the way which they hoped. Indeed, government policy under Harold Macmillan as Chancellor of the Exchequer (December 1955 – January 1957) was moving the other way. An essential part of Macmillan's April 1956 budget was the cutting of food subsidies, which resulted in rises in the cost of bread and milk.

At the 1956 TUC, when the General Council's annual report on economic policy was being considered, Frank Cousins, the new Secretary of the Transport and General Workers' Union, moved successfully a composite resolution which was vigorous in condemning government economic policy. Much of the resolution is printed below.

This Congress recognises the critical weakness of the national economy and places a large measure of responsibility for recent inflationary trends on the government's failure, after 1951, to maintain and improve the export trade. By abandoning economic controls on the plea of setting the people free, the government left the economy to drift and deprived themselves of the most effective means of recovering control in a crisis.

Congress asserts the right of Labour to bargain on equal terms with Capital, and to use its bargaining strength to protect the workers from the dislocations of an unplanned economy. It rejects proposals to recover control by wage restraint, and by using the nationalised industries as a drag-anchor for the drifting national economy.

Congress warns the government that major reliance on monetary controls cannot increase production where it is most needed, but must inevitably lead to erratic markets and damage over wide fields of industry. In this menacing situation, technological developments (including automation) must aggravate unemployment, unless there is re-established the foundations of a planned economy.

Part of composite motion, in TUC, *Report of Proceedings at the 88th Annual Trades Union Congress*, 1956, p. 398.

The motion does not portray a sudden upheaval of thought within the trade union movement. It is a cumulative development....

We accept ... that in a wage scramble some of the small unions would be distressed. But we suggest that they are distressed now.... We are a big union. We recognise ... that it brings its responsibilities. We shall play our part in helping those who may not be so numerically strong....

Now if you turn to the second paragraph of the motion.... We assert that right. We say that we want to preserve that right. We accept that in a period of 'freedom for all' we are part of the 'all'....

In the period while high profits are being taken and prices are being raised without any regard for the overall economic problem of the country – export markets – we shall do all we can to protect the rights of the people we represent.... Prices of bread and milk have gone up [for old age pensioners and] those on the unemployed register.... We will do everything we can to ensure that the benefit scales for those groups are improved....

In the second paragraph we say that we are determined to reject proposals to recover control by wage restraint.... We are not going out on a rampage....

The government has exerted an influence on the nationalised industries, particularly through the British Transport Commission, an organization which is running into debt. It has said to them, 'You must not put fares up, and the way to do it is not to give way to wage demands'. Let us tell them we are not playing. Let us say deliberately, 'This is ... not the view of the Transport and General Workers Union only ... this is the view of the whole trade union movement'.

Frank Cousins, 5 September 1956, in TUC, *Report of Proceedings at the 88th Annual Trades Union Congress*, 1956, pp. 399–400.

2.4   Calls for an impartial body to comment on wage claims

In 1954 a Court of Inquiry into engineering and shipbuilding disputes commented that such wage claims in themselves were not a threat to the economy but needed to be seen as part of a general annual pattern of wage settlements. These suggestions were repeated in two Courts of Inquiry in 1957 in the same industries (Cmnd 159 and 160).

144. We would ... add that during this Inquiry it has been borne in upon us that some of the issues that have been raised are essentially part of much wider problems affecting the national economy....

145. ... We do not believe that the sort of increase which we think is justified in this particular claim could by itself have disastrous effects, but it is part of a more general movement of wages, costs and prices.

146. Such a movement if continued, and particularly if accelerated, could conceivably undermine our whole economy. And there is apparently being established something very like an annual cycle of wage claims – a process which must surely tend to accelerate the movement. The circumstances that give rise to this and its probable effects might well be examined.

147. We feel, therefore, that it might be a most valuable contribution to a solution of the wider problems to which we have referred if an authoritative and impartial body were appointed to consider them and the complex and sometimes conflicting economic arguments which surround them, to form a view upon their implication for the national economy and our ability to maintain our present standards, and to give advice and guidance as to broad policy and possible action.

Court of Inquiry into a dispute between employers who are members of the Engineering and Allied Employers' National Federation and workmen who are members of trades unions affiliated to the Confederation of Shipbuilding and Engineering Unions, *Report* (Cmd 9084), 1954, pp. 47–8.

2.5 The Council on Prices, Productivity and Incomes

This was set up by Peter Thorneycroft, Chancellor of the Exchequer. It consisted initially of a judge, Lord Cohen, an accountant, Sir Harold Howitt, and an economist, Sir Dennis Robertson ('The Three Wise Men'). Before accepting appointment Robertson made it clear to Thorneycroft that his views were likely to be highly controversial, that unemployment would need to rise in order to maintain price stability. Thorneycroft was equally emphatic that he had no difficulties with this. Harold Macmillan in his memoirs (*Riding the Storm*, London, 1971, p. 707) compared this policy with Harold Wilson's later use of the National Board for Prices and Incomes: 'In each case the government tried to rely upon the authority of these supposedly impartial men to sustain their policy'.

[Terms of reference, August 1957]

1. ... Having regard to the desirability of full employment and increasing standards of life based on expanding production and reasonable stability of prices, to keep under review changes in prices, productivity and the level of incomes (including wages, salaries and profits) and to report thereon from time to time.

[Analysis]

2. ... we think it right to point out from the start that some of the phrases which they [the terms of reference] contain are not very precise in meaning, and also that not everything which is 'desirable' is always fully attainable....

89. We do not believe that it is necessary, or even possible, to give confident answers to such questions as the following: What would have happened to wages in Britain during the last twelve years if, other things being unchanged, trade unionism had been non-existent or weak? What would have happened if, other things being unchanged, Britain had been self-supporting in food and raw materials? But it does not seem that policy need now be stultified by such inability to perform a completely satisfactory *post mortem* on the past. We have laid greater stress on the demand side of the story than some whose opinions we have studied. But we are well aware that, whatever *might* have been the case, the wage advances were in fact secured by workpeople organised in powerful trade unions and using, among many other weapons in their armoury, arguments based on preceding movements of the cost of living. That such unions exist and such arguments are used may have great importance for the near future even if it should be of less importance than some people suppose in explaining the recent past. Whatever its initiating cause, the habit of demanding large and frequent increases in monetary rewards grows by what it feeds on, and may be found to persist after any technical justification for it in the state of the labour market has passed away.

[Summary]

5. The increase in the cost per unit of home-produced goods and services and imports for the year 1956 compared with 1946 is attributable as to 49 per cent to extra wages, 19 per cent to extra profit income, 19 per cent to higher import prices and 13 per cent to extra

indirect taxes....

23. We consider the measures taken in September 1957 [a substantial rise of the Bank Rate and other squeezes on credit] ... were justified and indeed overdue....

27. The September measures must ... tend to lead to some rise in unemployment, but the figures available do not suggest that the rise has been such as to afford an argument for any general relaxation of the restrictive pressure. The percentage of unemployment has risen only from 1.2 per cent in January 1956 to 1.8 per cent in January 1958. It would not be alarming if it went somewhat higher.

28. We believe that the decline in intensity of demand will tend to moderate the insistence with which wage-claims are pressed.... We would ... hope that if any wage increases are granted in 1958, they will be substantially below the average of the last few years....

32. We have considered, but we cannot in present circumstances recommend, the reintroduction or introduction of physical controls over investment, price controls, subsidies or legislation enforcing dividend limitation or the repeal of the Rent Act of 1957.

Council on Prices, Productivity and Incomes, *First Report*, London, 1958, pp. 1, 27–8 and 52–3.

2.6 Responses to the *First Report*

> Those favourable saw the report as strengthening Thorneycroft's monetarist emphases in the government's policies, and some saw it as putting pressure on Macmillan to keep public expenditure in check after Thorneycroft's resignation. Others took a more critical view of the Council, one summed up by Sidney Pollard as a body 'to find respectable reasons for refusing wage increases' (*The Development of the British Economy 1914–1990*, London, 1992, p. 284).

... their counsel should not, for the moment, embarrass the government: it provides indeed a more effective justification of the policy of the last Chancellor of the Exchequer than he or its inheritor [Thorneycroft or D. Heathcoat Amory] ever has done....

Upon the issue that was presumably in the government's mind in appointing it, the council offers the required advice. A rise in wage rates in the current year sufficient fully to offset last year's rise of 4.6 per cent in retail prices would be much bigger than the increase in productivity in 1955, 1956 or 1957; it would therefore be more than the country can afford.

The Economist, 22 February 1958.

The only satisfactory feature of the report is the clear indication that the Tory policy of free for all only works if it is combined with unemployment. [At Eastleigh]

The 'three wise men' have produced not a scientific report analysing the situation objectively and presenting facts and figures. What they have done is to produce a political tract and because of that I say that what they have declared in this document has no authority whatever.... The views of the council on such matters as the appropriate level of dividends and rents and on the use of controls and subsidies have no greater validity than the views of any other citizen. [At Southampton]

Hugh Gaitskell, Leader of the Labour Party, speaking at Eastleigh and Southampton on 21 February 1958; *The Times*, 22 February 1958.

The council were given a difficult task for the question of what causes prices to rise happens to be one on which economists are at presently deeply divided.... Prices have (as the report itself points out) been rising since 1934. Yet in the first years of this period unemployment was between 10 and 15 per cent. It follows then, that even a level of demand low enough to cause very heavy unemployment is not by itself, and in all circumstances, sufficient to prevent prices rising. Does it not also follow that the report should have explained how a low level of demand would help now; and how much it would help? And if, indeed, it is not a reduction of demand alone which is going to make all the difference, should not more of the emphasis have gone on other things that have to be done also?

J. C. R. Dow (an economist), Letter, *The Times*, 9 April 1958. (Dow also wrote 'The Cohen Council On Inflation', *Economic Journal*, September 1958, pp. 610–27.)

What we condemn, above all ... is the view of the Council that we should as a nation try to remedy rising prices by consciously and deliberately cutting down our national production and leaving more of our national resources unused, and more of our people unemployed. That after all is what is meant by the damping down of demand which the Cohen Council has advocated and approved. We do not believe that in order to keep prices stable we have got to accept more unemployment. Moreover, we cannot accept the way in which the predominant emphasis has been put by the Council upon the influence of wages. Virtually everything else in the two reports is hedged around with 'ifs' and 'buts' or is the subject of vague recommendations and pious hopes, but the references to wages are quite specific and quite clear. They are likely to influence negotiations and arbitration and, indeed, it is the express hope of the Cohen Council that they will influence negotiations and arbitration.

C. Smith, Post Office Engineering Union, in the debate at the TUC on the *First Report*, in TUC, *Report of Proceedings at the 90th Annual Trades Union Congress*, 1958, p. 429.

2.7 The TUC on the economic situation in 1959

The 1958 TUC debate on the Council on Prices, Productivity and Incomes ended with a motion instructing the General Council 'to have prepared a report upon the economic condition of the country which recognises the need for maintaining full employment and improving the real standard of life of the people'. Hence in 1959 the General Council of the TUC prepared the report 'The Economic Situation'. The following passages are extracts from this report.

1. The objective of the Trade Union Movement's economic policy is ... to secure conditions in which working people can get, and be reasonably sure of keeping, suitable employment, and in which they can obtain real increases in their wages and real improvements in their working and living conditions. Its two elements are interdependent and the reason why trade unionists have on occasion put more emphasis on employment than on getting immediate improvements in wages....

2. There are other objectives of national policy which the Trade Union Movement may support either for their own sake or because they are linked with the Movement's essential aims. They include such aims as ... the more equal distribution of wealth, the narrowing of the gap between standards of living of recipients of social benefits and those of other people, paying our way abroad, the improvement of the living standards of the peoples of the under-developed countries, the maintenance of adequate national defence, and the extension and consolidation of social ownership....

3. Neither full employment nor improved living standards nor other desirable aims can be secured unless certain conditions, which are not for the most part within the control of trade unions, are satisfied. Essentially we must be able to buy necessary imports of food and raw materials, we must have an adequate rate of investment and must use our capital resources efficiently, and the government, employers and trade unions must want full employment and must therefore pursue active employment policies....

79. The economic crisis of September 1957 was the signal for a new policy of active and open intervention by the government in the course of wage negotiations. This new attitude was clearly stated by the Minister of Labour [Iain Macleod] in October 1957: 'Let me make it quite clear that we are not attempting to instruct arbitration tribunals ... but we do believe that the government has a duty to make plain to everyone concerned with these grave decisions what we believe to be the true economic facts that confront us'. This and other government statements at that time were widely regarded as an attempt to persuade arbitration bodies to accept the government's interpretation of the national interest when adjudicating on wage claims. There can be little doubt that speeches of this kind were designed as much for foreign as for home consumption: foreign holders of sterling had to be convinced that the new policy symbolised by the 7 per cent Bank Rate would be pressed home as forcefully as might be necessary to protect the reserves.

80. The full effects of this policy fell mainly upon the public services....

88. ... Perhaps the most alarming of its [government economic policy] consequences, apart from the fact that it must involve considerable numbers of people in spells (and not necessarily short ones) of unemployment, is that it must periodically destroy the confidence of industry and interrupt the process of economic growth....

96. ... The real danger is that Britain will be left behind in the competitive race for increased efficiency based largely on investment. It is clear that a higher rate of investment in private industry in the immediate future will depend on a higher level of demand, and that in fact there is room for increases in real consumption without putting undue strain on the economy.... There is enough industrial capacity lying idle now and enough potential for higher productivity to make possible particular improvements in wages and working conditions without fears of inflation....

101. One British worker in five, one in three in manufacturing industry, depends directly on overseas markets for his livelihood. Indirectly our dependence is much greater than this, for half our food and most of our raw materials come from abroad. More positive action is needed to increase exports, and the diversity of the experience of exporting industries in similar overseas markets, and of similar industries in the same markets, calls for a full inquiry by the government into UK export performance to find out where industry is failing to take advantage of its opportunities. Detailed study is necessary of such factors as delivery dates, sales techniques and the commercial policies of our competitors, as well as of relative prices.

TUC, 'The Economic Situation', *Report of Proceedings at the 91st Annual Trades Union Congress*, 1959, pp. 485–511.

2.8 Proposals for achieving wage restraint

The Council on Prices, Productivity and Incomes in its *Third Report*, July 1959, reviewed proposals that had been made for restraining the rise of money, pay and profits. These included price controls and a price commission to investigate price increases as well as setting up a national conference representing employers' associations, trade unions, the nationalised industries and the government. A further group of recommendations dealt with improving negotiation procedures.

Proposals for improving negotiating procedures in particular industries

(i) by restricting industry-wide bargaining to minimum rates and leaving each individual management to negotiate rates above this with the unions representing its employees;

(ii) by some means for automatically relating rates of pay to, e.g., productivity or profitability in particular industries;

(iii) by widening the terms of reference of Courts of Inquiry to enable them to take account of the effects of particular settlements on the public interest;

(iv) by drawing up a code of principles for the guidance of those concerned in pay settlements.

Council on Prices, Productivity and Incomes, *Third Report*, London, 1959, p. 53.

2.9 Wage drift and national plans

The Council on Prices, Productivity and Incomes included in its *Fourth Report* the following suggestions.

63. From the standpoint of the need to adjust the rise of money incomes to that of productivity, there are two areas on which we would focus attention, because it is in them that the traditional ways have in some cases lost control of present movements. One is the uneven rise of particular earnings and the distortion of the pay structure at the place of work. The other is the linking of settlements at the national level in an 'annual round'....

65. In the first area, we would call attention to two lines of development which have been suggested. One is to recognise the extent to which earnings are actually being fixed locally, and the greater bargaining power on the floor of the shop that goes with this, and make constructive use of them so as to provide a more orderly wage structure.... The other line is to increase the coverage and authority of national agreements....

66. The second area is that of the general rise of money incomes, both pay and profits, year by year. It is right that there should be such a rise so long as productivity is rising too, for higher money incomes are a way of distributing the gains of higher productivity.... The need, then, is not to stop the rise, but to see that it does not exceed the rise in productivity.

67. One suggestion is to have a projection, for a period ahead, of the extent to which productivity in the national aggregate may be

expected to advance. This projection would cover the production of goods and services of all kinds by the whole working population, and not the industrial sector alone. Such a projection could be related to a planned investment programme, and to forward assessments of manpower needs and resources. It could be an indicator of the anticipated pace of growth of the whole economy, and would be a guide for those responsible in their own particular fields for the planning of production, the fixing of prices and profit margins and the settlement of wages and salaries.

Council on Prices, Productivity and Incomes, *Fourth Report*, London, 1961, pp. 27–8.

2.10   Responding to Selwyn Lloyd's pay pause

> On 25 July 1961 the Chancellor of the Exchequer announced in the House of Commons that for wages and salaries 'a pause is essential as a basis for continued prosperity and growth' and would be applied by the government to the public sector. He went on to state, 'During the pause we must work out methods of securing a sensible long-term relationship between increases in incomes of all sorts and increases in productivity'. The next day the TUC responded by issuing a statement.

The result of the government's abdication from its duty to direct Britain's economic fortunes is that once more events have overtaken it, and a limited period of expansion is again to be checked by an uninspired formula of rebukes, threats and cuts....

The General Council are convinced that Britain's economic problems will not be solved except on the basis of planned expansion at home reinforced by rational measures to protect the balance of payments. They, therefore, welcome the Chancellor's insistence on the need to maintain productive investment and such steps, hesitant as they are, as the Chancellor is taking towards the selective limitation of bank advances and of private investment overseas and towards the reduction of military expenditure abroad....

The General Council have noted with interest the Chancellor's statement that he intends to discuss with both sides of industry the implications of setting targets for planned increases of output.... If the government is at last willing to give a positive lead towards the achievement of this objective the General Council will readily take part in a collective examination of how Britain's great potential can more effectively be harnessed to the service of its people.

TUC, *Report of Proceedings at the 93rd Annual Trades Union Congress*, 1961, pp. 257–8.

2.11 Forming the National Economic Development Council

From March 1962 the TUC joined the government and employers in discussing the running of the economy.

At the meeting between representatives of the General Council and the Chancellor of the Exchequer on August 23 [1961] ... the Chancellor sought to draw a distinction between the government's action to solve Britain's short-term economic problems, which he knew the TUC resented, and its longer-term proposals.... There were two alternative types of machinery. The first was a body with its own resources which could work and put forward a national plan. The second was a council of trade unionists, employers and independent persons under the chairmanship of the Chancellor and including some ministers, with an independent technical staff. The Chancellor said that he favoured the second type of organisation....

TUC General Council's Report, *Report of Proceedings at the 94th Annual Trades Union Congress*, 1962, p. 252.

I believe that the time has come to establish new and more effective machinery for the co-ordination of plans and forecasts for the main sectors of our economy. There is a need to study centrally the plans and prospects of our main industries, to correlate them with each other and with the government's plans for the public sector, and to see how in aggregate they contribute to, and fit in with, the prospects for the economy as a whole, including the vital external balance of payments....

I am anxious to secure that both sides of industry, on whose co-operation the fulfilment of our objectives must significantly depend, should participate fully with the government in all stages of the process. I hope they would ... obtain a picture, more continuous and comprehensive than has hitherto been available, of the long-term problems in the development of our economy; and this should enhance the value of new advice on, and efforts in, the search for solutions. They would also have better opportunities to help in the moulding of the economic policies of the government at the formative stage.

Letter from Selwyn Lloyd to the TUC and employers' organisations, 23 September 1961, reprinted in D. R. Thorpe, *Selwyn Lloyd*, London, 1989, Appendix B, pp. 458–60.

[Meeting with the Chancellor on 28 November 1961.] The Chancellor said that he was disturbed by the effects of the pay pause on industrial relations but he still believed that the policy was necessary. The sooner long-term planning got under way the sooner the policy of restricting demand could end and he hoped that the TUC would join the council which would enable it to have more influence on government policy....

[General Council's meeting, January 1962.] In deciding whether to accept the Chancellor's invitation the General Council considered carefully whether they would best serve the interests of the Movement by doing so. They were well aware that the government's proposal to set up the NEDC did not prove that the government was committed to economic planning as Congress understands it. Nevertheless, the General Council eventually decided that they should put to a practical test the question whether participation would give them a genuine opportunity of influencing the government's policies in ways which would help trade unionists.

TUC General Council's Report, *Report of Proceedings at the 94th Annual Trades Union Congress*, 1962, p. 254.

2.12   The creation of the National Incomes Commission, 1962

Faced with the failure of deflationary measures to lessen wage pressures in the economy, Macmillan decided in June 1962 to move to a formal incomes policy. After sacking his Chancellor of the Exchequer (Selwyn Lloyd) and six other Cabinet colleagues in July, Macmillan stated in the House of Commons (26 July 1962), 'An incomes policy is ... necessary as a permanent feature of our economic life' and announced the setting up of the National Incomes Commission to provide 'an impartial and authoritative view on the more important or difficult pay questions given by a body which can see the questions both as they affect individual interests and the nation'.

The parties concerned in a pay claim, including the government, could refer the matter to the National Incomes Commission, or the government could refer for retrospective examination any particular settlement.

In considering any such reference the Commission is ... required to have regard both to the circumstances of the case concerned and to the national interest, including in particular:

(a) the desirability of keeping the rate of increase of the aggregate of monetary incomes within the long-term rate of increase of national production;

(b) the desirability of paying a fair reward for the work concerned;

(c) the manpower needs of the service, industry or employment concerned, taking into account any regional or local differences in such needs, and the importance of securing the most efficient deployment and use of national resources including manpower;

(d) the policies and practices in the service, industry or employment concerned in such matters (where appropriate) as pricing, profit margins, dividends, efficient use of manpower and equipment, and organisation;

(e) the repercussions which a particular settlement in the case concerned might have in other employments.

National Incomes Commission (Cmnd 1844), 1962.

The Government was now attempting to expose the TUC to the attack that, in rejecting the proposal, it was acting without regard to the national interest or the interest of economically weak groups in the community. In fact the proposal was open to fundamental criticism on a number of grounds. First, it was based on a wrong assumption – that general restraint was needed on wages as part of a general anti-inflationary policy.... Second, the proposal was obviously aimed at maintaining the government's restrictive policies under a different guise and, at the same time, shifting on to the shoulders of a group of independent persons the opprobrium that attaches to such policies. Third, the proposal involved the Commission either acting as the government's agent or itself defining the national interest. But nobody can attempt to define the national interest without necessarily becoming involved in argument, in general and in particular terms, about a whole range of highly contentious issues. The Commission could not do that, nor could it apply in particular and often unique industrial situations, except in an unacceptably crude form, criteria of the national interest. Finally, the operations of such a Commission could have most undesirable effects on industrial relations by introducing hesitancy and uncertainty into voluntary negotiations, and limiting or even undermining independent arbitration.

While condemning the government's proposals the General Council did not deny that it is possible for incomes to get so much out of line with output as to raise costs and prices, or that at any one time some groups of people have a greater claim than others to improvements in their incomes. Nor is any group of trade unionists entitled (or indeed able) to pursue its own interests with complete disregard of the interests of the rest of the community – or of other trade unionists.

The TUC's response to the setting up of the National Incomes Commission, as formulated by the General Council's Economic Committee on 8 August 1962, in TUC, *Report of Proceedings at the 94th Annual Trades Union Congress*, 1962, pp. 469–70.

The Donovan Commission and diagnosing ailments of British industrial relations in the mid to late 1960s

The Donovan Commission represented a watershed in post Second World War trade union and industrial relations history. That something should be done appeared to be a political necessity to Conservatives and many Labour politicians. Agreement on what should be done was another matter.

The Donovan Report placed a strong emphasis on maintaining voluntarism and so on persuading people to change their procedures for dealing with industrial discontent. Unlike the Conservative Party's proposed remedies (see 3.9), the majority of the Donovan Commission called for government action but not the use of the law.

The Donovan Commission's proposal for the creation of an administrative body, a Commission for Industrial Relations (CIR), was taken up by Harold Wilson's Labour government and such a body was created (see 4.4). This was succeeded from 1974 by the Advisory, Conciliation and Arbitration Service (ACAS).

One area which received scant attention from the Donovan Commission was that of industrial democracy. This is discussed along with the Bullock Report in Chapter 6.

3.1 The Donovan Report on the system of British industrial relations: (a) the problem

1007. Britain has two systems of industrial relations. One is the formal system embodied in the official institutions. The other is the informal system created by the actual behaviour of trade unions and employers' associations, of managers, shop stewards and workers.

1008. The keystone of the formal system is the industry-wide collective agreement, in which are supposed to be settled pay, hours of work and other conditions of employment appropriate to regulation by agreement.

1009. The informal system is often at odds with the formal system. Actual earnings have moved far apart from the rates laid down in industry-wide agreements; the three major elements in the 'gap' are piecework or incentive earnings, company or factory additions to basic rates, and overtime earnings. These are all governed by decisions within the factory (or other establishment ...). At the same time, disputes procedures laid down in industry-wide agreements have been subjected to strain by the transfer of authority to the factory and workshop.

1010. The bargaining which takes place within factories is largely outside the control of employers' associations and trade unions. It usually takes place piece-meal and results in competitive sectional wage adjustments and chaotic pay structures. Unwritten understandings and 'custom and practice' predominate.

1011. These developments help to explain why resort to unofficial and unconstitutional strikes and other forms of workshop pressure has been increasing.

1012. This decentralisation of collective bargaining has taken place under the pressure of full employment, which in Britain has had special consequences because of the way our industrial organisations have reacted to it.

Royal Commission on Trade Unions and Employers' Associations 1965–1968, *Report* (Cmnd 3623), 1968, p. 261.

3.2 (b) The remedy (according to the Donovan Commission)

1019. The central defect in British industrial relations is the disorder in factory and workshop relations and pay structures promoted by the conflict between the formal and informal systems. To remedy this, effective and orderly collective bargaining is required over such issues as the control of incentive schemes, the regulation of hours actually worked, the use of job evaluation, work practices and the linking of change in pay to changes in performance, facilities for shop stewards and disciplinary rules and appeals. In most industries such matters cannot be dealt with by means of industry-wide agreements.

1020. Factory-wide agreements can however provide the remedy. Factory agreements (with company agreements as the alternative in multi-plant companies) can regulate actual pay, constitute a factory negotiating committee and grievance procedures which suit the circumstances, deal with such subjects as redundancy and discipline and cover the rights and obligations of shop stewards. A factory agreement can assist competent managers, many current industry-wide agreements have become a hindrance to them.

1021. Industry-wide agreements should be limited to those matters which they can effectively regulate; but there would be advantage in agreements between employers' associations and trade unions which set out guide-lines for acceptable company or factory agreements.... But if the basis of British industrial relations is to become the factory agreement, the change must be accomplished by boards of directors of companies....

1022. The Commission recommends that boards of companies should review industrial relations within their undertakings with six objectives in mind: [1] to develop comprehensive and authoritative collective bargaining machinery; [2] to develop joint procedures for the rapid and equitable settlement of grievances in a manner consistent with relevant collective agreements; [3] to conclude agreements regulating the position of shop stewards; [4] to conclude agreements covering the handling of redundancy; [5] to adopt effective rules and procedures governing disciplinary matters; and [6] to ensure regular joint discussion of measures to promote safety at work. In pursuit of these policies companies should welcome the exercise by employees of their right to join trade unions, develop positive management policies [on such matters as recruitment, promotion, training and retraining] and collect systematic information, which should be made available to workers' representative in so far as they may reasonably require it....

1024. An Industrial Relations Act should be passed. Companies of a certain minimum size [5,000 initially was suggested, but then progressively reduced] should be obliged to register their collective agreements with the Department of Employment and Productivity or if they have none to state why. This requirement would have a dual purpose: to emphasise that the primary responsibility for the conduct of industrial relations within a concern ... lies with the board of directors and to draw attention to the aspects of industrial relations which the public interest requires should be covered wherever possible by clear and firm company and factory agreements....

1025. The Act should provide for the establishment of an Industrial Relations Commission.... The Commission would, on a reference from the Department of Employment and Productivity, investigate and report on cases and problems arising out of the registration of agreements.... The Industrial Relations Commission should also consider problems referred to it concerning companies not large enough to be covered by the obligation to register agreements as well as carrying out inquiries into the general state of industrial relations in a factory or industry.... There would be no penalties for non-compliance with the Commission's recommendations, though this question would have to be reviewed in the light of experience.

1026. These proposals will assist an incomes policy to work effectively by exposing the whole process of pay settlement to the influence of policy. The functions of the Industrial Relations Commission and the Prices and Incomes Board are different but the work of each will assist the other.

Royal Commission on Trade Unions and Employers' Associations 1965–1968, *Report* (Cmnd 3623), 1968, pp. 262–4.

3.3 Donovan and multi-unionism

The Donovan Report discussed the problems arising from multi-unionism, which it stated took two forms (paragraph 672), and objections to the often suggested solution of industrial unionism, 'one union for all employees in the same industry regardless of occupation' (paragraphs 674–8). Alternative ways of responding to multi-unionism than industrial unionism are drawn from the Donovan Report's summary (1075–77).

672. ... First there is the common situation in which each one of the main occupational groups in the factory is organised by a different union – e.g., technicians, supervisors, clerks, operatives and various craft groups. Its essential characteristic is that while there are many different unions, each has a monopoly of a given group of work-

ers. The second type of multi-unionism arises when there is more than one union competing for membership within a given group of workers within a factory. Both types of multi-unionism are found together, but the second is less common than the first and mainly affects non-craft workers.

674. [Problems with industrial unionism].... In practice sectional claims can still arise within so-called industrial unions. Demarcation problems can exist within one union – as is still ... demonstrated by the Boilermakers Society. The absence of competition between unions is no guarantee of responsibility or against informal, unconstitutional, shop floor organisation divorced from formal union influence – as can be proved from the example of the docks....

675. ... Many workers, such as craftsmen, clerks or technicians, have an obvious interest in combining on an occupational rather than an industrial basis, so that they are free to take their transferable skills from job to job while remaining within the same union. Occupational unions, for groups of this kind, may in fact facilitate and encourage labour mobility....

676. Special problems arise if industrial unionism is taken to the point where it includes white-collar workers. White-collar workers appear to be more readily organised on an occupational basis. Moreover, an industrial union which represents workers in an industry which is contracting must inevitably decline along with the industry.... It can also be argued that new technologies are breaking down conventional industrial classifications, and many large companies now straddle traditional industry boundaries.

677. ... the really decisive objection to industrial unionism is a practical one. However defined, industrial unionism would involve a drastic upheaval in the structure of almost every major union in the country and virtually all expanding unions. It would, for example, mean the dismemberment of craft unions and of both the giant general unions (the Transport and General Workers' Union and the General and Municipal Workers' Union) and the cutting off of large sections of the membership of the Amalgamated Union of Engineers and Foundry Workers, the Union of Shop, Distributive and Allied Workers and the Electrical Trades Union....

678. It is certain ... that the trade unions will not voluntarily adopt the attainment of industrial unionism as it exists in the Federal Republic of Germany, for example, as their objective; and indeed the Trades Union Congress recently rejected it. Nobody has seriously sug-

gested to us that this reform can be imposed compulsorily by means of legislation, which would mean the end of free trade unions....

1075. There is scope for many more mergers between trade unions. It would in particular be useful to work towards the goal of one or at most two unions for the great bulk of craftsmen in engineering and in construction, and of one union for the printing industry.

1076. Apart from union mergers, the most practical way to reduce competition between unions for members in the same group of workers in a factory is for the unions concerned to conclude agreements on rights of representation. The major task here falls to the unions themselves, although they will need the co-operation of employers where questions of recognition are involved....

1077. It is suggested that the TUC should intensify its efforts to encourage the unions concerned to adopt closer working arrangements. The TUC should also consider adopting the principle of 'one union for one grade of work within one factory' as a guide for the future development of structure....

Royal Commission on Trade Unions and Employers' Associations 1965–1968, *Report* (Cmnd 3623), 1968, pp. 179–81 and 271.

3.4 Donovan and shop stewards and full-time union officials

> The Donovan Report proposed that the role of shop stewards in industrial relations should be more fully recognised and regularised.

1078. Trade unions should provide constitutionally recognised committees to perform many of the functions now carried out by unofficial shop stewards' 'combine' committees.

1079. The processes of union government should be altered to accommodate shop stewards and work groups more adequately. It is desirable for union branch organisation to be based on factories and for branch meetings to be held at the place of work. This will require the co-operation of employers. Union rules relating to shop stewards should also be revised in relation to such matters as elections, term of office, the filling of casual vacancies, the bounds of the shop steward's jurisdiction, his relations with other union officials and his place in the union's organisation.

1080. The reconstruction of industrial relations (and especially the growth of factory bargaining) will mean that more full-time union officials are required....

1081. So far as training is concerned, trade unions are urged to concentrate on developing courses for junior full-time officers ... and for shop stewards....

Royal Commission on Trade Unions and Employers' Associations 1965–1968, *Report* (Cmnd 3623), 1968, pp. 271–2.

3.5 Donovan and the problem of unofficial strikes

As with much else, the paragraphs concerning strikes argued for more information and for reform of procedures for dealing with industrial relations issues.

1044. Official strikes tend to be much more serious individually than unofficial strikes in terms of working days lost, but they are relatively infrequent and their number shows no consistent tendency to grow.

1045. Some 95 per cent of stoppages are unofficial, and unofficial strikes are becoming more common. About half concern wages and over 40 per cent concern 'working arrangements, rules and discipline' and 'redundancy, dismissal, suspension etc.', matters usually dealt with at workplace rather than at industry level.

1046. Investigation of unofficial strikes in the motor industry shows that the causes are complex and that employers and unions both bear a considerable responsibility. Above all, they have failed to develop adequate institutions in changing circumstances. Wages structures, the engineering industry's disputes procedure and trade union communications are all defective.

1050. The tendency to appoint inquiries into industrial relations problems which are able to examine long-term problems as well as immediate causes of dispute is welcomed, but in future the resources available to the bodies concerned will need to be increased. The Department of Employment and Productivity should have its own industrial relations research section....

1052. By far the most important part in remedying the problem of unofficial strikes and other forms of unofficial action will ... be played

71

by reforming the institutions of whose defects they are a symptom....

Royal Commission on Trade Unions and Employers' Associations 1965–1968, *Report* (Cmnd 3623), 1968, pp. 266–7.

3.6 Donovan and restrictive practices and training

> The problem of restrictive practices, part of the wider matter of the efficient use of labour and training, was also seen by the Donovan Commission as a matter which would be improved if the procedures of industrial relations were reformed.

1036. The formal system of industrial relations is especially ill-fitted to accomplish improvements in the use of manpower, since it offers no means for negotiating about the relaxation of restrictive practices enforced by work groups.

1038. Experience of productivity bargaining shows what can be accomplished by the conclusion of company and factory agreements. The proposals made for the reform of the collective bargaining system are therefore fundamental to the improved use of manpower. They will put in management's hands an instrument – the factory agreement – which, properly used, can contribute to much higher productivity; and the work of the Industrial Relations Commission can give an impetus to change and progress which has been lacking hitherto.

1039. Training is an area in which restrictive traditions have especially deep roots in British industry and where the pressure of technological advance makes the need for a radical change in outlook particularly urgent. The present craft system can be very prejudicial to efficiency and to the needs and aspirations of workers outside the craft, and the gathering speed of technological change will make it still more obsolete.

1040. Certain specific obstacles in the way of access to skilled work must be removed. 'Dilution' agreements, under which if craftsmen are not available other workers may do skilled work, should be revised so that 'dilutees' can become skilled workers for all purposes. As regards the training of women, a revolution in attitudes and in practical performance is needed from all concerned – education authorities, the Youth Employment Service, industrial training boards, the Department of Employment and Productivity, employers and trade unions.

1042. Once objective standards have been laid down, trade unions should revise their rules as necessary to ensure that no qualified worker is arbitrarily denied admission or the right to use his skills; any worker alleging that he is denied admission although qualified should have a right of appeal to an independent review body.

Royal Commission on Trade Unions and Employers' Associations 1965–1968, *Report* (Cmnd 3623), 1968, pp. 265–6.

3.7 The TUC's response to the Donovan Report

The General Council gave preliminary consideration to the Donovan Report before the 1968 Congress and held a meeting with Barbara Castle, the Secretary of State for Employment and Productivity, in July 1968.

[On the central thesis of the two systems of industrial relations.] Well-founded generalisations about particular industries became generalisations about the whole field of collective bargaining....

Another consequence of the adoption of this main thesis was ... that the Royal Commission had become primarily a Royal Commission on collective bargaining, very little was said about the role of trade unions in relation to the formulation of economic planning, or in general in relation to their wider social purposes.

The value of the central thesis was in pointing to the need to extend collective bargaining, in terms not only of the number of workpeople not yet covered by collective bargaining, but also in terms of extending the scope of collective bargaining itself....

A further positive merit of the general thesis was that if the emphasis was to be put on the reform of procedures and institutions, correspondingly less importance could properly be attached to the potential value of making existing procedures enforceable by law. That was precisely the view the TUC had expressed on the same question.

TUC, *Report of 100th Annual Trades Union Congress*, 1968, pp. 408–9.

The General Council's representatives said that the TUC attitude to the CIR [Commission for Industrial Relations] would be influenced by its powers and terms of reference. It was doubtful if the General Council would favour the establishment of a CIR if it were to be linked with the use of sanctions ... reliance on sanctions was not a viable alternative to reliance on the good sense of industry. A collective bargain was between employers and trade unions and its content could not be determined and imposed by a statutory body. If it were, it would no longer be a civil contract and a move in that direction would entail the creation of a whole labour code, with the State deciding the substantive terms of employment.

Representatives of the TUC General Council meeting with the Secretary of State for Employment and Productivity, July 1968, in TUC, *Report of 100th Annual Trades Union Congress*, 1968, p. 410.

3.8   The Engineering Employers' Federation's response to the Donovan Report

12. The Federation's main objection to this diagnosis [Donovan Report's] is the dramatic nature of the antithesis which is made between the formal and the informal system....

13. ... The purpose of recent national wage agreements in the industry is to establish reasonable minimum standards of pay for a standard working week. It has always been recognised and accepted as normal practice that actual wages paid will be fixed in the factories. The arrangements for collective bargaining over wages nationally and domestically are complementary, not conflicting. It is true, of course, that a greater difference exists today between nationally agreed minimum rates and actual earnings than was the case pre-war. The difference, however, is not, as the Commission suggests, due to any weakening in the authority of the Federation to control earnings (which it has never possessed), but rather has been created by economic circumstances and by the competition for labour at factory level in a period of full employment. Unregulated trade union activity at plant level has had a part to play in this situation.

14. In the Federation's view it is also strange to label as informal a system of negotiation which is provided for in the industry's formal procedure agreements, and which, in many factories, is indeed highly

formalised.

25. ... [The Federation] does not believe that the need for national agreements has in any way diminished. The disappearance of agreed standard conditions for the industry on such matters as working hours and holidays would greatly increase the disorder in industrial relations of which the Commission complains....

33. Comprehensive and more orderly factory agreements are unlikely to flow from a system of competitive bargaining in which one union is always trying to go one better than the other unions in the same plant. An essential prerequisite to orderliness is the existence of a workers' negotiating body which subordinates sectional interest or pressure to the interests of the workpeople as a whole.

44. Industrial agreements are rarely ideal in form but they are the best that can be achieved in a given set of circumstances. An agreement forced upon an unwilling party cannot in the long run be calculated to improve industrial relations.

45. The Federation's welcome for the CIR is only qualified by its apprehensions as to what this body might become if it were given legal powers....

Engineering Employers' Federation, *The Donovan Report: An Assessment by the Engineering Employers' Federation*, January 1969, pp. 10, 16, 19 and 21.

3.9 The Conservative Party and its alternative remedies

The Conservative lawyers' evidence to the Donovan Commission represented a Conservative view which wished to place industrial relations (and the trade unions in particular) into a firm legal framework. Many of the points made in their evidence went into the Heath government's 1971 Industrial Relations Act.

1. There should NOT be *compulsory* 100 per cent membership either of trade unions or of employers' associations. But maximum voluntary membership of both is supported.

2. The test of the existence in law of a trade union or of an employers' association should be whether or not it is registered with the Registrar ... there would be substantial inducements to register....

6. Trade unions and employers' associations should no longer remain exempt in fields outside trade disputes from the ordinary liabilities incurred either in contract or through committing, by themselves or by their servants or agents, some tort [tort is a private or civil wrong]....

8. The Registrar should be under duty to refuse to accept for registration, any trade union or employers' association whose constitution and rules failed, or ceased to comply either with the basic principles of being 'fair, reasonable and in the public interest' or with the prescribed specific minimum requirements....

10. There should be new industrial courts: (i) a National Industrial Court presided over by a High Court Judge or lawyer of equivalent or higher standing, sitting with an equal number of lay members taken from panels nominated by the Confederation of British Industry and the Trades Union Congress. (ii) Regional Industrial Courts....

11. Suggestions ... as to the working and the functions of these courts ... include, *inter alia*, suggestions that the court should (i) have power to grant injunctions for sixty day 'cooling off' periods at the instance solely of the government in a 'national emergency'; (ii) adjudicate on breaches of collective agreements; and (iii) hear and determine complaints by employees who allege that they have been unjustly dismissed.

12. The definition of a 'trade dispute' – upon which depends immunity for tortuous acts committed in contemplation or furtherance of a 'trade dispute' – should be narrowed to exclude 'sympathetic' strikes or lock-outs....

13. There should be no immunity for action taken in furtherance of trade disputes between workmen and workmen (demarcation disputes) unless and until such disputes had been referred to and investigated and reported upon by the new industrial courts.

14. The rights of 'peaceful picketing' should be clarified so as to prevent its use for the purpose of intimidation....

16. It should be possible for an employer or employers' association to make a collective agreement with a trade union to operate a 'closed' or 'union shop', but certain terms necessary for the protection of individuals should be implied by law into any such agreement.

19. There should be no protection under the Trades Disputes Act 1906 for those who broke or induced a breach of or combined to break a 'collective agreement'.

20. As a first step restrictive practices preventing the efficient use

of labour should be investigated and reported upon by a Commission similar to the Monopolies Commission in its early days. At a later stage the Industrial Court might be given jurisdiction to condemn such practices and to issue injunctions. The protection of the Trades Disputes Act should be removed from anyone acting so as to continue or preserve a condemned practice....

22. There should be a legal duty on employers to recognise and negotiate with a trade union which so desired, if the result of a secret ballot (held at the request of the employer) showed that a substantial proportion of his employees, of a particular grade or class, wished to be represented by that union. It is suggested that a 'substantial proportion' should be at least 30 per cent.

Summary of conclusions, *The Memorandum of Evidence Presented to the Donovan Commission by the Inns of Court Conservative and Unionist Society*, February 1966.

We intend to reform both British management and British trade unions.

Everyone is fed up with pointless strikes and outdated management. We reject the argument that there is a clash between the interests of management and workpeople. Higher wages, good profits and competitive products are in the interests of both. Efficient production and stable prices are what the customer wants.

First, we will be transforming industrial relations by introducing a new Act covering the trade unions and employers' associations.

Second, we will be turning the heat on restrictive practices by both management and labour so that men and women can do a decent job unhampered by the fears and restrictions which belong to another age.

Third, we want to see better job prospects with greater security of incomes and pensions in the new high-wage, low-cost economy.

Action Not Words: The New Conservative Programme, 1966.

4

Governments, legislation and the trade unions after Donovan, 1969–1976

The Industrial Relations Act 1971 stemmed from the Conservative policy developments of the 1960s rather than from the Donovan Report. *In Place of Strife* had its roots mostly in the Donovan Commission. After the Wilson government's failure to carry this policy in 1969, the aspects of reform which enhanced trade unionism and the voluntaryist conduct of industrial relations provided much of the content of the labour legislation of Harold Wilson's 1974–76 government.

The Industrial Relations Act 1971 attempted to bring about changes on a broad front all at once. This failed. The Conservative Party's legislation in this area under Margaret Thatcher and John Major, passed between 1980 and 1993, in contrast brought about legal changes in eight smaller measures which individually did not produce the scale of opposition that the 1971 Act had aroused.

4.1 *In Place of Strife*: its broad arguments

> *In Place of Strife* was a much talked about document, with a small part of it arousing hostility on the Left. Yet most of it appears to have been little read at the time or subsequently.

8. More recently [state] intervention has become much more necessary and pronounced. The State has laid down minimum periods of notice in contracts of employment in the Act of 1963. Action has been taken to serve improvements in the quality and use of labour by creating Industrial Training Boards and the Redundancy Payments Scheme, both financed by compulsory levies on industry. The government has

increasingly had to play a part in helping to tackle the industrial problems of the motor industry. Far-reaching reforms have been initiated in worker-management relations in the docks.

9. As a result of these and other developments both management and unions have come to accept, and in many ways positively to welcome, government involvement.... While often still voicing the doctrine of non-intervention, managements and unions have entered into a positive and mutually beneficial partnership with the state to secure common objectives. Indeed in their evidence to the [Donovan] Commission ... and in their representations to government, bodies representing both employers and trade unionists have urged further intervention and involvement – at least where they see it as advantageous to them. Demands have been made by employers for new laws to discourage strikes; requests have been put forward on behalf of trade unionists for minimum wage legislation and government action to force employers to recognise trade unions. In short the doctrine of non-intervention is not, and never has been, consistently preached. The need for state intervention and involvement, in association with both sides of industry, is now admitted by almost everyone....

12. It is not even true to say that the [Donovan] Royal Commission's inquiries and surveys reveal a state of general complacency and disinclination to change. Managements have in recent years successfully carried through some remarkable experiments in the field of collective bargaining – many of them connected with the growth of productivity agreements. Changes are taking place in trade union organisation. Indeed, there has probably never been a time when more amalgamation schemes and mergers have been under discussion by the trade unions of this country.... The government's proposals are designed to assist the forces of change and to direct them into the most constructive channels....

15. The deficiencies of Britain's system of industrial relations are reflected in the character of our strike problem. It is true that, in comparison with many other countries, Britain's strike record, if measured by the number of employees directly involved and the number of working days directly lost, is relatively good. But this does not mean that the industrial effects may not be more serious.... The typical British strike is unofficial and usually in breach of agreed procedure. Although it is often soon over, it comes with little warning and the disruptive effect can be serious. It is commonest in a small number of industries such as motor assembly and components, the docks and

shipbuilding. Other industries often have long periods without strikes, but they may suffer indirectly because of a strike at a key point of their supplies or services. This type of strike can cause far-reaching dislocation of work and at times takes place in complete disregard of its consequences for the community. These indirect effects are not reflected in the strike statistics.

17. The combined effect of such [unofficial strikes and a range of other problems] defects is to increase the feeling of many employees that they have no real stake in the enterprise for which they work. There are of course other factors too. Britain is passing through a period of rapid technological change. New processes and methods of production are combined with changing patterns of company owner-ship and management structure. Established jobs and ways of work are disappearing to be replaced by unusual and unfamiliar tasks in surroundings often equally strange. This naturally reinforces feelings of insecurity among employees and even management itself, and re-sults in lack of co-operation and resistance to change, especially if systems for dealing with legitimate grievances and problems of all kinds do not adapt themselves to the demands placed upon them. Efficiency suffers and the community pays.

18. Yet there can be no reversal of the forces of change. On the contrary, the government has taken action to accelerate change. This is necessary if Britain is to survive and prosper. But it means that we must make sure that employees have the opportunity to participate in influencing the direction of change, that we must overhaul arrange-ments for dealing with the consequences of changes as they affect all who work in industry, and that we must remedy the defects [in the system of industrial relations]. This requires policies to secure four objectives:

(i) the reform of collective bargaining;
(ii) the extension of the role and rights of trade unions;
(iii) new aids to those who are involved in collective bargaining; and
(iv) new safeguards for the community and individuals.

In Place of Strife: A Policy for Industrial Relations (Cmnd 3888), Janu-ary 1969, pp. 6–9.

4.2 *In Place of Strife:* proposals for an Industrial Relations Act

The White Paper included the statement that the government intended 'after further consultations, to introduce an Industrial Relations Bill' which would include 25 provisions, the most significant in the list are below.

1. To put a Commission on Industrial Relations on a statutory basis.

2. To require employers to register certain collective agreements and arrangements with the Department of Employment and Productivity.

3. To modify ... the Trade Union Act, 1871, to facilitate the direct legal enforcement, where parties wish, of agreements between trade unions and employers' associations, and to provide that agreements should only be legally binding if they include an express written provision to that effect.

4. To give trade unions the right to have certain sorts of information from employers, subject to safeguards for confidential commercial information.

5. If necessary, to facilitate the appointment of workers' representatives to boards of undertakings.

6. To establish the principle that no employer has the right to prevent or obstruct an employee from belonging to a trade union.

8. To empower the Commission on Industrial Relations to look into recognition disputes, and to arrange a secret ballot if it thinks this desirable.

9. To enable the Secretary of State, where the Commission on Industrial Relations recommends that an employer shall recognise a union ... but there is continuing difficulty, (a) to make an Order requiring the employer to recognise and negotiate with the union and, in default, giving the union the right to take the employer to arbitration at the Industrial Court; (b) to make an Order giving the union a similar right against an employer who is refusing negotiating rights and (c) if necessary to make an Order excluding one or more unions from recognition, with penalties for breach of the Order by either the employer or a union.

12. To provide for the Commission on Industrial Relations to make grants and loans for trade union development.

13. To enable the Secretary of State by Order to require those in-

volved to desist for up to 28 days from a strike or lock-out which is unconstitutional or in which for other reasons adequate joint discussions have not take place, and to require the employer to observe specified terms or conditions.

14. To empower the Secretary of State, where an official strike is threatened, by Order to require a ballot.

16. To introduce safeguards against unfair dismissal.

19. To require trade unions and employers' associations to have rules on certain subjects and to register.

20. To create a new Registrar of Trade Unions and Employers' Associations – the post to be combined for the present with that of Registrar of Friendly Societies.

In Place of Strife: A Policy for Industrial Relations (Cmnd 3888), January 1969, pp. 36–7.

4.3 Some responses to *In Place of Strife*

Many of them [the government's 25 proposals] meet long-standing demands of trade unionists and will definitely assist in improving industrial relations. Very few trade unionists could object to the setting up of a Commission on Industrial Relations.... It is time that workers received greater protection, especially if they are active trade unionists. The idea of worker-representatives on boards of directors is a step towards greater industrial democracy, although it is a far cry from full democratic management. Trade unionists certainly should have the right to more information, so that negotiations can be more meaningful....

The offending proposals come broadly under three headings:

1. Compulsory Strike Ballots for some official strikes. 2. The so-called 'conciliation pause' for unofficial strikes.... 3. Fines for trade unionists that can be paid on the basis of attachment to wages.

These proposals add up to a new type of interference by government in industrial relations. They signify a departure from previous cherished methods. In a sense, it is an extension of the state intervention begun in the Prices and Incomes Act, and is in line with the new concept of state control.

Eric Heffer, MP, in *New Outlook*, February 1969 and reprinted in his *The Class Struggle in Parliament: A Socialist View of Industrial Relations*, London, Victor Gollancz, 1973, pp. 112–13.

This may be a late conversion, almost a death-bed repentance, perhaps. But we do welcome it, and we shall support it.... We designed a complete set of clothes. We see that the government has taken some of the outer clothing, but we think that they have left off many of the most important foundation garments.

Robert Carr, Conservative spokesman on Employment and Productivity, *The Times*, 20 January 1969, p. 2.

---

1. The conciliation pause for dealing with unconstitutional strikes is totally inadequate. 'Fire brigade' actions of this kind can never be as effective in preserving order in industrial relations as the selective enforcement of procedure agreements in certain key industries, which is what the CBI advocated.

2. There are many proposals which will reduce management's ability to carry on its prime function – to manage. For example, the proposal that the status quo ante should be maintained when a dispute takes place will prevent a manager from getting on with his job and will provide an easy way of putting pressure on management to make unjustified concessions.

3. There is no strategy for reforming trade union organisation, structure and behaviour other than persuasion....

4. In considering trade union recognition problems the CIR should be as much concerned with producing an efficient trade union structure as with satisfying the demands of particular groups of men....

9. The government's proposal to encourage experiments in the appointment of workers' representatives to boards of companies is misconceived.

From the CBI list of nine deficiencies of the White Paper, *The Times*, 18 January 1969, p. 13.

4.4   The Commission on Industrial Relations

6. ... Our principal concern is not ... with finding an acceptable formula for the quick settlement of an immediate dispute but rather with the means, and methods and attitudes which will provide a permanent basis for resolving conflicts constructively.

7. Secondly, although we firmly believe that improved industrial relations can make a big contribution to better economic performance, we are not directly concerned with specific measures designed to secure improvements in productivity and efficiency or to relate pay to performance. Our aim is to promote orderly and reasonable ways of resolving the issues which constantly arise in regulating working relationships.

15. Two leading considerations govern our approach to our work. The first is our acknowledgement of the final responsibility of the parties for conducting their own industrial relations; the second is our conviction that change can often be secured by the availability of more factual information and by a deeper knowledge of the attitudes and beliefs of the other party....

31. [Trade union recognition].... Employees naturally have a collective interest in such matters as pay and conditions. In our view the task of management is most effectively and acceptably performed by recognising that interest, allowing for its organisation and expression and seeking to reconcile the interests of the employees with other aspects of management responsibility. We do not believe that where pay and conditions are determined solely by the management this means that there is no conflict of interest; it merely means that the method of resolving the conflict is by unilateral management decision. Such a system may produce good pay and conditions and be accepted without overt protest, but we think that more is to be gained in terms of efficiency and satisfaction when the employees concerned are actively associated with management in joint consideration of these matters.

Commission on Industrial Relations, *First General Report* (Cmnd 4417), July 1970, pp. 2, 5 and 9.

---

25. Our enquiries have underlined the need for more training of shop stewards, supervisors and other members of line management with the specific purpose of improving their understanding of the pro-

cedures they are required to use.

27. Most of our reports have recommended that the pattern of trade union organisation and activities within the establishment concerned should be rationalised. We have underlined the importance of clear definition by unions of the powers and duties of shop stewards and their relationship to full-time officers, in particular where several unions are represented and the pattern of trade union organisation is complex. We have also urged that communications between full-time officials, shop stewards and shop floor members should be improved; this may assist in particular a clear understanding by trade union members of the advantages and commitments flowing from agreements entered into on their behalf. We have also stressed that where negotiating rights are held by several unions they should co-ordinate their activities, particularly through the union side of joint negotiating committees.

Commission on Industrial Relations, *Second General Report* (Cmnd 4803), November 1971, p. 8.

4.5   The Industrial Relations Act 1971

Barbara Castle, speaking at the American Bar Convention in July 1971, described the Industrial Relations Bill as 'one of the longest and most complicated in the history of the British Parliament'. The Act itself had 170 sections and nine schedules (with a later Code). It repealed the whole of the Trade Union Act 1871, the Trade Union Amendment Act 1876, the Trade Disputes Act 1906 and the Trade Disputes Act 1965, as well as part or all of fourteen other Acts.

The 1971 Act was intended to improve industrial relations and thereby assist British industry's competitiveness. A (or perhaps the) major target of the Act was strikes, both unofficial and inter-union. By creating the Sole Bargaining Agency, which in certain circumstances gave a registered trade union sole and legally enforceable negotiating rights, it was intended to cut out many inter-union disputes and strikes over trade union recognition. Legally binding agreements were expected to strengthen centralised trade unionism by deterring shop stewards or other activists from overturning them locally. There were also two defined 'unfair industrial practices' which were so because they were 'unofficial' – i.e. not decided upon by trade union officials – as well as one (section 98) which aimed to outlaw sympathetic action. Strike-prone workplaces could be referred by employers, the government or the unions to the National Industrial Relations Court. The Commission on Industrial Relations would then seek to find a voluntary solution, but if it did not succeed in that a legally binding procedure could be imposed on that workplace.

5. Every worker shall, as between himself and his employer, have ... the right to be a member of such trade union as he may choose ... to be a member of no trade union or other organisation of workers or to refuse to be a member of any particular trade union or other organisation of workers; where he is a member of a trade union, the right, at any appropriate time, to take part in the activities of the trade union ... and the right to seek or accept appointment or election, and ... to hold office....

11(1) In this Act 'agency shop agreement' means an agreement made between one or more employers and one or more trade unions ... whereby it is agreed, in respect of workers of one or more descriptions specified in the agreement, that their terms and conditions of employment shall include a condition that every such worker must either (a) be or become a member of that trade union or of one of those trade unions ... or (b) agree to pay appropriate contributions [to it or them] ... or ... agree to pay equivalent contributions to a charity....

(3) [If the Industrial Court is satisfied that the application is *bona fide* and is not excluded by other aspects of the Act, it] shall request the Commission [on Industrial Relations] to proceed ... to the taking of a ballot....

13(1) If the result of the ballot ... is that either a majority of the workers eligible to vote in the ballot or not less than two-thirds who voted in it have voted in favour of an agency shop agreement, then it shall be the duty of the employer to take all such action as is requisite on his part....

34(1) Every collective agreement which (a) is made in writing after the commencement of this Act, and (b) does not contain a provision which ... states that the agreement or part of it is intended not to be legally enforceable, shall be conclusively presumed to be intended by the parties to it to be a legally enforceable contract....

37(1) The Secretary of State ... may make an application to the Industrial Court with respect to any particular unit of employment on the grounds that the unit suffers from one or both of the following defects ... : (a) the absence of a procedure agreement, or the unsuitability of such procedure agreement as may exist for the purpose of settling disputes or grievances promptly and fairly; (b) where a procedure agreement is in existence, recourse to industrial action (whether consisting of lock-outs, strikes or irregular industrial action short of a strike) contrary to the terms or intentions of that agreement....

(5) [If the Industrial Court believes that there is a case for believing that the unit is so affected, so that] (a) the development or maintenance of orderly industrial relations in that unit has been seriously impeded, or (b) there have been substantial and repeated losses of working time in that unit, the Court shall refer to the Commission the question whether the unit does suffer [from such defects] ... and, if so, what remedy ... is to be recommended....

41(1) At any time before the end of the period of six months beginning with the date on which a report [made by the Commission] ... is transmitted to the Industrial Court, any employer or trade union included among the parties to the reference may apply to the Industrial Court for an order....

(2) [The] Court shall make an order ... that ... those provisions [in the Commission's report] shall have effect as a legally enforceable contract, as if a contract consisting of those provisions had been made between those parties....

45(1) An application may be made to the Industrial Court for the reference to the Commission, for examination by them, of the following two questions relating to the employees of an employer ... : (a) whether a specified group of those employees should, as a whole, be recognised (or, if already recognised, should continue to be recognised) by the employer or employers as a bargaining unit ... ; and (b) whether ... a sole bargaining agent should be recognised by the employer or employers and, if so, what joint negotiating panel ... should be the sole bargaining agent in that bargaining unit....

49(1) Where ... the Commission have recommended ... that a particular organisation of workers or joint negotiating panel should be recognised by one or more employer as sole bargaining agent for a bargaining unit ... [either side can apply to the Industrial Court for such recognition, and the Commission would hold a ballot which would need a majority of those voting to be in favour]....

61(3) In this Act 'trade union' means an organisation of workers which is for the time being registered as a trade union under this Act....

67(1) ... [Any] organisation which (a) is an independent organisation of workers and (b) has power, without the concurrence of any parent organisation, to alter its own rules and to control the application of its own property and funds, shall be eligible for registration as a trade union under this Act....

78(2) The registrar shall ... enter in the provisional register every organisation which, immediately before the passing of this Act, is for the time being registered as a trade union under the Trade Union Acts 1871 to 1964.

79(1) In the case of each organisation which is entered in the provisional register, the registrar shall consider whether it appears to him to be eligible as a trade union or employers' organisation ... ; and if ... the registrar is satisfied that it is so eligible, he shall cancel that entry and register the organisation under this Act ... and shall issue to it a certificate of such registration....

96(1) It shall be an unfair industrial practice for any person, in contemplation or furtherance of an industrial dispute, knowingly to induce or threaten to induce another person to break a contract to which that person is a party ... [unless acting for a trade union or employers' association]....

97(1) ... it shall be an unfair industrial practice for any person, in contemplation or furtherance of an industrial dispute, to take or threaten to take ... steps....

(2) (a) calling, organising, procuring or financing a strike; (b) ... [or] any irregular action short of a strike; (c) ... [or] a lock-out [unless acting for a trade union or employers' association].

98(1) It shall be an unfair industrial practice for any person, in contemplation or furtherance of an industrial dispute, to take or threaten to take any of the steps specified [above] in section 97(2) of this Act if (a) he knows or has reasonable grounds for believing that another person has entered into a contract (not being a contract of employment) with a party to that industrial dispute; (b) his purpose or principal purpose ... is knowingly to induce that other person to break that contract ... ; and (c) that other person is an extraneous party in relation to that industrial dispute.

HMSO, *Industrial Relations Act 1971,* Chapter 72, pp. 3–4, 9–10, 11, 27, 29–30, 33, 36, 41, 54, 58, 65 and 76–8.

4.6   Responses to the Industrial Relations Act 1971

The Industrial Relations Act enraged the trade unions and was received coolly, or at least cautiously, by many employers, including the CBI.

The Labour Research Department (a left-wing body funded largely by the trade unions) produced detailed critiques of the initial Consultative Document (O. H. Parsons, *The Tory Threat to the Unions*, 1970), the Bill (O. H. Parsons, *Tory War on the Unions*, 1971) and the Act (LRD, *Industrial Relations Act 1971: Trade Unionist's Guide*, 1971).

The Bill ... makes legal provision for:

[a] a list of actions which are deemed 'unfair' and made unlawful, a list embracing a very wide range of normal industrial behaviour;

[b] a ban on the right to call unofficial strikes, prohibiting the calling of strikes on a number of 'unfair' issues and imposing severe limitations on official and 'fair' strikes as well;

[c] provision for collective agreements to be legally enforceable;

[d] severe restrictions on the rights of trade unions to organise and manage their own affairs and their relations with their members, rendering them liable to harassment by outside quasi-legal government bodies;

[e] a tight system of registration of unions, with a severe limitation on a wide range of normal industrial activity by groups of workers acting otherwise than by or with the authority of a registered trade union;

[f] severe restrictions on closed shops;

[g] a charter for the non-unionist;

[h] provision for setting up a new system of law courts to carry out the provisions of the Bill, with power to award damages against unionists and unions (such penalties to be enforced as civil debts with the ultimate sanction of imprisonment in default), to issue injunctions and to imprison for contempt of court.

Summary assessment of the Bill, O. H. Parsons, *Tory War on the Unions: An Analysis of the Industrial Relations Bill,* 1971, pp. 3–4.

Section 96 does not apply to a registered trade union.... The section is designed to catch the leaders of unofficial strikes and also affects unregistered unions and their officials, even if these officials are acting within the scope of their authority. It deprives these unions and their officials and members of the immunity which they have had for over 60 years under the Trade Disputes Act, 1906.

The cause of the strike is irrelevant provided that it is an industrial dispute. However outrageous or provocative the behaviour of the employer may have been, he has the right to sue the strike leaders in the NIRC [National Industrial Relations Court] and claim compensation for any loss he has suffered. [However, where] the court finds the action by the employer to any extent caused or contributed to the strike, it can reduce the compensation to the extent it considers fair.

Labour Research Department, *Industrial Relations Act 1971: Trade Unionist's Guide*, 1971, p. 10.

The Industrial Relations Act is a classic case of overkill, and consequently it will collapse....

The Industrial Relations Act is seeking to replace the sociological approach to industrial relations with a system of legal regulation which is irrelevant to the problems which actually exist in industry.

Vic Feather, Secretary of the TUC, speech to an industrial relations conference, London Graduate School of Business Studies, 20 December 1971; *The Times*, 21 December 1971, p. 13.

Mr Heath has followed a policy of provocative confrontation, calculated, contrived slogging matches, in order to buttress a disastrous ... economic policy.... Instead of seeking the path of reconciliation he has deliberately set out to channel all the problems, industrial and human, into a rigid pattern of misconceived and irrelevant industrial law. In place of conciliation and understanding, ministers taking a lead from him were acting as agents provocateurs seeking to involve judges and the majesty of the law in the consequences of unnecessary and dangerous confrontation deliberately provoked for political purposes....

His policy of gladiatorial bullfights with union after union has been ground into the blood-soaked sands with his inglorious defeat at the hands of the miners and railwaymen.

Harold Wilson, speech to the Conference of the Furniture, Timber and Allied Trades Union, 15 June 1972; *The Times*, 16 June 1972, p. 2.

The main effect of the legislation should be to stimulate the improvement of industrial relations by voluntary arrangements.... Resort by employers to the legal processes in the Act may well be less effective than good voluntary practices.... Only on rare occasions would you wish to involve the remedies available under the Act.

CBI, booklet for members, July 1971; *The Times*, 22 July 1971; also quoted in R. Taylor, *The Trade Union Question in British Politics*, Oxford, 1993, p. 192.

4.7   Responses to the Employment Protection Act 1975

The Industrial Relations Act 1971 was repealed by the Trade Union and Labour Relations Act 1974, which also enacted updated versions of measures dating from 1871–1964 repealed by the 1971 Act. As Harold Wilson's government was a minority ministry until the second general election of 1974, Wilson had to carry some of his proposals in a second measure, the Trade Union and Labour Relations (Amendment) Act 1975.

The Employment Protection Act 1975 provided some of the measures favourably discussed by the Labour ministers and the trade unions in 1969–70 and afterwards. It aimed to provide legal support for strengthening collective bargaining as well as to extend the employment rights of employees.

Were Mr Ted Heath to become Prime Minister in October, his government would immediately face a trade union crisis on top of the existing economic one....

Because a new Heath government is going to have to adopt a tough wages policy, it is right to be as generous as possible to the unions on all other fronts. Mr Jim Prior ... announced [on 21 August 1974] that the Industrial Relations Act will not be reintroduced, and that a new Tory government would not seek to change Mr Michael Foot's new Trade Union and Labour Relations Act....

Mr Prior also announced that a new Tory government would introduce a Charter of Rights at Work. This would give all workers statutory new rights, and is designed as a rival to Labour's planned Employment Protection Act, which will be unveiled in mid-September. The main difference between the two is that the Tories will give rights to all workers which Labour would confine to trade union members only. The Tories will also include measures to encourage higher voting turnouts in union elections. The main Tory rights will be:

[a] Union officials and other workers allowed time off during working hours.

[b] Unions to hold meetings during working hours on the employer's premises. The aim is to raise the numbers attending....

[c] Members to have more control over their unions. The Tories will probably retain their February plan for a postal ballot for union elections.... A desirable carrot here: the Tories should say that government will make cash available to finance electoral reform in unions, maybe meeting 60 per cent of the cost of postal ballots....

[d] Workers will have to be consulted by employers on all redundancies, sackings, mergers, takeovers, welfare schemes and disciplinary rules. This is to be the main thrust of the Tories' approach to workers' participation. All major companies will have to devise some machinery to carry out this consultation, although variations will be allowed. The operation will probably be supervised by an Industrial Co-operation Commission.

The Tories have, however, gone cold on the idea of worker-directors.... The Tories would encourage more experiments, perhaps in nationalised industries, but they reckon that companies have enough on their hands already without having to cope with worker-directors.

'How should the Tories handle Hughie?' [Hughie being Hugh Scanlon, Secretary of the Amalgamated Union of Engineering Workers], *The Economist*, 24 August 1974, pp. 64–5.

Whilst recognising that parts of the ... Bill gave legislative effect to good industrial relations practice, [he] declined to give a Second Reading to a Bill which makes no attempt to establish a fair balance between the rights of management and unions, adds a heavy burden of cost without proper consideration of how it should be shared by employer, employee and state, and takes no account of the particular problems of small business....

The Bill contained no obligations on unions to avoid strikes, to keep to contracts, to respect the public interest, to promote greater efficiency through increased productivity, to provide more flexible training methods or to provide greater mobility of labour....

A more appropriate name for the Bill would be the Trade Union Benefits (No. 2) Bill.

Jim Prior, speaking in the House of Commons on the Second Reading of the Employment Protection Bill; *The Times*, 29 April 1975, p. 8.

─────────

The Employment Protection Act which was enacted on November 12 1975 contains a number of important provisions concerning remuneration during suspension from work on medical grounds; guarantee payments during short time working; maternity pay and leave ... ; guarantee of unpaid employers; contributions to pension schemes in cases of insolvency; and the administration of trade dispute disqualifications for unemployment and supplementary benefit.

The Act has also amended the Health and Safety at Work Act 1974, so as to bring agriculture within its remit and within the scope of the Health and Safety Commission.... The Health and Safety at Work Act is amended so that only independent recognised trade unions may appoint safety representatives at the place of work.

Summary of the Act in TUC General Council's Report, *Report of 108th Annual Trades Union Congress*, 1976, p. 136.

─────────

[Meeting of CBI, Small Firms Council, Engineering Employers' Federation and construction organisations with government representatives at the Department of Employment.] [They] accused the government of being totally under the influence of union interests. The Bill was described as 'completely one-sided'....

The clear suggestion from the employers was that what was happening to them under the Bill's present provisions looked like the reverse of what happened to the unions under the Industrial Relations

Act now repealed.

Fierce objection was taken to the clauses relating to recognition disputes taken by unions to the Advisory, Conciliation and Arbitration Service. The subsequent award would be binding on employers, but not on unions. This was unfair.

The sheer cost of providing new benefits and meeting clauses on low pay was ... attacked as inflationary. [So was] placing the burden of new maternity benefits ... on employers who had a high proportion of female labour.

The Times, 31 May 1975, p. 15.

5

Incomes policies, 1964–1979

The era of prices and incomes policies began with Selwyn Lloyd's 'pay pause' in 1961 (see 2.10), though there had been earlier attempts with the 'wage restraint' of 1948–50 (see 1.5–7) and the 'price plateau' policy of 1956–57 (see 2.2–5). The National Economic Development Council, set up under the Macmillan government, was consulted during the preparation of the Labour government's National Plan, published in September 1965. The economic assumptions behind the National Plan provided the framework for the trade union movement's co-operation with the Wilson government's prices and incomes policies. Initially, in 1964–65, these were voluntary. But from the autumn of 1965 the government decided to make notification of pay and price increases compulsory. After the sterling crisis of July 1966 the government imposed a six-month pay freeze and then a 'period of severe restraint'. From June 1967 the policy became less severe and the statutory controls were ended in January 1970.

Edward Heath's Conservative government (1970–74) came to office committed to not having a formal incomes policy. Nevertheless it did set pay norms and purposefully tried to reduce public sector pay rises (the 'N-1' policy). After the 1972 coal-mining strike, the government tried to secure TUC and CBI consent to a prices and incomes policy. When the TUC declined to be involved in working such a policy, the government in November 1972 introduced a statutory policy in three stages, beginning with a complete freeze. The policy ran into major problems, notably rapid rises in international oil and other prices and a further coal-mining dispute as the miners' pay improvements of 1972 had been eroded by inflation. The Heath government lost the February 1974 general election, at a time of soaring prices and wages.

The Wilson government (1974–76) reached agreement with the TUC to limit wage increases as part of a wider package of social measures, 'the Social Contract'. The TUC supported Phase 1 and Phase 2 of the policy but James Callaghan's government (1976–79) unilaterally set further wage limits under Phases 3 and 4 (1977–79). The policy crumbled in the winter of 1978–79, the so-called 'winter of discontent'.

5.1 The voluntary prices and incomes policy, 1964–1965

> After winning the 1964 general election, Harold Wilson formed a government which was committed to economic planning to secure greater growth combined with lower inflation. This it intended to achieve through consulting and securing the consent of the trade unions and the main employers' associations. A prices and incomes policy was a part of this strategy, and initially it was voluntary.

We, the representatives of the Trades Union Congress, the Federation of British Industries, the British Employers' Confederation, the National Association of British Chambers of Commerce accept that major objectives of national policy must be:

[a] to ensure that British industry is dynamic and that its prices are competitive;

[b] to raise productivity and efficiency so that real national output can increase, and to keep increases in wages, salaries and other forms of incomes in line with this increase;

[c] to keep the general level of prices stable.

We therefore undertake, on behalf of our members:

[a] to encourage and lead a sustained attack on the obstacles to efficiency, whether on the part of management or of workers, and to strive for the adoption of more rigorous standards of performance at all levels;

[b] to co-operate with the government in endeavouring, in the face of practical problems, to give effective shape to the machinery that the government intend to establish for the following purposes:

(i) to keep under review the general movement of prices and of money incomes of all kinds;

(ii) to examine particular cases in order to advise whether or not the behaviour of prices or wages, salaries or other money incomes is in the national interest as defined by the government after consultation with management and unions.

Joint statement of intent on productivity, prices and incomes, in TUC, *Productivity Prices and Incomes. Report of a Conference of Executive Committees of Affiliated Organisations held on 30 April 1965*, 1965, pp. 9–11.

---

3. The ascertainment of the relevant facts will require considerable statistical and economic expertise as well as complete impartiality. This work will be done by the National Economic Development Office and government departments ... and the results embodied in reports submitted ... to the National Economic Development Council....

5. The government have discussed with management and unions the practical problems involved in establishing machinery to investigate particular cases of price and income behaviour and with their agreement now propose the setting up under Royal Warrant of a National Board for Prices and Incomes working in two separate divisions, to be known as the Prices Review Division and the Incomes Review Division respectively....

18. The government intend to give the voluntary method every chance of proving that it can be made to work. Accordingly, in the case of both prices and incomes, persuasion and the pressure of public opinion will be relied upon to ensure that the findings and recommendations of the Board are accepted by the parties concerned. The government would resort to other methods only if they were convinced that the voluntary method had failed.

Machinery of Prices and Incomes Policy (Cmnd 2577), 1965, pp. 2 and 4.

---

11. The development of an effective policy for keeping increases in money incomes in line with increases in real national output will call for considerable efforts on the part of unions and management and all others concerned with the determination of incomes. The object must be to increase productivity and efficiency as rapidly as possible to raise real incomes and to avoid, wherever possible, increases in money incomes that push up costs and prices. An important step will be to lay down a 'norm' indicating the average rate of annual increase of money incomes per head which is consistent with stability in the

general level of prices. In present circumstances the appropriate figure for this purpose is 3–3½ per cent....

15. Exceptional pay increases should be confined to the following circumstances:

(i) where the employees concerned, for example, by accepting more exacting work or a major change in working practices, make a direct contribution towards increasing productivity in the particular firm or industry. Even in such cases some of the benefit should accrue to the community as a whole in the form of lower prices;

(ii) where it is essential in the national interest to secure a change in the distribution of manpower (or to prevent a change which would otherwise take place) and a pay increase would be both necessary and effective for this purpose;

(iii) where there is a general recognition that existing wage and salary levels are too low to maintain a reasonable standard of living;

(iv) where there is widespread recognition that the pay of a certain group of workers has fallen seriously out of line with the level of remuneration for similar work and needs in the national interest to be improved.

Prices and Incomes Policy (Cmnd 2639), 1965, pp. 7–9.

The General Council [of the TUC] asked the conference of executives [on 30 April 1965] to endorse their approval of the Joint Statement of Intent on Productivity, Prices and Incomes and the succeeding statements on Prices and Incomes Policy because of their conviction that the economic circumstances of the country and the wider interests of workpeople established the imperative necessity of these measures.

In reaching that conclusion the General Council were guided by two major considerations. The government had declared its clear commitment to a plan for the revival of the British economy. The economic objective of that plan is to achieve and maintain a rapid increase in output and real incomes combined with full employment. Its social objective is to ensure that the benefits of faster growth are distributed in a way that satisfies the claims of social needs and justice. In this context the General Council took account of the fact that successive Congresses have accepted that, in conditions of full employment, it is possible for incomes to get out of line with output with the result that costs and prices go up. Whereas Congress has rejected solutions based on deflation and the creation of unemployment, it has recognised that a continued failure to keep costs down would itself inevitably result in unemployment. In view of the government's declared economic and social objective the General Council considered that it would be in keeping with the aims of the trade union movement to underpin the programmes by working out a policy for prices and incomes.

TUC General Council's Report, *Report of 97th Annual Trades Union Congress*, 1965, p. 292.

---

9. ... the Government, with the agreement of the General Council, issued the following statement on 2 September:

It is a matter of overriding importance that the policy on productivity, prices and incomes, which has been agreed with both sides of industry, should be effective....

Prices are still rising and pay claims are being settled well above the norm. There are too many indications of restrictive and wasteful attitudes on both sides of industry. From now on the policy must be applied more vigorously and with a greater sense of urgency.

To this end, the government propose to give the National Board for Prices and Incomes statutory power to collect all necessary information and call witnesses to give evidence ... they will introduce legislation as soon as possible after Parliament resumes which will give them powers by Order in Council:

(1) to require notification of intention to increase prices or charges, and to require notification of claims relating to pay, hours or other major improvements and prospective terms of settlement;

(2) to refer to the National Board for Prices and Incomes in the national interest (a) any price, whether existing or proposed and (b) any claim or settlement;

(3) to require the proposed price or pay increases to be deferred until after the Board has reported.

The government's proposal will leave intact the essential voluntary principle upon which the policy is based. Settlements will continue to be reached voluntarily and prices determined by those concerned, but all responsible for taking those decisions will be expected to have regard for the national interest....

The General Council ... are prepared to recommend Congress to agree to the government introducing legislation ... [to] take power by

Order in Council to secure items (1), (2) and (3) ... The General Council agree that in the meantime they will use their best endeavours to make the prices and incomes policy more effective.

The First Secretary [George Brown] stated that the government would not make an Order to bring these provisions into effect unless they were convinced that they were necessary to make the prices and incomes policy more effective....

12. The General Council will ... proceed on the basis that effective action on their part involves the acceptance by affiliated unions of two specific obligations – to provide the TUC with the necessary information and to discuss with the TUC the action they propose to take in the field of wages.... The General Council wish to emphasise that, after the claim has been examined by the TUC, the union or unions will be free to proceed with it, but they will be expected to take into account such broader considerations of the national interest and of its possible effects on other unions as the General Council may draw to their attention.

Productivity, Prices and Incomes: TUC General Council's Supplementary Report, in TUC, *Report of 97th Annual Trades Union Congress*, 1965, pp. 565–7.

Clive Jenkins (Association of Supervisory Staffs, Executives and Technicians): Our problem is productivity, and every attempt to restrain incomes aggravates and adds to this inflamed, long-standing and neglected problem. Britain is a low-wage, high-cost economy. We want a high-wage, high-productivity, low-cost economy.

... Checks will be only on affiliated unions ... and every anti-union house union and staff association in the country can go merrily along with their wage claims.

... And some people will escape the net. All of us with long-term contracts will be all right.... And all of us with a cost-of-living escalation clause are all right.

... From voluntary inside the TUC we move to statutory notification, and a short step away from statutory notification of wage claims is statutory enforcement of wage and salary levels. I believe that that is unacceptable to free men, freely bargaining in a free society dominated by private enterprise still.

Joe Gormley (National Union of Mineworkers): We ought not to be discussing this question of wages policy in the light of the Labour government being in control, because whichever government is in control you are going to need a wages and incomes policy; you are going to need a national planned economy. I disagree entirely [with a previous speaker] ... that the only function of this Movement is to look after the people who are employed.... I thought we were here to try to raise the living standards of everyone, including those of our members who are no longer able to work because of illness, injury or even old age.

If we firmly believe this, we must do something about stopping the rapid increase in the cost of living which goes on year after year and which is never made up, however large the increases you get for the people who are working.

... People in the world will not just lend this country money to increase the social benefits which do not exist in their own countries.... We do not want this country continually running in the red and trying to live on borrowed capital which can mean that your policies are dictated to you as a result.... It is our job to get this country living within its means....

I think sincerely some of the statements that have been made are a shock to the whole trade union movement, because you are saying in essence that we have no intention of having a plan, we just support the free-for-all arguments ... which we have condemned so much from this platform.... If you support [a motion opposed to the General Council's policy] you are asking that we continue with the free-for-all society, the 'I'm all right, Jack' kind of person. If you want a planned economy, if you want something you can grasp with a view to trying to get the wherewithal to create the social benefits we so much need, then you will support the plan and support the Supplementary Report because it seeks to do it by voluntary means.

[The General Council's Report and Supplementary Report were adopted by 5,251,000 votes to 3,312,000.]

TUC debate, 8 September 1965, in TUC, *Report of 97th Annual Trades Union Congress*, 1965, pp. 482 and 485.

---

16. [Following the TUC's adoption of the General Council's recommendations the TUC received details of impending claims.] These

claims are examined by a special committee established for this purpose, consisting of one General Council member from each of the 19 Trade Groups of Congress.

17. ... In the great majority of cases, not more than five weeks or so at the most should elapse between receipt of notification and completion of the procedure. Until then unions will be expected to refrain from proceeding with the claim but thereafter they will be free to proceed, taking account of such consideration as the General Council may draw to their attention....

19. Unions and staff associations etc. not affiliated to the TUC will be expected to follow the same procedure, except that notification of all claims should be to the Ministry of Labour....

Prices and Incomes Policy: An 'Early Warning' System (Cmnd 2808), 1965, p. 6.

5.2   The National Plan (September 1965)

> The National Plan – 'prepared in the fullest consultation with industry' (as George Brown, First Secretary of State and Secretary of State for Economic Affairs, stated in its Foreword) – incorporated in its strategy a prices and incomes policy.

The most serious economic problem facing us at the present time is the balance of payments. We have to eliminate the deficit and repay the debts incurred in financing past deficits. This must be regarded as a first priority in any programme for greater economic growth. We shall only get the exports which we need to do this by becoming more efficient and competitive.... [The] immediate situation makes it essential that industry must plan its investment, manning and training in order to achieve this result. If industry is to do this, it must have a clear picture of the potential growth of the economy four or five years ahead.... Only in this way can Britain break out of the vicious circle of balance of payment difficulties and restrictions of output that keep plaguing us....

To make the plan work requires above all an acceptance of change. For the manufacturer, changes in what he makes, what he sells, and where he sells it; for the worker, changes in what he does, where he does it, and how he does it, and for all of us a different approach to prices and incomes. Change will often mean disturbance, and we must take care of the effect it has on individuals. But without change there can be no opportunities and no rewards.

George Brown, 'Foreword', *The National Plan* (Cmnd 2764), 1965, p. iii.

---

1. Planning for economic growth requires policies for price stability and for the orderly growth of money incomes....

2. Price stability requires that the growth of money incomes should keep in line with growth in real output. Over the last 10 years total output in the United Kingdom rose by an average of rather less than 3 per cent a year whilst money wages and salaries rose by 6½ per cent on average and gross profits and other incomes by 6 per cent. As a result the general price level rose by an average of 3 per cent a year. The rise in prices would have been greater still had not the terms of trade worked in our favour over the greater part of the period.

3. Over the same period of 10 years, the United Kingdom's share of world exports of manufactureds declined in value from 20 per cent to 14 per cent. Wage costs per unit of output in manufacturing rose faster than in the economies of several of our main competitors. Many industrialised countries are, with varying success, currently pursuing policies designed to secure price stability and to keep increases in money incomes in line with real output....

12. The scope for applying the prices and incomes policy in the remainder of 1965 is limited by past decisions or existing commitments. However, the machinery is now operating and the following references have been made to the National Board for Prices and Incomes: bread and flour prices; soap and detergent prices; road haulage charges; printing wages, costs and prices; salaries of clerical and administrative workers in electricity supply; salaries of Midland Bank staffs; London Electricity Board tariffs....

15. To be successful a policy for prices and incomes requires the co-operation of management and workers throughout industry. It needs to be accepted by all organisations and individuals concerned with prices and incomes decisions or being both in their interests and in the interest of the community as a whole.... The government recognise that a revolution in traditional practices and habits of thought cannot be accomplished overnight. There are transitional problems in moving from a state of affairs in which all are primarily concerned

with money incomes to one in which they are primarily concerned with real incomes.... The essential need is to ensure that the policy acquires increasingly greater momentum, and the government are continuing to discuss with both management and the unions ways of achieving this. The government have made clear that they will take any further steps which may prove necessary to ensure that the objectives are realised.

The National Plan (Cmnd 2764), 1965, pp. 65 and 67–8.

———————

George Brown: ... The Plan is designed to achieve four main objectives. The first is to put right the balance of payments. Everything else we hope to do depends on this. The second is to speed up the rate of growth. Our target here expressed over the period 1964–70 is ... a 25 per cent increase....

The third objective is to secure a better regional balance of development, to put an end to the situation in which some parts of the country suffer from lack of jobs while others suffer from problems of congestion and overcrowding. The fourth objective is to ensure that the fruits of future growth are used in accordance with the needs of a civilised and just society.

House of Commons Debates, 5th Series, 718, cc. 1042–3; 3 November 1965.

5.3   The 1966 standstill

With the sterling crisis of July 1966, a statutory prices and incomes policy became an integral part of the government's emergency package of measures. The government had been moving this way as the voluntary approach had not been slowing down the rises in prices and incomes. In December 1965 George Brown had informed the General Council of the TUC that the government would be introducing its Bill to provide for a statutory warning system for intended pay and price rises. This Bill, however, fell with the dissolution of Parliament for the 1966 general election.

Another Bill was subsequently introduced, becoming the

Prices and Incomes Act 1966. At the 1966 TUC the debate on the government's policy illustrated well the clash between those adamantly in support of unrestricted free collective bargaining and those supporting planning (and a Labour government in economic difficulties).

[After the announcement on 20 July 1966 of the 'July measures', the General Council of the TUC saw the Chancellor of the Exchequer, James Callaghan, and then the Minister for Economic Affairs, George Brown, on 24 July.] The Minister [George Brown] stressed the importance of ensuring that the government's measures did not prevent the development of a planned economy, the attainment of more rapid growth and a long-term policy for productivity, prices and incomes. The main problem was to operate the wage standstill without prejudicing the prices and incomes policy. Had the voluntary policy been made to work the present difficulties would have been avoided.

The General Council's representatives drew attention to the inequities which the standstill would create and the difficulties it would face. It would perpetuate anomalies and unfairness between groups of workpeople and between wage and salary earners as a whole and people who received income by way of dividends, rents and so forth. It would lead to the dishonouring of agreements already made, including long-term agreements under which increments were due.... It would be bound to hit the hardest the lowest paid, many of whom had received no increases for 18 months, during which time the cost of living had risen considerably. If it applied to productivity agreements it would also impose a standstill on growth and modernisation, as well as on wages and salaries. Most important of all, it was unlikely to work. It would serve little purpose for the TUC to accept it if it was rejected in practice by groups in strong local bargaining position over whom neither the TUC nor the unions might be able to exercise control. If a sufficient number of such groups broke the standstill, perhaps by the threat or implementation of unofficial action, the sense of injustice on the part of the other workpeople would become so great as to make the standstill impossible to maintain. Even if it produced short-term advantages it ran the risk of prejudicing the voluntary incomes policy.

TUC General Council's Report, *Report of 98th Annual Trades Union Congress*, 1966, pp. 321–2.

[After two meetings with the Prime Minister on 25 and 26 July 1966 the General Council issued a lengthy statement of its policy.]

11. The choice before the General Council ... was to recognise that, whether or not they acquiesced in it, the government intended to proceed with the standstill, and to agree, albeit with some misgivings, to do what they could to make it effective; or to reject, or at least wash their hands of, the proposal, and leave or perhaps even compel the government to impose it, which might well necessitate the use of more statutory sanctions and – which to the General Council was the most compelling consideration of all – lead to more extensive unemployment....

12. ... the main reason why the General Council decided that they should not leave the government to act unilaterally was that they believed that this was the best way in which they could best protect and advance the interests of trade unionists. The General Council believe that the operation of the policy must take account of the need to promote social equity, and in particular to protect groups of very low paid workers, that it must not inhibit the development of industrial arrangements which genuinely increase productivity and reduce costs, that it must involve at least as rigorous treatment of all forms of non-wage incomes, and that the government must deal firmly with unpermissable, open or concealed, attempts to increase prices.

13. The General Council therefore accepted the government's invitation to discuss how the problems which would arise from the imposition of a standstill could best be dealt with, and what amendments should be made to the Prices and Incomes Bill....

TUC General Council's Report, *Report of 98th Annual Trades Union Congress*, 1966, p. 326.

---

2. The country needs a breathing space of twelve months in which productivity can catch up with the excessive increases in incomes which have been taking place. The broad intention is to secure in the first six months (... the period to the end of December 1966) a standstill in which increases in prices or incomes will so far as possible be avoided altogether. The first half of 1967 will be regarded as a period of severe restraint in which some increases may be justified where there are compelling reasons for them, but exceptional restraint will be needed by all who are concerned with determining prices and in-

comes....

18. It is not intended that the standstill should be regarded as applying to

(i) increases in payments made in specific compensation for expenditure incurred, e.g. travel and subsistence allowances;

(ii) increases in pay resulting directly from increased output, e.g. piece-work earnings;

(iii) increases in pay genuinely resulting from promotion at work....

(iv) it is not intended that the standstill should interfere with the normal arrangements for increasing pay either with age, as with apprentices or juveniles, or by means of regular increments....

19. At the time of the Prime Minister's statement at least six million workers – one in every four – were expecting an increase in pay or a reduction in hours (or both) during the next twelve months as a result of a long-term agreement or other type of settlement made at some time in the past ... [These cannot go ahead.] Apart from the unfairness to other workers for whom no such future commitment at present exists, it would in practice have been bound to jeopardise the effectiveness of the standstill from the outset....

21. In all these cases the operative date should be deferred by six months....

Prices and Incomes Standstill (Cmnd 3073), 1966, pp. 2 and 4–5.

[Prices and Incomes Act 1966]

1(1) There shall be established a body to be called the National Board for Prices and Incomes....

2(1) The Secretary of State, or the Secretary of State and any other Minister acting jointly, may refer to the Board any question relating to wages, salaries or other forms of incomes, or to prices, charges or other sums payable under transactions of any description....

5(3) ... any report of the Board ... must be published ... within three months....

6(1) Her Majesty may by Order in Council....

(a) bring the provisions of this Part [Notices and Standstills] into force for a period of twelve months....

(b) from time to time extend or further extend that period by a further period of twelve months....

16(1) It shall be an offence for an employer to implement an award or settlement in respect of employment at a time when implementation of the award or settlement is forbidden under ... this Act....

(4) If any trade union or other person takes, or threatens to take, any action, and in particular any action by way of taking part, or persuading others to take part, in a strike with a view to compel, induce or influence any employer to implement an award or settlement ... at a time when [that] ... is forbidden under ... this ... Act, he shall be liable

(a) on summary conviction to a fine not exceeding one hundred pounds and

(b) on conviction an indictment to a fine which, if the offender is not a body corporate, shall not exceed five hundred pounds. [The same penalties were applied to subsection 1, the employer.]

The Public and General Acts, 1966, 33, pp. 1–2, 5–6 and 16–17.

Harold Wilson: If these measures [the government's economic policies] are to be truly used as a springboard for further expansion, if they are to be decisively differentiated from the stop–go routine, two conditions are essential, productivity and the prices and incomes policy.

... the biggest challenge facing the trade union movement in the productivity drive is the elimination of every avoidable restrictive practice, whether at national or workshop level. And the biggest problem here is overmanning, deliberately employing more men than are needed to do a job. In the long years of the depression, work-sharing, spinning out the work to make it go further, these were understandable. In the conditions we face today, so far from being a protection against unemployment they are the surest road to it. Equally they are the most effective bar to rising living standards. In a full employment economy, or near full employment economy, living standards can rise only by more output per man. This is a basic reality in any system of economic society, capitalist, democratic socialist or communist....

And what is true of overmanning ... applies equally to demarcation, the problem of qualitative manning. Here it is right to pay tribute to the largely unchronicled record of individual unions on demarcation problems in these past two years.... But there are still scandalous cases of who-does-what holding back production, and even frustrating the installation of new and revolutionary techniques in production....

The second condition of success is an effective prices and incomes policy. And productivity, here again, holds the key....

The period of restraint which follows the standstill must be governed by criteria which have still to be discussed with both sides of industry ... those discussions ... must cover, amongst other things:

[a] the role of pay and productivity agreements, where there is real productivity and not just a pious declaration of intent;

[b] they must cover the problems of those in public service, for example, where productivity tests are not appropriate;

[c] the problem of lower paid workers – in the interests of lower paid workers, not using lower paid workers as stalking horses to enable differentials to be invoked;

[d] the role, for wages as well as prices, of the newly strengthened Prices and Incomes board....

... Restraint in incomes, an incomes policy related to productivity, is our only guarantee against unemployment. If incomes ... rise faster than productivity, we are back in the old dilemma when industrial expansion and full employment go under as a result of a balance of payments crisis.... Over the past ten years every stop phase in the stop–go rhythm was marked by higher and higher unemployment figures....

A free-for-all is one thing. But full employment means planning.

The Prime Minister's address to the TUC, 5 September 1966, in TUC, *Report of 98th Annual Trades Union Congress*, 1966, pp. 397–9.

[Frank Cousins had resigned from the Cabinet in July 1966, when it had decided on a statutory prices and incomes policy.].

Frank Cousins (General Secretary, Transport and General Workers' Union): ... We are asking Congress to declare its opposition both to the freeze and to the Prices and Incomes Act under which this freeze is established. We also say that the procedures under this Act would impose penalties on trade union officers in the discharge of their normal trade union duties....

... I think it would be a tragedy if it [the debate] came down to one of personalities, if it came down to a question of whether it was the Labour Party versus the TUC or Harold Wilson versus Frank Cousins. It is nothing of the sort. It is in fact the continuation of a policy which my union put forward in the days of Ernest Bevin and Arthur Deakin, that you cannot control by legislation the activities of the trade union movement.

A. R. Akers (Confederation of Health Service Employees): ... We in the National Health Service have lived with a pay policy for more years than we can remember. The prescription was very simple: you got as little as possible as seldom as possible....

My national executive committee decided that the present scheme with regard to pay that we are suffering from in the National Health Service can be no worse, and in fact the prices and incomes policy can give us the long overdue justice to which we have looked forward for so many years....

My union is satisfied to trust this government, the General Council and all those concerned to see that when the freeze ends, as it will shortly, justice is done to the people who want it most.

[The General Council's Report on Prices and Incomes Policy was adopted by 4,567,000 votes to 4,223,000.]

TUC debate, 7 September 1966, in TUC, *Report of 98th Annual Trades Union Congress*, 1966, pp. 463 and 469–70.

5.4 The easing of the prices and incomes policy, 1967–1970

The Incomes policy was exceedingly unpopular among many trade unionists and Labour Party supporters. It was eased in stages, and lapsed in January 1970.

3. The national response to the call for a standstill has been extremely encouraging. Management and unions, with very few exceptions, have done their utmost to support the standstill....

26. During the first six months of 1967 ... the 'norm' for the annual increase in money incomes per head must be zero. Increases in incomes during this period will be justified only in exceptional cases where they can be shown to meet the following criteria for exceptions, and even then only on a severely limited scale....

27. [Productivity and efficiency.] ... the employees concerned should make a direct contribution towards increasing productivity, for example, by accepting more exacting work or a major change in work-

ing practices and some of the benefit should accrue to the community as a whole, in particular, in the form of lower prices or improvements in quality....

28. [Lowest paid workers.] Improvements of the standard of living of the worst-off members of the community is a primary social objective.... It will be necessary to ensure that any pay increases justified on this ground are genuinely confined to the lowest paid workers and not passed on to other workers....

29. [Distribution of manpower.] During the severe restraint period only in the most exceptional cases can a pay increase be justified in order to attract or retain manpower....

30. [Comparability.] Similarly, pay increases will not in general be regarded as justified ... on the grounds of comparison with the level of remuneration for similar work or on the grounds of narrowing of differentials. There may be exceptional circumstances in which some immediate improvement in pay is imperative to correct a gross anomaly....

40. [Criteria after June 1967.] ... it is the government's view that the country cannot at present afford any further reduction in the standard working week or general movement towards longer hours.... The recent tendency to seek improvements in pay or hours (or both) at intervals of 12 months or even less has added considerably to our economic difficulties.

Prices and Incomes Standstill: Period of Severe Restraint (Cmnd 3150), 1966, pp. 3, 7 and 9.

---

4. In considering the future development of the productivity, prices and incomes policy, the government have two main objectives:

(i) to create conditions favourable to sustained economic growth and to avoid the 'stop–go' cycle;

(ii) to work as quickly as possible, consistent with the considerations set out in (i), towards the operation of an effective policy on a voluntary basis in agreement particularly with the CBI and TUC.

5. The government have therefore welcomed the undertaking given by the CBI and TUC in their recent consultations with these bodies to play their full part in the development of an effective voluntary policy.... It is agreed ... that there will be need for continued moderation especially during the twelve months following June 1967....

20. In the present economic situation priority must continue to be given to economic recovery and the strengthening of the balance of payments.... Over the twelve months' period beginning 1 July 1966, no-one can be entitled to a minimum increase; any proposed increase ... will need to be justified....

21. The government consider that in applying the criteria to proposed increases ... the objectives of the policy will be best furthered if the following additional considerations are taken into account:

(i) ... For the future, twelve months should be regarded as the minimum period which should normally elapse between the operative dates of successive improvements for any groups of workers;

(ii) In some cases it will be appropriate for substantial improvements in pay or conditions, which may be justified under the criteria, to be achieved by stages;

(iii) the parties concerned should not seek to make good increases foregone as a result of the standstill and severe restraint....

37. ... experience of the standstill and severe restraint has shown the importance of having some limited reserve powers available. [These were developed in the Prices and Incomes Act 1967, and included powers to delay for up to a year some wage and price increases.]

Prices and Incomes Policy After 30 June 1967 (Cmnd 3235), 1967, pp. 2, 5–6 and 8.

---

3. Over the next two years it is of paramount importance for the national economic strategy after devaluation [the pound was devalued on 18 November 1967] to raise productivity and efficiency and to obtain substantial restraint from all sections of the community in order to keep incomes more in line with the expected growth of national output and prevent them from rising with the cost of living....

6. The new feature of the policy will be a ceiling of 3½ per cent on wage, salary and dividend increases. But the government wish to encourage agreements which genuinely raise productivity and efficiency, thereby helping to stabilise or reduce prices, and the policy provides for an exception to the ceiling for such agreements....

10. ... The government have decided to introduce legislation [which became the Prices and Incomes Act 1968] to replace the powers under the expiring sections of the 1967 Act so as to:

(i) lengthen the maximum delaying power on price and pay increases to 12 months in the context of reference to the NBPI [National Board for Prices and Incomes];

(ii) require reductions in existing prices where this is recommended by the NBPI;

(iii) moderate and phase housing rent increases;

(iv) require notification of dividend increases, and prevent excessive distributions.

The powers will be sought for eighteen months....

11. All these powers will be held in reserve, and will only be used to the extent necessary where the voluntary arrangements are not being properly observed. The notification arrangements for price, pay and dividend increases will be on a voluntary basis provided that they operate satisfactorily.

Productivity, Prices and Incomes Policy in 1968 and 1969 (Cmnd 3590), 1968, pp. 3–4.

---

10. The lesson of the past few years is that the use of a productivity, prices and incomes policy for short-term purposes can only have a short-term effect. The long-term role of the policy is essentially an educational one: designed to bring home the fact that continuing steady expansion of the economy depends on our striking the right balance between an immediate increase in consumption and the long-term needs of economic development. In doing so it widens the area of democratic choice....

35. In the next few years output per worker is likely to go up by about 3 per cent a year. Therefore, if we are to avoid a sharp increase in the cost of living money incomes should only rise at about this rate.... If productivity rises faster than expected then so can incomes.

36. This means that most wage and salary settlements fall in the range of 2½–4½ per cent increase in a year if this aim of greater price stability is to be achieved.... The appropriate level for a particular settlement within this range will depend on a variety of factors....

40. The factors are Productivity and Efficiency Agreements; Reorganisation of Pay Structures; Low Paid Workers; Equal Pay for Women; Labour Market Requirements; [and] Pay in the Public Services.

Productivity, Prices and Incomes Policy After 1969 (Cmnd 4237), 1969, pp. 6 and 13–14.

5.5 The Heath government's prices and incomes policies

The trade unions were not likely to support a Conservative government's prices and incomes policies after their increasing disenchantment with the Wilson government's policies. This was even less likely given the bitterness aroused by the 1971 Industrial Relations Act (see 4.5 and 4.6). However, Edward Heath was willing personally to consult the trade unions on economic policy and to go a considerable way in reassuring them of his concern to limit the rise of unemployment. The TUC attempted to resolve the 1973–74 dispute with the miners by undertaking to treat a settlement as an exceptional case.

At a meeting with the Prime Minister and other Cabinet Ministers on December 1 [1971], the General Council pointed to the need for a considerable increase in the rate of economic growth if the rise in unemployment was to be reversed.... Unions would not co-operate in productivity arrangements if these were only to result in further unemployment.

... [Early March 1972] The Prime Minister described the government's objectives as a sustained and steady expansion of the economy, with the prime need to maintain competitiveness and bring price rises under control. The latter point raised difficult questions in the field of collective bargaining and ways of settling disputes. The government had no preconceived notions about this and they were willing to discuss any proposals the General Council might make, including those set out in the TUC *Economic Review*....

The General Council replied that they were always willing to have discussions with the government, but that it was hard to see any meaningful dialogue taking place in the context of the Industrial Relations Act. Their main concern on the economic front was the high level of unemployment and the need for economic growth. Other countries had been able to sustain higher growth, not because of any restraint on incomes but because of a more effective investment policy and manpower policy....

... the General Council met the Prime Minister and other Ministers in July and urged him to repeal or suspend the Industrial Relations Act.... The Prime Minister suggested that a small working group of TUC representatives and government ministers should discuss, as a matter of urgency, the problems of conciliation, low pay, a link in collective agreements with the cost of living, and an improvement in the UK's competitive position.

... The General Council took the view that the proper forum for discussion of the economic situation was the National Economic Development Council, of which the Prime Minister was the chairman. In response, the Prime Minister called a special meeting of the NEDC on July 18 [1972].

TUC General Council Report, *Report of 104th Annual Trades Union Congress*, 1972, pp. 250–1 and 256–7.

At a meeting [of the NEDC] on September 26 [1972] the Prime Minister presented a statement on proposals on which he invited discussion. The government proposed to increase its commitment to achieve a 5 per cent rate of growth to cover the next two years, and would aim to keep the growth of retail prices resulting from cost increases within a limit of five per cent; manufactured goods would be kept in a price limit of four per cent. The government would be prepared to consider further action to limit price increases, where it had the ability to influence them.

On pay the government proposed that increases for a normal working week should be kept within a cash sum of £2 per week. In industries with incentive arrangements any changes negotiated should be so designed that pay did not rise by more than £2 a week for the same output. A new body should be set up to help the traditionally low-paid industries to achieve greater efficiency as a basis for higher wages. To deal with once-and-for-all factors which in 1973 could cause prices to rise by more than five per cent, the government proposed threshold agreements with a flat-rate amount of 20p for each increase of one per cent above a threshold of six per cent.

The Prime Minister said that pensioners should benefit from the reduced rate of inflation and that the government would be prepared to take appropriate action to ensure that in the coming year pensioners also had the benefit of a share in the nation's increasing prosperity....

... on October 10 [1972], the General Council drew up a set of counter-proposals....

The statement set out the need for price control ... plus effective price surveillance; the abandonment of the Housing Finance Act rent increases; measures to check the growth of house prices and halt land speculation; and renegotiation of the Common Agricultural Policy, concentrating on price reductions for cereals and holding down the price of potatoes and milk. The General Council said that the economic arithmetic produced a higher figure of £3.40 if the share of the gross national product going to wages and salaries was 62 per cent (the average of 1971 and 1972) and if a higher productivity figure were assumed.

The threshold trigger assumed by the government should be five per cent and, given the level of earnings, the compensation should be higher. The General Council outlined the problems for negotiators in applying the government proposals....

The General Council argued that more equity should be introduced by a wealth tax and a surcharge on capital gains; limitation of dividend payments; the prevention of betterment profits accruing to private property developers; and the reversal of the 1972 Budget concessions on investment and high earned income and estate duty. They stressed the need for higher pensions and a move away from means-tested benefits in favour of substantial increases in family allowances. The General Council asked the government to give an assurance of non-operation of the Industrial Relations Act....

... The Prime Minister stated that any agreement would have to be statutory on both prices and wages or voluntary on both prices and wages....

On November 2 [1972] at the NEDC meeting the Prime Minister reiterated his original proposals of September 26 and outlined a number of additional possibilities: a 50p increase in the needs allowance for the calculation of rent rebates; an extension of the award period for Family Income Supplements, free school meals and welfare milk from six months to one year ... ; a lump sum payment to those receiving national insurance retirement and supplementary pensions; and government consultation with local authorities on moderating the growth of local rates. The Prime Minister emphasised that there were certain matters such as accession to the EEC, the Housing Finance Act and the Industrial Relations Act which were essentially matters of government responsibility.

The TUC representatives ... said that there had been virtually no movement in the government's position since September 26. They told the Prime Minister that they could not make a positive recommendation to the General Council on the possibilities he had outlined.

On November 6 the Prime Minister announced that the government would be taking statutory powers to freeze prices and incomes.... The Counter-Inflation (Temporary Provisions) Act [1972] ... set out measures for an interim 90-day standstill (from November 6) on increases in wages, prices, rents and dividends.

TUC General Council's Report, *Report of 105th Annual Trades Union Congress*, 1973, pp. 274–7.

Stage Two [of Heath's prices and incomes policy]

[The General Council saw the Prime Minister on 4 January 1973] to protest at rising prices and to urge a return to normal collective bargaining.... He said that the government would take serious account of the TUC points, although any proposals for the second stage of the government's legislation would necessarily involve some limitation on the size of wage increases and impinge on the process of negotiation. The government were drawing up suggestions on the second stage which would be sent to the TUC.

These were considered by the Economic Committee [TUC] on January 10 and detailed criticisms were made to the Prime Minister at a meeting the following day, when the Economic Committee emphasised a number of general objections, in particular the combination in the freeze of strict control on wages and ineffectual control of prices....

[The Counter-Inflation Act 1973.] Two new agencies were set up – a Pay Board and a Price Commission – to regulate pay and prices according to a Pay and Prices Code, to be introduced by Order....

Prices. Most manufactured goods and services would be subject to control except exports.... Net profit margins would also be controlled. Distributors would be required to maintain their gross percentage margins rather than controlling prices as such.

Pay. In the Stage Two period total annual increases in pay for any one group of employees must not exceed the sum which would result from the payment of £1 a week plus 4 per cent of the current pay bill of the group excluding overtime. Within the total, negotiators would be free to decide how best to distribute the amount within the group covered by the settlement, but with an absolute limit of £250 per annum for any individual. Increases on payments by results and similar schemes due to increased output were to be allowed, but new productivity and restructuring schemes would have to be implemented within the limit. Settlements must not be made more frequently than at 12-month intervals. As a movement towards equal pay, settlements which are outside the limit but reduce the differential up to one third were allowed.

Dividends. Dividends declared for a company's account year would not be permitted to exceed dividends for the previous year by an amount greater than five per cent.

TUC General Council's Report, *Report of 105th Annual Trades Union Congress*, 1973, pp. 277–8.

Stage Three [of Heath's prices and incomes policy]
[In February 1973] the General Council agreed to accept an invitation from the Prime Minister ... to discuss recent developments in the economic situation. The General Council told the Prime Minister that they wished the government to reconsider its inflexible position on Stage Two. The Prime Minister said that there would be no exceptions in Stage Two. Any hardships or anomalies would be dealt with in Stage Three. He said that he was not seeking a confrontation with the trade union movement, and he accepted that the trade union movement was not seeking a confrontation with the government.

[Following a special Trades Union Congress held on 5 March 1973] the General Council wrote to all affiliated organisations on April 5 inviting them to join a day of national protest and stoppage on May 1 as part of a nationwide campaign on prices, pensions and pay.

[After an invitation from the Prime Minister, the General Council's National Economic Development Council members met him on 17 May 1973. Afterwards the General Council adopted a statement which included:] ... the General Council believe it is right to make further representations to the government for the restoration of voluntary collective bargaining to replace the present statutory framework. The lack of similarity between processes determining wages and salaries on the one hand and prices on the other has been vividly demonstrated by the period of the freeze. In the six months of the wages and salaries freeze, prices overall increased by nearly 4½ per cent, and food prices rose by no less than 9 per cent....

The modernisation of industry cannot develop without some incentive being allowed in payment systems, for example, in the context of restructuring industries and jobs....

[The Prime Minister met the General Council's NEDC representatives again on 13 June 1973.] On voluntary collective bargaining the government had to assess how far this was compatible with restraining inflation. On the problem of the low paid, the £1 plus 4 per cent formula was designed to help them, but it might be opportune to take up the proposal which had been in the 1972 tripartite talks for special machinery to examine low-paid industries.... The TUC said they were looking for a clear indication that progress was possible on the basis of the General Council's statement.

The Prime Minister said that the agenda was open and the government would be ready to introduce any agreed measures to Parliament.... The TUC would put forward its case under three main headings: the restoration of voluntary collective bargaining, including the non-operation of the Industrial Relations Act; prices, including food prices and rents; and social policy, including pensions and taxation.

[The TUC's proposals under these headings were put to the Prime Minister on 27 July and further discussed on 23 August 1973. There were two further meetings on 20 and 27 September, before the government on 8 October 1973 published a consultative document for Stage Three of its counter-inflation programme. A second Prices and Pay Code Order was made on 26 October covering prices for a year from 1 November and pay from 7 November 1973.]

On pay, the main proposals were: pay increases for the group up to seven per cent or, if negotiators preferred, up to an average of £2.25 a week per head for the group, with an individual maximum of £350 a year; a flexibility margin of a further one per cent which would be available for negotiators for use in settlements which removed anomalies and obstacles to the better use of manpower; extra payments under new efficiency schemes when they showed genuine savings and contributed to stabilising prices; to bring premium payments to those working 'unsocial hours' up to a minimum standard; to deal with anomalies created by the standstill; further progress towards equal pay; increases in certain types of London allowances outside the pay limit; a threshold safeguard to enable pay to be increased up to 40p a week if, during the year, the increase in the Retail Price Index reached seven per cent and by up to another 40p per week for every one per cent rise above that level.

[At the Prime Minister's request, TUC representatives met him on

22 October.] They explained why the government's proposals for maintaining statutory controls on collective bargaining were unacceptable to the TUC.

TUC General Council's Report, *Report of 105th Annual Trades Union Congress*, 1973, pp. 281 and 283–5, and *Report of 106th Annual Trades Union Congress*, 1974, pp. 218–19.

On December 13 [1973] the Prime Minister announced further restrictions on the use of electricity and a three-day week for much of manufacturing industry which was to come fully into effect on December 30.... At a special meeting of the NEDC on December 21 the TUC representatives tried unsuccessfully to get the government to abandon or at least postpone the introduction of the three-day week and in the meantime seek to obtain a settlement of the miners' dispute....

At their meeting on January 9 the General Council's Economic Committee decided to take an initiative to try and end the three-day week. They stressed the errors of the government's argument that a substantial improvement for the miners would automatically lead to similar increases throughout the whole of British industry. The pattern of wage settlements in other industries in the months succeeding the miners' settlement of 1972 was broadly what would have been expected if that settlement had not occurred. They further stressed that settlements have regard to the circumstances in particular industries and the merits of each case. However, to meet the government's fears ... the following assurance was put to the government at the NEDC meeting ... on the afternoon of January 9:

The General Council accepts that there is a distinctive and exceptional situation in the mining industry. If the government are prepared to give an assurance that they will make possible a settlement between the miners and the National Coal Board, other unions will not use this as an argument in negotiations in their own settlements.

[This was followed by a letter and by two meetings with the Prime Minister on 10 and 14 January 1974.] At the end of [the] second meeting on January 14 the government said it would take stock of the situation in the light of the TUC conference of union presidents and general secretaries which had been called for January 16 to discuss the oil crisis, the economic situation, the three-day week and the TUC's constructive alternative to the government's policies. This conference overwhelmingly endorsed the General Council's initiative. However, the Prime Minister told the TUC representatives at a meeting on January 21, that the government was unable to respond to the TUC initiative.... The Prime Minister would not indicate whether there were any circumstances in which the government would be prepared to use the powers it held in the Counter-Inflation Act to deal with a claim on an exceptional basis. The General Council said that the government had lost a major opportunity to get Britain back to work on a full-time basis.

TUC General Council's Report, *Report of 106th Annual Trade Union Congress*, 1974, pp. 219–21.

5.6 The Wilson government and the Social Contract, 1974–1976

In Opposition, Harold Wilson and his colleagues were left in no doubt as to the vigorous opposition of major trade union leaders to the advocacy of new prices and incomes policies. Jack Jones, General Secretary of the Transport and General Workers' Union, nevertheless pressed for greater dialogue between the TUC and the Labour Party. As a result the Labour–TUC Liaison Committee began meeting from 23 January 1972. After discussing industrial relations legislation it moved to discuss economic policy, including unemployment and regional policy.

In January 1973 the Committee issued a statement, *Economic Policy and the Cost of Living*, part of which included the proposals submitted to Edward Heath in late September 1972 (see 5.5, second extract). With the return of Labour to office, the General Council of the TUC published a statement, *General Bargaining and the Social Contract*, in which it listed the Labour government's extensive action on its programme of February 1973. It drew the attention of its affiliated trade unions to its recommendation to negotiators (paragraph 34). Led by Jack Jones, the TUC developed and supported the Social Contract.

6. The key to any alternative strategy to fight inflation is direct statutory action on prices – and, above all ... on ... food, housing and

rents....

13. ... wages and salaries in Britain have *not* increased faster than the average for industries countries. What *has* increased faster is wage costs *per unit of output* – a direct result of the small rise of output in Britain.

14. Both output and output per man depend very substantially ... on the quality and effective management of capital equipment, as well as up to date working methods. Yet Britain's capital equipment in many industries is rapidly falling behind the standard of our competitors. Fundamental to the British economic problem, therefore, is the problem of *investment* and, more generally, the problem of control and the disposition of capital....

17. A new approach is needed also towards much greater democratic control in all aspects of our national life and towards greater public accountability for decision-making in the economic field....

18. In some respects, as was pointed out by the Donovan Commission, the extension of collective bargaining to deal with questions of industrial efficiency must entail the further movement of bargaining in many industries from national to plant level. But equally there has to be a development of common lines of action at national level and, indeed, at international level in dealing with the great international corporations.

Liaison Committee with the Labour Party, *Economic Policy and the Cost of Living* (pamphlet), reprinted in TUC, *Report of 105th Annual Trades Union Congress*, 1973, pp. 312–13.

---

34. In summary, the General Council's recommendations to negotiators in the coming period are as follows:

(i) although the groundwork is being laid for increasing consumption and living standards in the future, the scope for real increases in consumption at present is limited, and a central negotiating objective in the coming period will therefore be to ensure that real incomes are maintained;

(ii) this will entail claiming compensation for the rise in the cost of living since the last settlement; taking into account that threshold agreements will already have given some compensation for current price increases;

(ii) an alternative approach would be to negotiate arrangements to

keep up with the cost of living during the period of the new agreement;

(iv) the twelve month interval between major increases should in general apply;

(v) priority should be given to negotiating agreements which will have beneficial effects on unit costs and efficiency, to reforming pay structures, and to improving job security;

(vi) priority should also be given to attaining reasonable minimum standards, including the TUC's low pay target of £25 minimum basic rate with higher minimum earnings, for a normal week for those aged 18 and over;

(viii) a continuing aim is the elimination of discrimination against particular groups, notably women; improving non-wage benefits such as sick pay and occupational pension schemes; and progress towards four weeks' annual holiday;

(viii) full use should be made of the conciliation, arbitration and mediation services of the CAS [Conciliation and Arbitration Service – soon set up as ACAS] to help towards a quick solution of disputes....

40. The General Council believe that much progress has been made in implementing the social contract, which was first envisaged in the TUC–Labour Party joint statement of February 1973. Since taking office, the government have demonstrated their commitment to implementing the agreed approach....

General Council, *Collective Bargaining and the Social Contract* (26 June 1974), reprinted as Appendix A to TUC General Council's Report, *Report of 106th Annual Trades Union Congress*, 1974, pp. 290–1.

Between May and July [1975] the General Council considered the form of a statement to Congress on the development of the Social Contract....

At their June [1975] meeting the General Council considered the first draft ... and they agreed six major points to be defined more specifically:

(i) a price target to be achieved by the middle of 1976;

(ii) a figure for pay, related to the achievement of this target in the form of a flat-rate money increase universally applied;

(iii) limits on very high incomes;

(iv) radical action to limit price increases involving the application of the Price Code, subsidies and action at the High Street level;

(v) a major reduction in the level of unemployment in 1976; and

(vi) the maintenance and development of the Social Contract as the fundamental basis of continuing unity between the trade union movement and the Labour government.

... A special session of the General Council was held on July 9 [1975] when proposals for the coming year and for implementing the Social Contract were approved. Those are contained in *The Development of the Social Contract* [selections as follows]....

49. Adopting a flat rate approach, fixing the pay limit at 10 per cent would give £6 a week to all full-time adults (aged 18 and above) up to a cut-off point, with pro rata payments for part-timers and juveniles. A flat rate approach has the advantages of focusing increases on the low paid and preventing unduly large cash increases being obtained by the high paid. It is clear and simple, most emphasises the General Council's view about the gravity of the economic and industrial situation and cuts through the complication of separate provisions for particular groups which, via comparability claims, has helped to weaken the previous policy....

58. ... those with incomes over £7,000 a year should forego any increase....

60. ... The aim should be that the Retail Price Index by autumn 1976 will be less than 10 per cent above the figure a year earlier....

91. It is not sufficient for the trade union movement at Congress to give formal endorsement to a report of this kind. Just as important as the formula itself is winning its acceptance by members and their negotiators. There is therefore a major job for everyone to do in ensuring that this understanding is disseminated to the ten million trade unionists.... There has to be an identification and a commitment to the action to follow.

TUC General Council Report and 'The Development of the Social Contract', *Report of 107th Annual Trades Union Congress*, 1975, pp. 272–3, 356–7 and 363.

Jack Jones (Transport and General Workers' Union): ... the General Council's policy and government policy has been to help the pensioners and help the low-paid workers and the housewives and ultimately to help ourselves and help the country in the battle against inflation and unemployment.... Prices are rising by 26 per cent per year.... It is estimated that our policy can reduce the rate of price increases to 10 per cent or less in 12 months....

Of course the economic mess we are in in this country is not all the fault of working people and the trade unions. Employers and governments over the years have been to blame in not dealing with the underlying economic weaknesses of our country. But that does not alter the need for us to help in breaking out from the disastrous trends facing the country. Let us face it, in recent months there has been a fantastic level of wage claims which would have meant 30, 40, 50 or 60 per cent in some firms. Arising out of fear for the future, yes, but they did affect prices and have affected jobs.

... Plenty of groups here in this Congress, including my own union, are well qualified and organised to look after themselves, but surely our policy is to use our general strength and influence to promote social justice, to bring about economic circumstances which will give all workers protection and the opportunities for advancement. Not a free for all but a fair for all – that is our policy. In my experience recently our best and most effective shop stewards and union officers up and down the country are increasingly accepting that these are times to moderate wage claims to preserve the unity of members, to avoid damaging setbacks and to save jobs....

The policy before you is an attack on low pay and at the same time it is a support for the Labour government.... It has tried to implement those sections of the social contract which formed the basis of its appeal to the electorate: to try to improve the lot of the pensioners, improve health and safety at work, improve the approach to sex discrimination and generally to move in the direction of social justice.

The policy before Parliament at the moment is also vital to us. The Employment Protection Bill is a workers' charter and the Industry Bill is essential; and real sacrifice would be justified to secure their enactment. At the same time there is a need to ensure that North Sea oil will serve the needs of the people and not the millionaires, and that requires the continuation of a Labour government. So I say to you we cannot afford the luxury of destroying the Labour government and handing power over to Mrs Thatcher....

[The Social Contract section of the General Council's Report and 'The Development of the Social Contract' were approved by 6,945,000 votes to 3,375,000.]

Jack Jones, 3 September 1975, in TUC, *Report of 107th Annual Trades Union Congress*, 1975, pp. 459–61.

5.7   The Callaghan government and the Social Contract 1976–1979

The £6 a week flat-rate policy of 1975–76 was the major contributor to reducing the rate of increase of earnings from an average of 26.9 per cent per annum in July 1975 to 12.9 per cent per annum a year later (while the Retail Price Index rose by 12.9 per cent over that year). In order to secure a second period of wage restraint Denis Healey, Chancellor of the Exchequer, offered £920 million of tax concessions if a pay policy in the area of 3 per cent was agreed by early June 1976. In the event a 5 per cent figure within a tighter package was agreed. The first extract provides the main elements of this. In the ensuing year earnings rose on average by 8.8 per cent while prices went up by 17.6 per cent. After this the trade union movement was unwilling, and probably unable, to agree to restrict its members to a third year of a fixed-wage policy, but it did provide guidelines for 'an orderly' return to collective bargaining: the second extract. In 1978 the General Council rejected the government's 5 per cent wage level and made clear its different views: the third extract.

18. The TUC's pay guidelines agreed with the government are set out below. These guidelines should be universally applied and the TUC will oppose any settlement in excess of them.

(i) It has been agreed that the guidelines for increases becoming operative in the period August 1, 1976 to July 31, 1977 should comprise a percentage increase of five per cent on total earnings for all hours worked with a cash minimum of £2.50 and an upper cash maximum of £4 per week. The figures will apply to all full-time adults (aged 18 and above) with pro rata payments for part-timers and juveniles.

(ii) This will be payable as an individual earnings supplement....

(iii) The twelve months' interval between major pay increases should continue to apply. Where no increase has been received since August 1, 1975 because of the cut-off requirements of the £6 policy, the normal negotiating date should apply.

(iv) All other improvements including non-wage benefits should be kept within the overall pay figure except as provided for in the current policy....

(v) Negotiators will be responsible for ensuring that earnings do not increase beyond these levels. Where unions experience difficulty in interpreting the guidelines in relation to their own negotiating situation, they should approach the TUC for guidance.

[A special Congress held on 16 June 1976 approved this Report by 9,262,000 votes to 531,000.]

TUC, 'The Social Contract 1976–77', printed in the General Council's Report, *Report of 108th Trades Union Congress*, 1976, p. 408.

---

1. For the past two years the trade union movement has operated an effective voluntary policy of restraint on wage settlements....

3. The reasons why the annual rate of increase of prices is still more than 17 per cent, nearly twice the rate the government had predicted, lie partly in the impact of international economic forces outside Britain's control ... but partly also in the government's inability to check the rise of prices in the shops....

5. The policy of restraint has itself given rise to problems in the field of industrial relations and wage structure.... Clearly action needs to be taken to relieve these strains, and the only way in which this can be done is through the process of voluntary collective bargaining.... There is no other method by which the necessary adjustments can be made to meet the complex and ever-changing requirements of industry and commerce ... both the TUC and the government have recognised that the withdrawal from the pay restraint policies of the past two years must be orderly and that a pay explosion must be avoided.

6. The basic way in which this can be ensured is by maintaining settlements made under the current policy of Congress. To re-open within the 12-month period settlements made under that policy would be a breach of the policy and unfair to other groups loyal to the Congress decision; it would also be a breach of the policy for negotiators to defer settlements due before July 31 [1977] in the hope of securing an advantage over other groups of trade unionists....

7. The General Council recognise that some unions may well come under pressure from sections of their membership to re-open existing settlements, but it is important that such pressure should be resisted

in order to avoid a possible chain reaction on other settlements made on the five per cent basis. Nor can there be any doubt that this basic requirement for the orderly restoration of collective bargaining could be put at risk if groups whose settlements still have some months to run were to see other groups demanding and achieving unrealistically high new settlements in the months after July.

8. It would certainly lead to great difficulties, both in terms of negotiations in the industry concerned and in terms of effects on other negotiations, if unions framed their claims on the basis of catching up, in money terms, ground which had been apparently lost since 1975 or 1974 – or, indeed, earlier....

14. The TUC has never equated the positive functions of the social contract with the negative features of wage restraint, and the restoration of voluntary collective bargaining must increase, not reduce, the determination of the trade union movement to continue to strengthen the framework of co-operation with this government on the basis of the foundations that have been jointly laid.

TUC, 'The Economic Situation and Pay', printed in the General Council's Report, *Report of 109th Annual Trades Union Congress*, 1977, pp. 227–9.

The General Council met the Prime Minister and other ministers on July 18 [1978]. The Prime Minister said that it was no part of the government's case that wages were the sole cause of inflation. Wages were one of a number of factors, including international pressures. Inflation would stay at 7–8 per cent for the rest of 1978 but what happened thereafter would depend on pay settlements.... He recognised that in view of TUC adherence to voluntary collective bargaining, there would not be a formal agreement or possibly even an understanding on the pay policy, but he hoped that the least that would emerge from the meeting would be a closer understanding of each side's positions and responsibilities.

The Chancellor of the Exchequer argued that current gains could only be maintained if inflation was kept down. Over the past year the UK's competitive position had deteriorated because of relatively higher UK pay rises and lower productivity. If pay rises remained at the current level inflation would almost certainly reach double figures, with consequent adverse effects on the £, interest rates, investment, output and jobs....

The Prime Minister ... said that there was not going to be any attempt to introduce pay legislation and the only weapons in the government's armoury were persuasion and public opinion. He took the view that each year it would be desirable for the government, the unions and the employers to reach an agreed view about the level of wage increases which would be appropriate.

On July 21 the government issued its White Paper, *Winning the Battle Against Inflation....* On pay the main points were as follows:

(i) apart from specified exceptions (below) the total increase in earnings for any group compared with the previous year should not be more than five per cent;

(ii) the 'kitty' principle is maintained to enable negotiators to shape their settlements in the best way suited to their needs, including restoring differentials where appropriate;

(iii) exceptional increases resulting from independent awards for a small number of public sector groups – firemen, policy, armed forces, university teachers and those covered by review bodies – can go ahead on the basis of the balance over the guidelines being paid in two equal stages at the next two annual dates;

(iv) there may also be a small number of other groups for whom similar treatment may be appropriate....

(v) to help the lower paid, higher percentage increases will be allowed where the earning outcome does not exceed £44.50 for a normal full-time week. This level represents the TUC minimum pay target of £30 in 1974–75 updated by the increases available under subsequent pay policies, including those in the present White Paper;

(vi) negotiators should respect existing annual settlement dates; although the government will be willing to consider synchronisation of highly fragmented bargaining situations in a few cases, provided the annual level of settlement takes account of the costs involved;

(vii) self-financing productivity schemes will be permitted....

(viii) the government welcome the TUC's initiative on overtime; and accept the scope for additional jobs in substitution for overtime at no increased costs and the scope for reductions in working hours without loss of earnings where revised shift arrangements or other working practices make possible the more extensive and effective use of existing plant....

(ix) improvements in other non-wage benefits must count towards the level of settlements, subject to the continuation of current exceptions for pension benefits, sick pay and job security.

The General Council considered the White Paper at their meeting on July 26 [1978] and issued the ... statement, 'Pay Policy After July 31': ...

2. The TUC fully shares the government's determination to win the battle against inflation but it does not accept the government's view of how this can be achieved. The objective of the trade union movement is to secure the maximum real increase in living standards for those in work and for people who are out of work and who have retired from work, at the lowest possible rate of inflation. Success in achieving a real rise in living standards in the coming year will depend not on pay guidelines or norms, but on the government's general economic and social policies and in particular on giving effect to the industrial strategy, and on the trade union response to those policies....

4. ... It has been on the achievement of higher levels of growth, productivity and real pay that stability in overseas countries has been based, not on policies which concentrate on restricting pay. The General Council are opposed to sanctions being applied to companies in the private sector which allegedly violate the guidelines. They are also opposed to the use of cash limits to restrict the pay of public sector employees.

TUC General Council's Report, *Report of 110th Annual Trades Union Congress*, 1978, pp. 289–91.

6

Workers' participation in industry

Workers' participation in the running of industry has been a major theme in British and continental European trade union history in the twentieth century. While those on the Left of Labour movements have derided anything short of workers' control, workers' participation has generally had much support in democratic socialist circles. Workers' participation has been advocated on the grounds of securing greater productivity, as part of workplace democracy and as a way of improving industrial relations in the workplace.

6.1   A critical appraisal of participation in a nationalised board

The Left has often seen workers' participation in running even nationalised industries as being detrimental, or irrelevant, to militant trade unionism securing the maximum for the workers.

Nationalisation from our point of view still presents us with the fact that the boards of nationalised industries in relation to the workers are the buyers of what we sell. The boards, in negotiating wages and conditions, are in effect buying labour as a commodity and we, the trade unions, are seeking to sell it under the best possible conditions. So that though the basic relationships as between the workers and the boards of nationalised industries may have been modified, the fundamental difference between the buyer and seller still remains after an industry has been nationalised: the boards must function as employers. We have had experience of three outstanding persons connected with this Congress, Walter Citrine, Ebby Edwards and Joseph Hallsworth, and we have no complaint to make against the manner in which they have endeavoured to interpret their trade union principles as functioning members of the National Coal Board. But in spite of their desire and inclination to be of service to the miners ... they, in the last analysis, are the employers and in relation to us have an entirely different function from that which we are called upon to perform.

Arthur Horner, leading Communist Party figure and secretary of the National Union of Mineworkers, 7 September 1949, in TUC, *Report of Proceedings at the 81st Annual Trades Union Congress*, 1949, p. 415.

6.2 The TUC and workers' participation in the control of nationalised industries

On 7 September 1948 the TUC debated and passed the composite motion reprinted below.

Congress welcomes the nationalisation of the basic industries of the country.

Congress expresses its concern, however, at the present composition of the boards of the nationalised industries and stresses the necessity for greater workers' participation, which can only be obtained from trade union ranks.

Congress believes that persons appointed to administer nationalised industries at all levels should be chosen on the basis of proved ability and belief in the policy of nationalisation. Extensive training schemes should be undertaken within the nationalised industries to develop administrative ability of a type which will ensure the success of nationalisation.

TUC, *Report of Proceedings at the 80th Annual Trades Union Congress*, 1948, p. 371.

[It is important] to see that we get the complete success of the nationalised industries for three very substantial reasons: (1) that we get as quickly as possible an economic reconstruction of the country so that we may be able to raise the standard of life of those we represent; (2) that we conclusively demonstrate the infinite superiority of nationalisation or national ownership and administration over a monopoly control; and (3) that we ensure the reaffirmation of the confidence of the people in the Labour Party at the next general election, because unless we do make a great success of nationalised industries we will leave ourselves open ... to a very serious attack on Labour's policy.

J. B. Figgins, National Union of Railwaymen, in TUC, *Report of Proceedings at the 80th Annual Trades Union Congress*, 1948, p. 371.

6.3   The revival of wartime joint production councils

The joint production councils of the wartime period were revived in order to assist economic recovery. The form of these councils was very explicitly voluntaryist, with very clearly limited remits. The General Council of the TUC approved in principle the revival with the following provisos.

(a) That such machinery should be purely voluntary and advisory in character;

(b) That it should not deal with questions relating to terms and conditions of employment which are normally dealt with through the ordinary machinery of joint negotiation; and

(c) That it should be left to each industry, through its ordinary negotiating machinery, to adjust the form of machinery best suited to its own particular circumstances and to decide, in particular, whether such machinery can best be established at the factory level or cover a wider area.

TUC, *Report of Proceedings at the 79th Annual Trades Union Congress*, 1947, p. 239.

6.4   A plea for extensive workplace democracy

In the post-war period the Union of Post Office Workers was in the vanguard of those wishing for greater workplace democracy. For postal workers this would have been to extend well-established consultation procedures. The union was among those civil service unions banned from membership of the TUC between 1927 and 1946 by the Trade Disputes and Trade Unions Act 1927. The union raised the issue of participation again at the 1956 TUC. In 1974–75 Tony Benn saw the Post Office as a good area for the extension of consultation.

[The trade union movement has to face] whether there is going to be control from the top downwards, or control from the bottom upwards. We believe that the workers of this country are capable of electing not only the political leaders, not only the trade union leaders, but also the leaders in industry, in the industry to which they belong. Out of their experience ... the workers have sufficient capacity to elect the best men for the job ... our people who have got to be at the [work] benches, who have got to do everyday work, are much more conversant with these things than they are with many of the more subtle questions of foreign policy.

G. Douglas, Union of Post Office Workers, 7 September 1948, in TUC, *Report of Proceedings at the 80th Annual Trades Union Congress*, 1948, p. 379.

6.5 The TUC and the development of workers' participation in the nationalised industries

After the 1962 TUC the General Council consulted the unions in the nationalised industries about their experiences of joint consultation and prepared a report in January 1963. In the report the General Council commented that 'one essential aim of joint consultation ... [was] improving relations between the workpeople and management at the workplace'.

3. ... Electricity supply and coal-mining ... have had very different experiences with joint consultation. The former has one of the best systems in the country, while the latter, largely because of its structure and history, has had a harder task in attempting to establish joint consultation as a dynamic process in the industry....

13. Although it is not possible to measure the success or failure of joint consultation in any but a rough and ready way most of the unions regard it as a useful device in promoting better industrial relations. Nevertheless it can hardly be said to have achieved all that was hoped for it at nationalisation.

14. The two chief complaints the unions make are of the

workpeople's apathy to consultation and the lack of influence which the unions are able to wield. To put these problems in their right perspective, it is necessary to recognise the limits of joint consultation as they have clearly revealed themselves during the past decade. Joint consultation is essentially an attempt to reconcile independent and to a considerable extent conflicting forces. (This has been recognised by the General Council in their rejection of more radical concepts of industrial democracy.) From this it is reasonable to infer that the area within which joint consultation takes place and the effectiveness of the process, at least from the unions' point of view, will tend to change as the balance of power between the two sides changes. The more powerful management becomes, the more likely it is that the joint consultative machinery will tend to become an instrument (perhaps a benign and paternalistic one) to dispose advice and information to the workers, while the more powerful the workpeople become the greater will be their authority in joint councils and the wider the area of consultation. As the NUM [National Union of Mineworkers] has put it, 'there is sometimes dissatisfaction that the joint consultation machinery is only advisory but the union is sure that its strength is taken into account by the NCB [National Coal Board] in arriving at its decisions'. It is true that enlightened management may under any circumstances draw on the experiences and seek the support of the trade unions and in the area in which the interests of both parties coincide realistic joint consultation may take place – that is, where the discussion turns on means rather than ends. But it cannot be assumed that all managements are enlightened and even where they are the interests of the two sides may conflict more often than they coincide. These considerations set the limits to joint consultation and show its relationship to collective bargaining.

TUC, *Report of 95th Annual Trades Union Congress*, 1963, pp. 276–9.

6.6   The 1964–70 Wilson government, workers' participation and improved productivity

Faced with serious economic problems, the Wilson government, like the Attlee government before it, had hopes that the widening of workers' participation would help it secure greater productivity in British industry. The economic development committees [EDCs], which had been set up under the National Economic Development Council, had their roles expanded, including being involved in implementing the government's National Plan. By 1967 these committees covered two-thirds of British manufacturing industry. In the EDC reports there was consideration of workers' participation along with greater job security being part of a package on offer in return for greater labour flexibility.

Having for some time been concerned about irregular attendance of some trade union members at meetings of certain EDCs, the General Council wrote to all trade union members in June [1965] emphasising the importance of ensuring that trade union interests are fully taken into account in the work of the committees.... Although they [the NEDC] recognised that it was desirable to establish EDCs first in the private sector, as it was there that machinery for consultation and a method of backing private decision-making with public purpose was largely lacking, the General Council have not regarded this as ruling out in principle the establishment of EDCs in the nationalised industries and other parts of the public sector. Their representatives have on a number of occasions raised this issue on the NEDC, citing in particular the case for establishing such a committee in the Post Office, which the unions concerned have strongly supported.

TUC General Council's Report, *Report of 97th Annual Trades Union Congress*, 1965, p. 300.

... [The] answer to our economic difficulties lies not in deflation to create unemployment but in the wisest use of our resources by economic planning for full employment....

The first essential of the realisation of that higher productivity ... may well lie in greater capital investment and in more efficient management, but neither of those will succeed unless those who are engaged within industry are themselves able actively to participate, appreciate and understand and have their place within the plan and within the economic development that is essential to higher productivity and to economic expansion....

R. Smith, Union of Post Office Workers, 9 September 1965, when moving a motion calling for an ECD in the Post Office, in TUC, *Report of*

97th Annual Trades Union Congress, 1965, pp. 529–30.

Although some have been more effective than others, the Committees [EDCs] have done a considerable amount of useful work, especially in defining some of the major obstacles to improved efficiency in their industries, and in publicising ways in which productivity can be increased. Weaknesses have also been revealed, however, especially with regard to the relationship between the EDCs and the firms in their industries. Communications between them is usually through the medium of trade associations, which in many cases are fragmented and inadequate for the purpose, and direct contact with individual firms is almost non-existent. Attempts have been made to correct these deficiencies by holding conferences attended by leading people in the industry and by developing less formal contacts. More thought, too, is being given to ways of improving contacts between the trade union members of the EDCs and the workpeople at shop-floor level in the industries....

[The Electronics EDC's] manpower working party has been particularly interested in seeing to what extent increases in productivity could result from the introduction of joint consultative practices and improved communications in firms, accompanied by greater job security, changes in job structure and measures to create a feeling of involvement amongst workers on the shop floor. The working party has called in various consultants to meetings to talk about experiments which they have undertaken in this direction....

[Paper and Board EDC.] A small working party was established to examine productivity and efficiency in the industry as a result of recommendations originally made in a paper by the trade union members. A report of its findings was published by the EDC, which made general recommendations about four-shift working, the limitation of overtime, the relationship between earnings and productivity, incentive bonus schemes, co-operation and communications between management and workers, methods of increasing the workers' sense of security in the face of change, and the establishment of an Industrial Training Board....

[The Chemicals EDC sent a team for three weeks to the USA and Canada.] The team concluded that output per head in the chemical industry in North America was three times as high as in Britain. The main reason for this is the much greater size of production units there, and the team recommended that British industry should urgently consider what steps it needs to take to rationalise itself in order to overcome this obstacle to higher productivity. Another important factor was the greater professionalism of American management, who operate with more precise objectives of performance than did British management.

The team found that on the labour side there was more flexibility between the various trades, and between craftsmen and production workers. American training is more effective than Britain's and there are no barriers to training or retraining up to ages as high as 45, even for craftsmen. The American worker also identifies more with his company than in Britain. Among the reasons for this are that the American chemicals industry offers a real career structure to its workers, pays more attention to safety, and devotes much more attention to keeping its workers informed. There are no barriers between staff and hourly-paid workers as are to be found in British industry.

TUC, *Report of 99th Annual Trades Union Congress*, 1967, pp. 344, 349 and 350.

[Jack Jones, Secretary of the Transport and General Workers' Union, ensured that there was a commitment to an Industrial Democracy Act in the Social Contract of 1974.] I wanted to avoid at all costs the sort of fiasco which occurred when Harold Wilson's government of 1966–70 experimented with industrial democracy in the steel industry. When the idea was first considered I personally urged on Barbara Castle and Dick Marsh, the two ministers involved, the need to ensure that the worker directors should be elected and accountable to the shop stewards, and through them to the workforce. Their reaction was that my idea was 'syndicalist', if not 'anarchist', and could not be entertained. In fact, as it worked out, the procedure became meaningless and patronising. The men who were appointed had to give up any active connection with their union. Indeed, in the early stages it was decided that the 'worker directors' should not operate in their own industrial group – as if a bus driver was appointed a director for the docks industry. As a result the 'worker directors' were virtually unknown to most of the workforce.

Jack Jones, *Union Man*, London, Collins, 1986, p. 313.

6.7 Jack Jones, the TUC and industrial democracy

Jack Jones, Secretary of the Transport and General Workers' Union, was the major trade union figure who took up the cause of industrial democracy. There were motions and resolutions calling for wider industrial democracy passed at the TUC 1967, 1968, 1971 and 1972. The second extract is the TUC General Council's comments on the report of a working party (which included Jones) on industrial democracy. The 1974 TUC adopted a final report, *Industrial Democracy*. Jack Jones and other leading TUC figures were influenced by the West German experience of industrial democracy and took pains to ensure that members of the Bullock Committee were aware of the system there.

[These are Jack Jones's comments when he moved a motion on 4 September 1968 which included 'Congress recognises that a much wider degree of industrial democracy ... can make a major contribution to higher living standards, employment security and industrial efficiency.']

Industrial democracy is a natural extension of trade unionism and starts with the right to negotiate on the issues I have mentioned ['Unfair dismissals, victimisation of active union members, arbitrary management decisions on promotion, discipline and redundancies ...'] and many others....

One weakness in labour relations has been the traditional distinction between consultation – telling people – as against negotiation. The drawing of a line between what unions can talk about and what they can negotiate about is quite inappropriate at a time when productivity bargaining has largely eliminated this division....

Workers are people on whom industry moves, not just voters to be called on at elections. Their interests, needs, skills, knowledge and intelligence could, and should, be involved in decision making. It is far too often suggested that they are not to be trusted to look rationally at the problems of a firm, that they are dominated by self-interest. What about the enormous number of directors representing financial interests, insurance outfits and the rest who sit on boards of private companies? They can be trusted. Apparently our people cannot.

TUC, *Report of 100th Annual Trades Union Congress*, 1968, pp. 531–3.

139

The [working party on industrial democracy] report begins by recognising that trade unions have already created a substantial measure of industrial democracy in this country, but new demands are now being made. Some of them can be met by establishing new areas of joint control and the extension of collective bargaining at the level of the workplace. Others require direct trade union participation in decision-making bodies at enterprise or national level.

Existing company law provides that management boards of companies are exclusively responsible to shareholders. This is out of date. The interests of workpeople are equally important and this should be recognised by fifty-fifty [per cent] representation on the supervisory boards of companies. The same principle should apply in the nationalised industries and there should be appropriate corresponding developments in the public services.

The central feature of all the report's recommendations is that progress in this field can only be made if representation is firmly based on trade union organisation. This is why the report comes out clearly against any general system of works councils, as these could only duplicate existing trade union arrangements at plant level or displace them.

TUC General Council's Report, *Report of 105th Annual Trades Union Congress*, 1973, pp. 304–5.

---

62. To be relevant, schemes of industrial democracy must be seen to be effective by workers at their own place of work. Yet some of the most basic aspects of the work situation, and the security of that employment, stem from decisions taken at extremely remote levels. This applies particularly to decisions on closures, redundancies, mergers and major redeployment. It is for this reason that any policy for the extension of industrial democracy must operate at *all* levels, from the shop floor to the board room, and indeed affect the process of national economic planning itself....

66. The main way to extend the area of joint control and limit managerial prerogatives of day to day management is to use the present structure of collective bargaining machinery to bring into the field of negotiations matters which are currently outside collective agreements. Coupled with parallel improvements in procedures, this can lead to a substantial extension of joint control over the immediate work situa-

tion. There is no logical reason why the collective bargaining process should only apply to the division of resources of the enterprise in terms of money wages. Already most collective bargaining agreements cover holidays and holiday pay. Plant, site and enterprise level bargains should be extended to cover recruitment, training, deployment, manning and speed of work, work-sharing, discipline, redundancy and dismissals; plus fringe benefits and aspects of job security such as pension rights (and the control of pension funds), sick and industrial injury pay, minimum earnings guarantees and so forth. Collective bargaining can also be extended to cover many aspects of work organisation and the working environment.

Industrial Democracy, in TUC, *Report of 106th Annual Trades Union Congress*, 1974, pp. 312–13.

When I visited the Federal Republic of Germany a little earlier this year, Chancellor Helmut Schmidt arranged a meeting which I could attend between members of the Bullock Committee ... and their German opposite numbers who already have 25 years' experience of worker participation. The Bullock Committee will reach its own conclusions and present them to the government. But I want to say that I came away from the meeting with the German Chancellor and the representatives of German employers and German workers convinced that the introduction of a system of industrial democracy into British industry must be given high priority when the Bullock Committee has reported.

James Callaghan, Prime Minister, 28 September 1976, in Labour Party, *Report of Seventy-Fifth Annual Conference of the Labour Party*, 1976, p. 187.

[Jack Jones, writing later about the Bullock Committee.] One of them [employer members], Barrie Heath, then chairman of GKN, enthusiastically backed a visit to Germany to study the operation of supervisory boards. He was not afraid of worker directors, at least of the sort he had on the boards of his German companies.

Jim Callaghan, I think, had similar views. He certainly admired Chancellor Schmidt, who in turn was enthusiastic about the German

141

co-determination system. They were both in Bonn at the time of the Committee's visit and arranged to meet us. Schmidt effectively refuted the idea that foreign investment would dry up if worker directors were introduced into Britain. On the contrary, it was clear to me that he thought the 'old school tie' was inimical to British interests and that worker directors would be a beneficial influence.

Jack Jones, *Union Man*, London, Collins, 1986, p. 314.

6.8 The Report of the Committee of Inquiry on Industrial Democracy (The Bullock Report)

Peter Shore, the President of the Board of Trade, announced in the House of Commons on 5 August 1975 his intention to set up a Committee of Inquiry 'to advise on questions relating to representation at board level in the private sector'.

[Terms of Reference]
Accepting the need for a radical extension of industrial democracy in the control of companies by means of representation on boards of directors, and accepting the essential role of trade union organisations in this process, to consider how such an extension can best be achieved, taking into account in particular the proposals of the Trades Union Congress report on industrial democracy as well as experience in Britain, the EEC and other countries. Having regard to the interests of the national economy, employees, investors and consumers, to analyse the implications of such representation for the efficient management of companies and for company law.

Committee of Inquiry on Industrial Democracy, *Report*, p. v.

---

3. The main TUC proposals are as follows:
(a) worker representation on the board to be a legal right which a recognised and independent trade union may demand;
(b) selection of representatives to be through trade union machinery;
(c) half the seats on the board to be occupied by worker repre-

sentatives;

(d) the provisions to apply (at least initially) to all companies and groups employing 2,000 or more people;

(e) responsibilities of worker representatives to be analogous rather than identical to those of shareholder directors, and their accountability and reporting back to their constituents to be safeguarded.

EEC policy

10. The view that social and economic changes require a new relationship between capital and labour has clearly played a major role in the development of industrial democracy in the EEC. The Green Paper [*Employee Participation and Company Structure*] said that 'employees are increasingly seen to have interests in the functioning of enterprises which can be as substantial as those of shareholders, and sometimes more so', and concluded that decision-making structures need to reflect this fact. Strong emphasis is put by the EEC Commission on representation of employees at the level of company boards as an integral part of a system of employee participation at all levels of the enterprise. The Green Paper puts forward no single blueprint for the form employee representation on boards might take, preferring a more flexible approach that might accommodate the different systems of member states. However, in the form of the Draft Statute for European Companies, a specific EEC Commission proposal for such representation does exist, and has stimulated comment in the evidence submitted to us.

11. ... The main provisions relating to industrial democracy in the Draft Statute are as follows:

(a) a two-tier system with a management board appointed and monitored by a supervisory board;

(b) the supervisory board to consist of one third shareholder representatives, one third employee representatives and one third members co-opted by the other two groups to represent general interests;

(c) the supervisory board to have rights of access to all management information and powers of veto over all proposals for closure or transfer of activities; curtailment, extension or modification of activities; major organisational changes and long-term co-operation with other enterprises;

(d) appointment of employee representatives to the supervisory board to be by a uniform system of indirect elections in all member states, with voting by all employees whether trade union members or not;

(e) a European Works Council on which all establishments within a company would be represented, with no functions overriding established collective bargaining machinery but with certain rights in relation to the management board: co-determination on matters of company employment policies and working conditions; prior consultation on matters subject to veto by the supervisory board; and information on a wide range of other matters.

12. ... In oral evidence to us, Commissioner Gundelach expressed the view that where more advanced types of industrial democracy had been implemented, the relationship between industry and the labour force had improved considerably and wasteful confrontation had been minimised....

The CBI proposal

13. The third proposal ... is different from those of the TUC and EEC Commission; in written and oral evidence to us the CBI was strongly critical of employee representation on the board based on any form of compulsion. The essence of the CBI's evidence, echoed in a number of other submissions, was a plea for flexibility in developing alternative forms of participation and for building on what had already been developed, free of any statutory right or obligation for employees to be represented on boards of directors....

15. Reflecting their concern with the different needs of companies, the CBI laid strong emphasis on the value of voluntary participation schemes:

[The following three quotations are from CBI evidence to the Bullock Report, paras 13, 19 and 21.]

'A fundamental principle ... on which proposals for greater employee involvement in company affairs must be based, is that participative arrangements must be designed to fit a company structure, and not vice versa. Moreover, such participative arrangements must be sufficiently flexible to accommodate the various forms of participation already in operation successfully, and to the satisfaction of all parties, in a number of companies.'

'Many large and small companies already successfully operate formal, but voluntary, consultative arrangements. The CBI favours this approach, and therefore proposes that the establishment of deliberative bodies representative of all employees should be actively encouraged in all firms of a size where they would be practicable and where the need for increased participation is felt.'

'The CBI recognises, however, that in larger firms where even over a reasonable span of time it might not be possible, for whatever reason, for voluntary agreement on the form of participation to be reached, it would be necessary for there to be a requirement of law to provide compulsory arbitration by an independent third party. This form of legislation would afford the maximum degree of flexibility possible, while providing considerable safeguards for the interests of industrial efficiency, as well as those of employees. The provision of an individual solution to the needs of the individual enterprise is essential.'

17. The CBI believe that the main focus of attention at present should be below board level participation. What is needed in their view is a gradual, organic development of industrial democracy from the shopfloor upwards. It is pointed out that the willingness of employees to participate needs to be nurtured at lower levels, where their interest and attention can be captured by discussion of ideas of immediate, direct import. The CBI evidence states clearly that in their view at the present time 'employee representation at board level will not usually be a suitable form of participation' [CBI evidence paragraph 28].

Summary of TUC, EEC and CBI proposals, Committee of Inquiry on Industrial Democracy, *Report*, pp. 26–31.

---

2. During our inquiry we found a widespread conviction, which we share, that the problem of Britain as an industrialised nation is not a lack of native capacity in its working population so much as a failure to draw out their energies and skill to anything like their full potential. It is our belief that the way to release those energies, to provide greater satisfaction in the workplace and to assist in raising the level of productivity and efficiency in British industry – and with it the living standards of the nation – is not by recrimination or exhortation but by putting the relationship between capital and labour on to a new basis which will involve not just management but the whole workforce in sharing responsibility for the success and profitability of the enterprise. Such a change in the industrial outlook and atmosphere will only come about, however, as a result of giving the representatives of the employees a real, and not a sham or token, share in making the strategic decisions about the future of an enterprise which

in the past have been reserved to management and the representatives of the shareholders.

4. In fact the debate about industrial democracy is much less about the desirability of moving in the direction of greater participation (which many would accept as inevitable), than about the pace of change and the need to extend such participation to the board. We fully accept the arguments about the necessity for participation at levels below the board.... Nonetheless, we believe that the crucial test which alone will carry conviction and create a willingness to share responsibility is an acknowledgement of the right of representatives of the employees, if they ask for it, to share in the strategic decisions taken by the board.

5. ... [We] believe it is membership of a reconstituted unitary board, rather than a supervisory board, which will provide for effective participation in decision-making, will foster the efficiency of British companies and, despite the changes involved, will be more compatible with our company law and administration.

6. We have deliberately avoided recommending a system which ... should have universal and immediate application. We believe that all employees should be involved in a ballot and that if a sufficient majority is obtained, then the process of reconstituting the board should take place. This is a half-way house between enabling legislation and universally mandatory legislation.

Majority Report, Committee of Inquiry on Industrial Democracy, *Report*, pp. 160–1.

---

4. ... We believe that those who work in industry are not ready for the radical changes which the Majority Report aims to achieve. In the Trade Union Movement itself there is abundant evidence of conflicting thinking on this subject....

5. ... [Large] numbers of employers are strongly – and, they believe, justifiably – opposed to precipitate action; and 'middle' management, a particularly hard-pressed element of immense significance in our society, regard with dismay developments from which they might be excluded and which in their view would be likely to affect adversely the speed and quality of decision-making in their companies.

10. This country needs a profitable and competitive private sector. Meeting that need must be a fundamental objective in the light of the

dismal economic performance of the UK in comparison with that of its overseas competitors in terms of industrial growth, productivity, share of world trade and rate of inflation.

11. Industrial democracy can play its part in this process if it enables a more open and effective sharing of the real and practical problems of industry to take place.... It must involve an increased accountability by management for the human, material and financial resources which the community makes available to industry and a more openly expressed concern for the rights and interests both of shareholders and of employees....

14. We believe that any legislation that the government wishes to introduce should:

(a) improve the effectiveness of companies in their task of generating wealth for the community as a whole;

(b) ensure that Boards of Directors are legally and demonstrably accountable for their actions to their employees as well as to their shareholders;

(c) satisfy the aspirations of employees for involvement in the formulation of decisions which closely affect their work.

35. Our recommendation, subject to the creation or existence of a suitable substructure, is that if there is to be employee representation at board level it should be on *Supervisory Boards*. We recognise the existence in this country of a wish (not confined solely to questions of industrial democracy) for the introduction of some appropriate form of monitoring device to ensure that directors discharge their duties properly. A Supervisory Board is an appropriate device for such a purpose. It is here that the voice of employees can most usefully be heard....

60. Fundamental to these [Minority Report] proposals are five issues to which we attach the greatest importance and on which we believe there should be no compromise:

(a) that where a secret ballot reveals a majority of employees in favour of representation at board level, such representation should be on Supervisory, not Unitary, Boards;

(b) that the employee representation should always constitute less than half of a Supervisory Board;

(c) that the employee representation should include at least one representative of all categories of employees – from the shop floor payroll, from salaried staff employees, and from management;

(d) that the issues of board level representation should not be voted

147

upon until a complementary 'substructure' of an Employee Council had been established and operated effectively for a specified number of years;

(e) that all employees (not just members of trade unions) should be involved in elections both to Employee Councils and to Supervisory Board appointments.

Minority Report, Committee of Inquiry on Industrial Democracy, *Report*, pp. 170–2, 177 and 183.

7

Strikes

Strikes became a political issue increasingly from the mid-1950s, with some seeing them as a peculiarly British phenomenon – 'the British disease'. In a period of near full employment, the trade unions' bargaining position was strengthened. Earlier fears that mass unemployment might return gave way among not only those of right-wing views to alarm about inflation and declining British competitiveness in export markets. Yet inflation hit hard low-paid workers (as noted by one Court of Inquiry, see 7.3, para. 111). It also built up expectations of an annual wage increase, something the Engineering Employers' Federation tried to resist in 1953 (see 7.3, para. 49). The number of strikes rose markedly from 1953 and there were several periods when the number of days lost through strikes rose sharply: 1953–62, 1968–72, 1978–81 and 1984–85 (the last being the huge mining dispute).

While coal-mining disputes were a high proportion of the number of strikes between 1945 and 1965, the industry had less effect on the totals of days lost through disputes until the early 1970s and the 1984–85 dispute. Before then, political and public attention was often focused on the docks, the car industry, engineering and building (for examples of these see 7.1–4). A feature of the strikes – as highlighted in the Donovan Report, *In Place of Strife* and the Industrial Relations Act 1971 (see 3.1, 3.2, 4.1 and 4.5) – was that a rising proportion of them was unofficial. Images of small groups of Communists conspiring to cause strikes became popular, not least with the Labour Prime Minister Harold Wilson in 1966 at the time of a merchant seamen's strike. In some cases Communist shop stewards or other activists played a role (see 7.4). However, poor working conditions and/or bad industrial relations provided the context in which such leadership could flourish.

There was also much concern in the 1950s and after about inter-union disputes. These were a concern of the Donovan Commission (3.3) and of the Industrial Relations Act 1971 (4.5). These disputes were usually to do with different skills or different levels of skill. In Loughborough in 1972 there was a notable dispute which involved rancour within one union and racial issues (7.6).

7.1 Unofficial strikes in the London docks

George Isaacs, the Minister of Labour, set up a Committee of Inquiry on 19 May 1950. This reported in May 1951.

14. During the three years, 1947–1950, there were four major un-official strikes in the London docks, each involving the majority of the workers in the Port, and a large number of smaller stoppages.... The outstanding feature of the major strikes is the extraordinary way in which they rapidly spread and assumed serious proportions, while at the same time the original issue became confused and distorted or was thrust into the background....

35. Any idea that the unofficial movement is a kind of 'ginger-group' devoted to the strengthening and reform of union organiza-tion and policy must be completely dispelled by the sustained and systematic attack by unofficial spokesmen and publications on all union action, paying no regard to the merits of any particular issue, and characterised by unrestrained personal abuse of union leaders....

81. The unofficial leaders ... exert their most powerful influence by their eloquence at mass meetings, and their activity at the place of work.... After the recent wage settlement, when unofficial strikes took place in Liverpool, Birkenhead and Manchester, the TGWU, in con-junction with other unions in London, succeeded in averting a serious stoppage there despite persistent efforts by the unofficial group to bring the men out. This was a considerable victory for constitutional procedure.... We would also emphasise the need for closer personal contact between national union officials and the men....

Ministry of Labour and National Service, *Unofficial Stoppages in the London Docks: Report of a Committee of Inquiry* (Cmd 8236), 1951, pp. 4, 11 and 28.

7.2   An early post-war car body dispute

In spite of the wartime ban on strikes still being in force, the strike at Duple Motors Ltd, Hendon, lasted from 19 October to 18 December 1950, and the strikers secured recognition from the National Union of Vehicle Builders, the National Union of Sheet Metal Workers and Braziers, the Amalgamated Engineering Union, the Amalgamated Society of Woodworkers and the Amalgamated Society of Woodcutting Machinists (with other affected unions paying strike pay to their members).

The employer's attempt to use redundancy as a weapon to smash trade union organisation within the factory was exposed and defeated.

A notable advance for trade unionists everywhere was achieved when the employers were forced to accept redundancy as a matter for negotiation through the normal channels of procedure, with no dismissal notices issued except by agreement, and until after a National Conference has considered the circumstances.

Thus the claim of the NUVB [National Union of Vehicle Builders] to apply the Avoidance of Disputes Clause in the National Coach Trade Agreement to questions of redundancy, was won by the united and determined stand of the 1,000 workers involved.

Duple Strike Committee, *How Duple's Won*, n.d. (1951?), p. 4.

The main reasons for this magnificent victory were:

First, the fact that the strikers, members of eight different unions and their officials, stood united....

Second, the really splendid and resourceful leadership of the strike committee and the unswerving determination of the workers. They built an organisation second to none, and consistently carried the fight forward. Their many-sided activities reached out to other sections of the movement and the general public on a scale seldom, if ever, reached in a dispute of this kind.

The financial and moral support thus won stiffened the fight considerably, and enabled it to be broadened at all stages. This form of action is of prime importance in every dispute and all should understand how essential it is to win the sympathy and support of the general public as well as that of organised workers.

W. A. G. Roberts, President of the National Union of Vehicle Builders, in
the Foreword to Duple Strike Committee, *How Duple's Won*, n.d. (1951?),
p. 3.

7.3 The official dispute in the Engineering and Allied Trades, 1953–1954

The Confederation of Shipbuilding and Engineering Unions
(CSEU) at a conference in April 1953 called for a 15 per cent
increase in wage rates. The Allied Employers' National Federation declined to concede any rise during negotiations between July and November. The CSEU called a one-day strike
on 2 December 1953 and the introduction of a ban on overtime and a limitation of piecework. Before the latter took place
the Minister of Labour set up a Court of Inquiry under Lord
Justice Morris. For its broader comments see section 2.4 of
this book. The following extracts are from the Court of Inquiry's Report. The trade union case (para. 32) gives the three
main trade union arguments in the post-war period for a rise
in wages.

5. The industries affected by this dispute constitute the largest group
in the British manufacturing industries and employ about one-sev-
enth of the country's total working population. One third of the industries' output ... is exported abroad. In 1938 engineering goods
constituted 26 per cent of the country's exports by value, but this
percentage rose to 38 in 1948 and 41 in 1952....
32. ... Mr Tanner [Secretary of the Amalgamated Engineering Un-
ion] explained that the claim was for a percentage increase in basic
rates rather than for a uniform advance, because it was desired to
prevent any further narrowing of existing differentials between skilled,
semi-skilled and unskilled workers. The unions based their case for
an increase on three considerations – firstly, the rise in the cost of
living during recent years which had led to a fall in the real value of
wages of the majority of workers in the industry; secondly, the very
great increase in productivity (as expressed by the rise in output per
worker) which had taken place in the industry since the war; and
thirdly, the large and continuous rise in the profits made by the indus-

try....

49. [The Employers' case was that orders had declined and they disputed the trade unions' statistics.] It had been observed that since the war many trade unions had adopted a practice of submitting a claim for a substantial increase in wages each year. The inflationary conditions which reigned for several years after the war were perhaps the reason for this practice, but undoubtedly the wage increases since the war had contributed to inflation.

111. [The Court of Inquiry's observations.] The perils of inflation and of adding impetus to its spiral effect are, of course, fully and widely recognised especially at a time when it was reasonable to hope that a halt had been called in the upward trend of prices.... Though there may be at any particular moment a difficulty in deciding whether wages have been chasing prices or whether prices have been chasing wages, we think that in the case of the lower wage earning groups the effect of a material rise in the cost of living is one to which great heed must be paid.

142. ... We cannot but be impressed by the fact that the minimum wage rates in the industry do appear to be relatively low as compared with those of some other industries, although average wage earnings in the industry compare favourably with those in industry generally....

143. ... we are agreed that there is justification for some increase in consolidated time rates but not to the extent claimed. We hope that the parties will resume negotiations with a view to agreeing to some increase.... As a pointer ... our view is that it should be something in the region of one-third of the amount claimed.

Court of Inquiry into a dispute between employers who are members of the Engineering and Allied Employers' National Federation and workmen who are members of trade unions affiliated to the Confederation of Shipbuilding and Engineering Unions, *Report* (Cmd 9084), 1954, pp. 4, 19, 24, 40 and 47.

7.4 London building trade strikes at the Barbican and Horseferry Road sites

Two major building contracts of £5.5 million and £5 million respectively were delayed by a series of disputes. These included a series of go-slows, work-to-rules and short strikes between January 1965 and November 1966. The disputes were complex in their causes, but in both cases unofficial action by workplace committees played a major role. The Court condemned the Joint Sites Committee as being 'associated with, if not controlled or directed by' the Communist Party. The firms concerned were Sunley's and Myton.

117. [Sunley's problems at Horseferry Road.] The Company stated that by October 1966 they had no confidence in the ability of the NFBTO [National Federation of Building Trades Operatives] or the unions to exercise effective discipline over their members on the site....

120. It was contended on behalf of Sunley's that by 20th October they had been provoked beyond reasonable endurance. Reference was made to the large number of strikes and other unconstitutional actions during the period of the contract; the breaches of the WRA [Working Rule Agreement, the framework of industrial relations within the London building industry] by the stewards which had led to complaints to the NFBTO; and the unsuccessful attempts to find a solution, first by raising bonuses and later reprogramming. Large numbers of employees had left the site during weeks when there were either strikes or overtime embargoes, and the atmosphere on the site had been so bad that the company had had difficulty in keeping its staff. In addition, the company had been convinced that they were the victims of a deliberate form of sabotage on behalf of the Joint Sites Committee....

135. [Works Committee.] The Committee claimed that many disputes on the site had been due to a lack of understanding and cooperation on the part of the firm. Considerable argument, and often the threat or carrying out of strike action, had been required before the firm had agreed to provide elementary safety and social amenities. The firm had persistently flouted the WRA and Site Procedure Agreement by taking decisions on bonus working, safety and working conditions without consulting the Works Committee. Sunley's had also failed to accept the findings of the Disputes Commissions on several occasions and had refused to use the disputes machinery except when it suited them; on no occasion had a Disputes Commission found in favour of the company.

181. [The Court of Inquiry's conclusions.] In acting as they did ... we are of the opinion that the company [Sunley's] were immediately responsible for bringing about this stoppage of work and were to

blame in certain important particulars. [These included undermining its own negotiator and points made in 135.] ...

183. At both sites the influence of the Joint Sites Committee was subversive and mischievous; at both sites the Works Committee operated without any sufficient supervision or effective union control.... There is no doubt that the Works Committees at both sites supported and led 'unofficial' strikes, partial and complete 'go-slow' procedures and refusals to operate bonus or incentive schemes. In both cases enough information was in the hands of the NFBTO to warrant withdrawal of credentials from the Federation steward ... but this was not done....

188. There was ... on both sites failure in communication and consultation due to faulty organisation of industrial relations for which the companies bear responsibility, mischievous and illegitimate exercise of power and pressure by the Works Committees influenced by the London Joint Sites Committee, failure by unions and Federation officials to exercise such control as they could over the illegal activities of the Works Committees, and the constitutional imperfections in the WRA.

Court of Inquiry into trade disputes at the Barbican and Horseferry Road construction sites, *Report* (Cmnd 3396), 1967, pp. 36–7, 40, 52–4 and 58.

7.5 1972 coal strike

After the National Union of Mineworkers submitted in July 1971 a pay claim of a weekly minimum wage of £26 surface (increase of £8), £28 underground (increase of £9) and £35 under the National Loading Agreement (increase of £5), there was an overtime ban and a ballot in which 58.8 per cent voted for strike action when the National Coal Board offered £1.80 increase to the surface workers and £1.75 to the others. The strike began on 9 January 1972 after some relatively minor improvements in the offer to the NUM were rejected. After the intervention of the Secretary of State for Employment on 9 February 1972 the offer was improved to £3 to surface workers, £3.50 to underground workers and £2.75 to face workers. This was rejected. Following this, on 11 February 1972, a Court of Inquiry was set up under Lord Wilberforce.

11. Since about 1957, when falling demand caused undistributed coal stocks to rise dramatically, the miners have wholeheartedly co-operated in a continuing programme of streamlining coal production. In that period they have seen their numbers working in pits reduced from over 700,000 to under 290,000 and the number of producing collieries fall from over 800 to under 300. This rundown, which was brought about with the co-operation of the miners and their union, is without parallel in British industry in terms of the social and economic costs it has inevitably entailed for the mining community as a whole.

12. During this period of concentrating production on fewer collieries, production methods became highly mechanised and the miners responded by learning new skills and by co-operating with the NCB in the further concentration of production on faces where machines could be used to the best advantage. The policy of concentration enabled productivity to rise year by year. In 1957 output per manshift stood at 25cwts; by 1971 it had climbed to 44.2cwts, an increase of 77.5 per cent....

34. ... we can sum up the main factors which have convinced us that the miners' claim should be given exceptional national treatment.

(1) The surface workers who are on the minimum rate of £18 are among the lower paid. Their opportunities for alternative work are limited because they may well live in isolated communities. In a number of cases they have suffered sickness and injury in the service of the mines.

(2) The large group of men underground but not at the face do work which is heavy, dirty, hot and frequently cramped. In this day and age when physical conditions in other jobs have improved greatly the relative discomforts of working below ground become greater. Other occupations have their dangers and their inconveniences, but we know of none in which there is such a combination of danger, health hazard, discomfort in working conditions, social inconvenience and community isolation.

(3) The men working on the face and associated with the face, who are in the key jobs winning coal, not only suffer the problems of other people below ground but they may need to work in dust masks and suffer considerable noise and are at maximum danger risk.

(4) There has been quite exceptional co-operation shown by miners in the last few years in moving from piecework schemes to day working schemes in the interest of greater efficiency. This co-opera-

tion has been a model to industry as a whole. The consequence of this change in pay structure has been to hold back the pay of most face workers in relation to the rest of industry, and to hold back the pay of some groups of face workers far more than others to the extent that some miners are now earning less than they were five years ago. It is normal in such cases elsewhere in industry at the time of major changes to the wage structure to inject a significant overall increase. No such injection has taken place in the case of the miners.

(5) Shift payments are minimal or non-existent, which has advantages in terms of efficiency by giving greater flexibility in the organisation of work.

[Paragraphs 45–7 recommended back-dated to November 1971 pay rises of £5 to surface workers, £6 to underground and £4.50 to face workers.]...

51. It is only by improving productivity that any long term increases in real wages can be obtained. Productivity in the industry has been steadily rising.... This trend will need to continue and the NCB talked of an expected increase due to technical and mechanical improvements of over 50 per cent in the next few years. The NUM did not disagree with these figures....

53. We heard from both the NCB and the NUM of their efforts to evolve a productivity payments scheme which would reflect increases in productivity. The scheme should be agreed nationally, and could be based on increases in productivity nationally or by individual pits, or by a combination of the two.

Court of Inquiry into a dispute between the National Coal Board and the National Union of Mineworkers under the Chairmanship of the Rt Hon. Lord Wilberforce, CMG, OBE, *Report* (Cmnd 4903), 1972, pp. 2–3, 8–9 and 11–12.

7.6 The Mansfield Hosiery Mills, Loughborough strike, 1972

This was a highly publicised dispute which involved racial issues. Evidence was given at the Committee of Inquiry by the Race Relations Board and the Runnymede Trust as well as by representatives of the employers, unions, strike committee and three other employees. While substantial numbers of workers (40 and 51 per cent) at the company's two factories in Lough-

borough were of Asian origin, the most skilled jobs (full-fashioned and non-fashioned knitters) were overwhelmingly occupied by white workers while less skilled jobs (notably bar-
loaders) and the better paid intermediate grade of runners-on
were predominantly carried out by workers of Asian origin.
The report was made by the Rt Hon. Kenneth Robinson, a
former Labour government minister.

2.25 ... In 1962/3 [the Company's] attempts to appoint Asians to
running-on posts had provoked a strike by workers already employed
on that operation. After the dispute had been taken through the NJIC
[National Joint Industrial Council of the Hosiery Trade] procedure,
the 'reluctant acceptance' of the established runners-on was given to
the promotion of Asians.

2.26 Until 1968 management did not train Asians as knitters 'ow-
ing to the complexity of the operation and the high cost of training'.
In 1968/9 they took the initiative in discussing with the union and
shop floor representatives the possibility of affording job opportunities as knitters to Asians. Strong resistance was encountered and the
company's proposals were rejected by both the full-fashioned knitters
and the union....

2.27 In subsequent negotiations with the union, the company secured their written agreement to the establishment of Asians in non-
fashioned knitting....

2.28 Early in 1972, management re-opened talks on the question
of introducing Asians on to the full-fashioned knitting with union officials and with shop committees, but there was opposition to the
proposal and it was made clear that if the company gave effect to it a
strike by knitters throughout the group would result.

2.35 At Mansfield Hosiery the discrimination appeared to be confined to the full-fashioned knitting section. The [Race Relations] Board
recognised the fears expressed by the knitters concerning the security
of their jobs but considered that any practice in pursuit of job security
must be applied regardless of race and colour.

2.37 [Mr D. Stephen, Runnymede Trust] ... pointed out that the
statement [made in a Runnymede Trust report] that 'almost all the
cream jobs were held by British workers' was based on an impres-
sionistic basis – in only 3 out of 17 firms were there Asian full-fashioned knitters.... Mr Stephen referred ... to a very rudimentary shop
floor participation by Asians in union affairs; immigrant workers had

158

not been involved in the rules of the game, which was ultimately responsible for disputes of the type under investigation.

3.4 [Verdict of the Committee of Inquiry.] I accept that the policies of the company in respect of racial integration have been generally enlightened. Unfortunately the implementation of these policies appears to have been frustrated or at best delayed by what can only be described as a racialist attitude on the part of some of their white employees. This attitude can be explained, though not excused, by a growing sense of insecurity – however ill-founded – resulting from the steadily increasing proportion of Asians employed in the factory....

3.8 The union leadership informed me, and I have no reason to doubt their sincerity, that they acknowledge precisely the same obligations to their Asian members as to the rest of their membership. Nevertheless their failure to press home this policy in the face of the resistance of some of their members has led them into conflict with the Race Relations Board.... I accept that the union faces difficulties such as the language barrier and the relative ignorance of union procedures and organisation on the part of the Asians, but there is clearly much the union can do to increase the confidence of the Asian members that it will in fact champion their legitimate aspirations....

3.14 ... I am satisfied that the bar-loaders' principal grievance is not the rate of pay attaching to their job but their virtual inability to progress beyond that job and to join the coveted ranks of the knitters, especially the full-fashioned knitters.

Department of Employment, *Report of a Committee of Inquiry into a dispute between employees of the Mansfield Hosiery Mills Limited, Loughborough and their employer*, 1972, pp. 11 and 13–17.

7.7   Strikes: a Conservative appraisal of the issue

This is an assessment drawn from a Conservative Party publication issued in 1977, when an early general election seemed imminent.

Britain's relatively poor industrial performance is frequently seen as stemming from its bad industrial relations. Recent well-publicised research by the Department of Employment has shown, at least during the period of the last Conservative government, that the proportion of plants where strikes actually occurred was very small. On average 98 per cent of manufacturing plants were free of stoppages in each year from 1971 to 1973. A total of 81 per cent of manufacturing employees, in an average year, worked in plants where no strike occurred. These statistics, however, hide both the incidence of industrial action short of strikes (go-slows, working to rule etc.) and the extent to which the threat of strike action hampers efficient decision-making in industry. The actual figures for the number of stoppages, workers involved and working days lost have been disturbingly high in Britain over a long period.

There has been a welcome improvement since 1974, almost certainly due to the existence of massive unemployment caused by Labour policies.

Conservative Central Office, *The Campaign Guide 1977*, London, 1977, p. 201.

8

Conservative governments' trade union legislation, 1979–1993

Between 1979 and 1993 the Conservative governments of Margaret Thatcher and John Major repeatedly introduced legislation affecting trade unions. Conservative victories in general elections were followed by measures which weakened trade union bargaining power. In this the various Acts were parts of the government's economic policies, notably those to reduce inflation and generally to try to keep British export prices from rising faster than those of her competitors. In doing this the Conservatives were also making an effective attack on the major economic supporters of their main political opponent, the Labour Party.

The legislation of the early 1980s tended to tilt the balance in industrial relations back in favour of the employers, and so moving against the strengthened trade union role of 1974–79, while also removing supports from those among the weakest in the labour market. After the bitter year-long miners' strike of 1984–85, the legislation took matters much further in an anti-trade union direction. This was so under John Major as much as it was under Margaret Thatcher.

From 1979 the trade unions were no longer consulted as contributors to gaining higher productivity and greater harmony in British industry. The tripartite bodies of the 1960s and 1970s were wound down and abolished. The trade unions were not seen as pillars of free collective bargaining. The legislation undercut their positions and weakened them in dealing with employers. Individual trade union members were encouraged to assert their individuality and to undermine collective action, even when it had been agreed upon by a majority in a democratic ballot.

161

8.1 *The Right Approach*

In Opposition in 1974–79 the Conservatives were wary of
alarming electors by appearing to be ready for another head-
on collision with the trade unions.

One of the main aims of all these [Conservative] policies is the creation of a high-wage, low-cost economy....

Monetary restraint, including the setting of targets for monetary
expansion, is a key feature of economic policy, though not the only
one. Excessive wage claims should clearly not be accommodated by
an easy expansion of bank lending. In the public sector this must be
supplemented by the use of cash limits. Every organisation (including
those in the public sector) should be put into a position in which workers and management are obliged to face together the inescapable choice
between realistic pay levels and job security, or excessive earnings
and a doubtful future....

Given the power that the leaders of trade unions wield, it is clearly
important that they should be as representative as possible....

The main drive for improvement in the democratic procedures of
the trade unions must come from union members themselves. But we
are ready to help. Public money should be made available for the
conduct of postal ballots for union elections when these are requested.
Firms should also be encouraged to provide time and facilities for the
conduct of union meetings....

We have emphasised on a number of occasions that on our return
to office we do not intend to introduce a major round of new industrial relations legislation. This in no way diminishes our opposition to
certain points in recent legislation ... we are in no way curbing our
right to amend provisions which prove in practice to be as ill-chosen
or wrong-headed as we have consistently argued. In particular, we
are concerned to protect individual rights, for instance, as they are
affected by the closed shop.

The closed shop (in one form or another) has been a feature of
British industrial life for over fifty years. Sometimes it has come about
through the mutual wish of employers and employees; sometimes as a
result of trade union or political pressure. Sometimes it has helped
put industrial relations on an orderly basis; sometimes its working
has threatened individual freedom. We believe a proper balance must
be struck. For example, it is *wrong* that people who have given years

162

of service can not only lose their jobs because they will not join – or are not accepted by – a union, but also receive no compensation.

Conservative Central Office, *The Right Approach: A Statement of Conservative Aims*, London, October 1976, pp. 37, 38 and 44–5.

Trade unions are historic institutions. They have many achievements to their credit. We Conservatives count millions of trade unionists among our political supporters, and an increasing number among the active workers for our cause. It is neither our purpose nor our interest to damage these institutions or their members.

However, there is no disguising the damage that some trade union practices and some trade union policies and some trade union leaders are doing to the nation – including many of their own members....

We will look at recent trade union legislation, in the light of experience, to see what amendments are needed. [Closed shop and secret ballot.]....

These things we will do, but we are well aware that many trade union leaders are conducting negotiations every day in the country with a complete sense of responsibility and a proper regard for the interests of the firms in which they work and of the future welfare of their own members. We will consult together in the knowledge that there are prizes to be won, not only by the public but by the unions themselves, if sensible reform can be achieved....

We shall invite the unions to join with us in building the new and prosperous Britain we all want. We shall not 'bash' the unions. Neither shall we bow to them.

Conservative Central Office, 'This is the Right Approach' (Margaret Thatcher, the Conservative Leader's Address to the Paddington Conservative Association), 18 December 1978, London, n.d. (1979), pp. 3–5.

8.2   The Employment Act 1980

Some of the main features of this are given below. Section 1 deals with funding for ballots, 4 with the closed shop, 6 and 7 with unfair dismissals, 11 with limiting maternity rights and 16 with removing illegal immunity from secondary picketing.

1(1) The Secretary of State may by regulations make a scheme ... providing for payments by the Certification Officer towards expenditure incurred by independent trade unions in respect of ... ballots....

(3) The purposes ... are:

(a) obtaining a decision or ascertaining the views of members of a trade union as to the calling or ending of a strike or other industrial action;

(b) carrying out an election provided for by the rules of a trade union;

(c) electing a worker who is a member of a trade union to be a representative of other members also employed by his employer;

(d) amending the rules of a trade union;

(e) obtaining a decision in accordance with the Trade Union (Amalgamations etc.) Act 1964 on a resolution to approve an instrument of amalgamation or transfer; and such other purposes as the Secretary of State may by order specify.

4(2) Every person who is, or is seeking to be, in employment ... shall have the right (a) not to have an application for membership of a specified trade union unreasonably refused; (b) not to be unreasonably expelled from a specified trade union.

[5 An Employment Appeal Tribunal or industrial tribunal to award compensation to be paid by the union.]

[6 Unfair dismissal: the burden of proof of acting reasonably removed from the employer.]

7(2) The dismissal of an employee ... shall be regarded as unfair if he genuinely objects on grounds of conscience or other deeply-held personal conviction to being a member of any trade union whatsoever or of a particular trade union....

[11 Introduced a right for women workers who were pregnant not to be unreasonably refused permission to attend ante-natal check-ups. This took up a recommendation made by the all-party Commons Select Committee on Social Services.]

16(1) For section 15 of the 1974 [Trade Union and Labour Relations] Act there shall be substituted: 15(1) It shall be lawful for a person in contemplation or furtherance of a trade dispute to attend

(a) at or near his own place of work, or

(b) if he is an official of a trade union, at or near the place of work of a member of that union whom he is accompanying and whom he represents, for the purpose only of peacefully obtaining or communicating information, or peacefully persuading any person to work or abstain from working....

(2) Nothing in ... the 1974 Act shall prevent an act done in the course of picketing from being actionable in tort unless it is done in the course of attendance declared lawful by section 15 of that Act.

Public General Acts of 1980, 42, pp. 825–6, 829–32, 837–42 and 844.

8.3 Responses to the Employment Act 1980

Let me reiterate that we have sought a balance. I do not believe that what we have witnessed in the last 20 years has been a balance. It is that which has worried successive governments and this House throughout this unsettled period. The changes we propose are limited to those where experience has shown that the law is not working well, where privilege is being abused and suffering results where the creation of new jobs is being inhibited by fear of the present law and what it means. Our proposals do not change the need for bargainers to behave sensibly, nor do they in any way absolve those who lead them from their responsibility of providing practical voluntary guidance on the use of the powerful weapons in their bargaining armoury.

Our proposals are designed to improve industrial relations, but to do so by working with the grain rather than against it. So let no one use them as an excuse for abandoning the search for the good voluntary procedures which are the best protection against tough laws.

James Prior, *House of Commons Debates*, 5th Series, 976, c. 60; 17 December 1979.

[Sir John Methven, Director General of the CBI.] 'We could have a disaster on our hands if we try in the present frenzied atmosphere [of the national steel strike] to put hasty legislation on the statute book without proper consultation.'

The CBI's official policy ... is that, apart from comparatively minor changes, it supports the Bill for the time being. The support, however, is conditional on ... attempt being made for stronger measures on trade union immunities and secondary picketing at a later date.

The Times, 9 February 1980, p. 17.

[The CBI urged James Prior to consider legally binding collective agreements and compulsory strike ballots.] In the past the law has played only a minor part [in industrial relations] but it is clear, as it is tacitly acknowledged in the Employment [Protection] Act [1975] that our traditional voluntary system is no longer adequate on its own to deal with recent developments in collective bargaining.

... [The CBI concedes that the 1980 Act] will severely restrict the immunity of individuals in respect of the inducement of secondary industrial action. Nevertheless, it will still leave scope for action which may result in disrupting production in companies which have no interest in the dispute in question.

The Times, 6 August 1980, p. 1.

The Employment Act 1980 has been put forward as a fairly modest Act to improve industrial relations. It is nothing of the sort.... Together with the codes of practice, which in effect can be extended at any time to make the Act more effective, it purported to deal with the bully boys, yet the more you examine it, the more you see that the people who are damaged the most are those with the weakest bargaining power in our society. The fact that Section 11 of the Employment Protection Act is now repealed sweeps away any statutory rights of [trade union] recognition, so that the only way you can get recognition is by agreement or through industrial action.... This [schedule] gives protection for minimum wages and conditions of employment for millions of people who are unable to exert the industrial strength to protect those minimum wages and conditions....

Unfair dismissal protection has been removed from hundreds of thousands of people. The only way they can now be protected is through industrial action, and the same is true of areas of special maternity rights for women.

Again, on picketing, secondary action, it is the weak who are made weaker.... If the Polish workers [Solidarity in the Gdansk shipyards, in particular] were to win Prior's law all those people acting in support of free trade union rights would be subject to heavy punitive damages. Yet we are in England, where trade unionism was cradled.

On union membership agreements: it is not the strong who will worry. There will be no 'free-riders' in the mining industry; there will be no 'free-riders' on the docks and the other strongly organised areas. Where the problems will arise, both on picketing, on secondary action, on union membership agreements ... will be in those huge areas of weak organisation, the hotel and catering industries, the multiple shops, the clothing industries, and so on....

But it is on immunities where the thrust is the most dangerous. Even the 'primary' right to strike is threatened. In Britain the right to strike is more narrowly defined than in any of the other democratic countries. It is related only to the furtherance of trade disputes, but now, as the result of Prior's Act, judges are to determine whether it is, in effect, a trade dispute, something that Lord Justice Scarman said was impossible to do.

C. H. Urwin, General Council, 1 September 1980, in TUC, *Report of 112th Annual Trades Union Congress*, 1980, pp. 389–90.

8.4   The Employment Act 1982

Even before the 1980 Employment Act had been passed Margaret Thatcher publicly aired the desirability of reconsidering trade unions' immunities from legal action, enacted in the Trade Disputes Act 1906. The two sides of the argument for keeping or removing such immunities were presented in January 1981 in the Green Paper, *Trade Union Immunities* (Cmnd 8128), prepared under James Prior's tenure at the Department of Employment. Norman Tebbitt took the view that his was 'a much tougher package' than his predecessor would have introduced. The extracts below indicate the main features of the 1982 Act.

2. [Provisions] enabling the Secretary of State to make payments towards compensating individuals who in certain past cases have been dismissed for failure to conform to the requirements of a union membership agreement. [This covered the period from 1974 to the operation of the 1980 Employment Act.]

[On the closed shop, in place of Clause 58A of the Employment Protection (Consolidation) Act 1978] ... a union membership agreement shall be taken ... to have been approved in relation to the employees of any class of employer if a ballot has been held on the question whether the agreement should apply to them and either

(a) not less than 80 per cent of those entitled to vote, or

(b) not less than 85 per cent of those who voted,

voted in favour of the agreement's application. [Where these conditions were not met, a dismissed worker could bring a claim for substantial damages against the union and the employer.]

12(1) Any term or condition of a contract for the supply of goods and services is void in so far as it purports

(a) to require that the whole, or some part of the work done for the purposes of the contract is to be done only by persons who are not members of trade unions or members of particular trade unions; or

(b) to require that the whole, or some part, of such work is to be done only by persons who are members of trade unions or members of a particular union.

13(1) Any term or condition of a contract for the supply of goods and services is void in so far as it purports to require any party to the contract

(a) to recognise one or more trade unions (whether or not named in the contract) for the purpose of negotiating on behalf of workers, or any class of worker, employed by him; or

(b) to negotiate or consult with, or with any official of, one or more trade unions (whether or not so named)....

15(1) Section 14 of the 1974 [Trade Union and Labour Relations] Act (immunity for trade unions and employers' associations from certain actions in tort) shall cease to have effect.

16(1) ... in any proceedings in tort brought against a trade union the amount which may be awarded against the union by way of damages ... shall not exceed the appropriate limit.

(3) The appropriate limit is

(a) £10,000, if the union has less than 5,000 members;

(b) £50,000, if it has 5,000 or more members but less than 25,000 members; and

(c) £125,000, if it has 25,000 or more members, but less than 100,000 members; and

(d) £250,000, if it has 100,000 or more members.

[18. The meaning of 'trade dispute' in the 1974 Trade Union and Labour Relations Act was amended to exclude inter-union disputes, solidarity strikes with other workers at home or abroad and any other sympathy action.]

Public General Acts of 1982, 46, pp. 1475–1518.

8.5   The Trade Union Act 1984

Like the 1982 Employment Act, this Act was preceded by a
Green Paper, *Democracy in Trade Unions* (Cmnd 8778), issued in January 1983, which aired the government's broad
intentions. The theme of both the Green Paper and the 1984
Act was 'handing the unions back to their members'. Trade
union collective power was to be restricted by ballots for union office, before industrial action and to maintain a political
fund.

[1. All trade unions must ensure that 'every person who is a voting
member of the principal executive committee' is subject to re-election
by secret ballot every five years.]

10(1) Nothing in Section 13 of the 1974 Act shall prevent an act
done by a trade union without the support of a ballot from being
actionable in tort ... on the ground that it induced a person to break
his contract of employment or to interfere with its performance.

[(3) A majority of those voting needed to be in favour of strike
action, and the strike needed to take place within four weeks of the
ballot to avoid ... being open to legal action for damages.]

[12. Decisions to establish political funds under the Trade Union
Act 1913 need to be renewed every ten years by secret postal ballot.]

Public General Acts of 1984, 49, pp. 1957–66.

8.6   Banning trade unionism at Government
Communications Headquarters (GCHQ)

The removal of trade union rights from the large number of
employees at the Government Communications Headquarters
at Cheltenham caused political uproar. The TUC and many
trade unionists saw those who subsequently lost their jobs,
rather than renounce trade union membership and take £1,000,
as comparable to the Tolpuddle Martyrs of 1834 (Methodist
farm workers who were transported because of their trade
union membership).

Sir Geoffrey Howe (Foreign Secretary): ... the Employment Protection Acts contain provisions that enable the government to except

Crown employees from the application of the Acts. These provisions can be used only for the purposes of safeguarding national security....

... I have today signed certificates [under the 1975 and 1978 Employment Protection Acts].... The certificates have immediate effect and new conditions of service are at the same time being introduced at GCHQ. Under these new conditions, staff will be permitted in future to belong only to a departmental staff association approved by their director.

... The government fully respect the rights of civil servants to be members of a trade union, and it is only the special nature of the work of GCHQ that has led us to take these measures.

... Those who decide to remain at GCHQ will each receive a payment of £1000 in recognition of the fact that certain rights that they have hitherto enjoyed are being withdrawn from them in the interests of national security. Those who do not wish to continue to serve at GCHQ will be offered the opportunity of seeking a transfer to another part of the Civil Service.

Denis Healey (Labour MP and Shadow Foreign Secretary): I found the Foreign Secretary's statement at once disturbing and perplexing. Government communications headquarters ... has performed an indispensable service to the nation since the war by providing vital intelligence with an efficiency and dedication that is the envy of the world. It is not, like some other branches of the security services, a small body of professionals. It is a large industrial enterprise employing thousands of skilled technicians. Any of the very few offences against security that have been committed by members of GCHQ have been dealt with under the law.... As far as I am aware, there has been no industrial action for the past three years, since 1981, by members of GCHQ.

The House must be told by the Foreign Secretary why the government have decided after all these years to deprive GCHQ employees of rights that are enjoyed by civil servants in the Ministry of Defence and the Foreign and Commonwealth Office, who are doing work of equal security and operational importance. Why is the Foreign Secretary depriving GCHQ employees of rights of industrial organisation that are enjoyed by employees of the royal ordnance factories and those in private firms such as Vickers and Plessey, who are doing work which is equally secret and equally central to the nation's security?

I wish to ask the Foreign Secretary two questions about how he took his decision. What consultations did he have, before taking his decision, with elected representatives of GCHQ employees? Secondly, did he discuss his decision with the Security Commission which, although it was not set up specifically to deal with a broad question of this nature, comprises people with deep and longstanding knowledge of the work of GCHQ and whose impartiality would be accepted on both sides of the House?....

Sir Geoffrey Howe: Members of the Security Commission were not consulted. It is not a matter for them. They are normally involved only in cases where there has been a breach of security. Nor was there consultation with the trade unions at GCHQ....

The debate which followed the announcement of the ban by the government, *House of Commons Debates*, 6th Series, 52, cc. 917–18; 25 January 1984.

8.7 The Wages Act 1986

This legislation was notable (Part 1) for abolishing the Truck Acts of 1831–1940 and similar legislation which ensured manual workers had to be paid in cash, and (Part 2) for the removal of workers under the age of 21 from the scope of wages councils and generally a weakening of the wages councils. The Part 2 changes were highly controversial.

The first objective is to promote employment. We will do this by simplifying the wages councils orders, by removing outdated restrictions on the method of paying wages, by ensuring that growing and prospering companies do not meet an unfair share of the costs of supporting those which run into difficulties, and by ensuring that young workers can get their foot on the employment ladder by accepting jobs at wages which employers are willing to offer and they are willing to accept, without wages councils preventing the jobs from being offered by insisting on higher rates of pay. We will also ensure that wages councils think about the employment effects when they take decisions.

The second major new reform is to provide major new rights to employees to ensure they do not suffer unlawful deductions from pay.

The third objective is to reduce barriers of status between manual and non-manual workers.... Finally, we aim, to a modest extent, to reduce crime by removing impediments to the growth of cashless pay, thus reducing opportunities for wages snatches and theft.

Kenneth Clarke, Paymaster General and Minister for Employment, when he introduced the Second Reading of the Bill, *House of Commons Debates*, 6th Series, 91, c. 797; 11 February 1986.

[Representatives of the General Council of the TUC saw Kenneth Clarke on 7 May 1986.] On Part 1 of the Bill, the General Council representatives stated that cashless pay should be introduced by agreement and negotiation rather than compulsion, and that the Bill did not seek to address many practical aspects of changing to cashless pay but merely allowed employers to impose cashless pay without any of the safeguards of the existing legislation....

As regards Part 2 of the Bill, the TUC representatives stressed that wages councils afforded essential statutory protection to millions of low paid and unorganised workers. Under the Wages Bill, however, not only were young workers to be denied any statutory minimum rates of pay, but the protection for the remaining workers covered by the wages councils – three quarters of whom were women – were also to be severely reduced. The TUC representatives pressed for suitable amendments to the Bill to ensure continued legal protection for young workers, to preserve a wider role for wages councils in determining terms and conditions other than pay, and to strengthen, not weaken, the existing enforcement mechanisms. They also pointed out that there was no evidence that wages councils had hindered job creation or caused unemployment, or that statutory minimum rates had prevented young people from getting jobs. Indeed, removing statutory protection destroyed rather than created jobs. They pointed out that, against the government's stated expectations, the contracting-out of public services to private contractors which followed the abolition of the Fair Wages Resolution had led in many cases to significant reductions in workforces and a marked worsening of pay and conditions for the workers concerned.

TUC, *Report of 118th Annual Trades Union Congress*, 1986, p. 35.

That [Wages] Act is now in force and for over half a million workers in hotel and catering these warnings [of the General Council] have become starkly true.... The wages council which covers these workers will no longer be able to offer any form of protection for young people under the age of 21, no longer will they be able to make provision for annual holidays or holiday pay and other very important conditions of service. The wages council will in future be restricted to setting just one single rate of pay.... [The employers] have made it clear they want to use the Act to cut the already desperately low rates of pay existing in the industry.

Workers in hotel and catering do represent a large proportion of those who need the protection ... [of] legal rights.... Are they working in an industry which is poor and declining? No, they are not. The total profits of the industry stand at over £1 billion.... It is an industry which is being hailed by government as a great growth industry and a shining example of economic recovery. It is indeed a successful and highly profitable industry, but it must be remembered that success has been achieved at the expense of the workforce who now face cuts in their already appalling levels of pay and also now face a loss of rights.

E. P. Newell, General, Municipal, Boilermakers and Allied Trade Union, 4 September 1986, in TUC, *Report of 118th Annual Trades Union Congress*, 1986, p. 605.

8.8 The Employment Act 1988

The coal-mining dispute of 1984–85 and the News International dispute at Wapping in 1985–86 were marked by mass picketing. The government included such action as one of several targets for police powers under the Public Order Act 1986. These events encouraged the government to take further action against the trade unions. Once more legislation was preceded by a Green Paper: *Trade Unions and their Members* (Cm 95), issued in February 1987. The re-election of the government in the 1987 general election further encouraged it to extend the scope of its measures against trade union power.

1(1) A member of a trade union who claims that the union has, without the support of a ballot, authorised or endorsed any industrial action in which members of the union (including that member) are likely to be, or have been, induced by the union to take part or continue to take part may apply to the court for an order under this section.

[(2) The court, if satisfied that the claim is true, shall order the union to stop the industrial action.]

3(1) An individual who is or has at any time been a member of a trade union shall have the right not to be unjustifiably disciplined by that union.

(3) Conduct by an individual falls within this subsection if

(a) it consists in a failure to participate in or support any strike or other industrial action (whether by members of the trade union in question or by others) or indicates opposition to, or lack of support for, any such strike or industrial action;

(b) it consists in a failure to contravene, for any purpose connected with any such strike or other industrial action, any requirement imposed on that individual by ... a contract of employment or any agreement between that individual and a person for whom he works [or other actions such as lodging a complaint against the union for its action].

10(1) Nothing in section 13 of the 1974 [Trade Union and Labour Relations] Act (immunity for acts in contemplation or furtherance of a trade dispute) shall prevent an act being actionable in tort where the reason, or one of the reasons ... is the fact or belief that a particular employer

(a) is employing, has employed or might employ a person who is not a member of any trade union ... ; or

(b) is failing ... to discriminate against any such person.

11. In the 1978 [Employment Protection (Consolidation)] Act, the ... provisions (which enable an employer to take action in certain circumstances to enforce trade union membership) shall cease to have effect....

12(1) In ... Section 1 of the 1984 [Employment] Act (duty to hold election of voting members of a trade union's principal executive committee), the word 'voting' ... shall be omitted....

19(1) The Secretary of State shall appoint an officer to be known as the Commissioner for the Rights of Trade Union Members....

[20 and 21 The Commissioner was given the task to assist trade union members to take legal action against their unions, with public funds available for legal advice and representation.]

24(1) The body ... established by ... the 1973 [Employment and Training] Act with the name of the Manpower Services Commission shall be known instead as 'the Training Commission'....

[24–29 The responsibility for Job Centres and other employment services were returned to the Department of Employment. The Secretary of State was given powers to increase the membership of the Commission from ten to 'not less than ten or more than sixteen'].

Public General Acts of 1988, 19, 1988, pp. 1369–1400.

8.9   Reponses to the Employment Act 1988

> The following extracts are from the House of Commons debate on the Second Reading of the Bill, including a joke by the former Leader of the Labour Party, Michael Foot.

Eric Heffer (Labour MP): The government insist that there must be a ballot. A majority decide to take certain action, and a minority may decide not to do so. [Why then introduce clause 3?]

Norman Fowler (Secretary of State for Employment): The union member has many obligations. Under his contract of employment he certainly has an obligation to his trade union, but he also just as certainly has an obligation to his employer. Of course, he has a wider obligation to the community and, indeed, to his own family. Such separate duties and obligations can obviously pull an individual in different directions. Our view is that, in coming to a decision, he should not be influenced by the fear of disciplinary action being taken against him by his own trade union.

Michael Meacher (Labour MP and Shadow Secretary of State for Employment): It is the government's hypocrisy, above all, that stands out so sharply in all this. They are happy, indeed anxious, for union members to take their unions to court to uphold the rule book. However, as soon as the union seeks to apply the contents of that same rule book, the government will not have it....

There is not a golf club in the country – let alone organisations responsibly representing millions of workers – that operates on the principle of requiring a secret ballot and then encouraging people not to abide by the outcome. Even the government's staunchest supporters – the CBI, the British Institute of Management, the Conservative trade unionists, the Engineering Employers' Federation and even the Freedom Association – cannot stomach that principle. I hope that there will be enough fair-minded Conservative hon. Members … with the decency and honesty to recognise that this clause represents a standing repudiation of democracy so that we can defeat it in the House.

Michael Foot (Labour MP): … I shall call clause 3 the 'wager clause'. I believe that there was a wager between the lawyers who were advising the Secretary of State. I believe that one of them said to the other, 'I bet you cannot introduce or frame a clause of such anti-trade union dedication that it would be opposed by the Conservative Trade Unionists' National Committee'. That was the wager and it was accompanied by another wager that they could get such a clause past the new Minister. Perhaps they thought that wager was a good deal easier.

Cyril Smith (Liberal MP): Clause 3 states that a vote on whether to strike can be taken. However, if people do not want to strike, they should not worry because, whatever the result of the vote, they can please themselves and ignore it with total immunity. That is shaking the shilling…. I would have thought that a union should at least have the right to expel a member or refuse continued membership to someone who, after a ballot had been taken, refuses to accept the ballot's result. I should have thought that that refusal of membership could be carried out bearing in mind clauses 10 and 11 about the closed shop. Therefore … we must conclude that the clause displays the government's hatred of the trade union movement.

House of Commons Debates, 6th Series, 121, cc. 819–21, 825-6, 833–4 and 843; 3 November 1987.

8.10   The Employment Act 1989

This, like the Wages Act 1986, was part of the government's moves to deregulate industry. Lord Young, as Secretary of State for Employment, brought forward the White Papers, *Lifting the Burden* (Cmnd 9571) in July 1985 and *Building Businesses … not Barriers* (Cmnd 9794) in May 1986 which in effect argued for as little employment protection legislation as possible.

The 1989 Act also followed the 1986 Sex Discrimination Act in responding to the employment law of the European Community. A large part of the Act repealed legislation (including Factory Acts protective of women and young workers) which required discrimination in either employment or training. The Act also made more restrictive the range of trade union duties for which employers must give time off work, it extended from six months to two years the period of employment before an employee was entitled to a written statement of reasons for dismissal and it abolished the Training Commission as well as providing exemption for Sikhs from wearing hard hats on building sites.

The following extracts are from the debate on the Second Reading of the Bill on 11 January 1989.

Norman Fowler (Secretary of State for Employment): This Bill is about the widening of employment opportunities for women and young people and the removal of unnecessary burdens on employers.... The Bill is about ... taking further action to bring down the barriers standing in the way of developing employment....

The Bill ... tackles some of the issues of sex discrimination in circumstances where discrimination is not only unfair to its victims but damaging to the economy....The Bill sweeps away a number of archaic restrictions on women's employment. It introduces a general rule that equal opportunity takes precedence over restrictions on women's employment. Restrictions are retained only where they can be strictly justified. The Bill also gives women the right to statutory redundancy payments up to the same age as men – a further step towards equality.

Clare Short (Labour MP): Will the Secretary of State confirm that the overwhelming majority of working women work in low-paid employment, and that their position is getting worse? Will he tell us whether he has any proposals to improve that position, if he wants to invite more women into the labour market? Why is he suggesting that wages councils might be abolished, when that would make the position of those women worse?

Michael Meacher (Labour MP and Shadow Employment Secretary): As the Secretary of State said, it [the Bill] is a deregulatory measure. It will enhance the power of employers to hire and fire at will but will do nothing to provide the increased work force that the economy needs for the 1990s. It is a Bill not about increasing employment but about diminishing employment rights....

The second object of the Bill is to get what young people there are to work longer hours – 54 hours a week – and to allow 16-year-olds to work nights. Mr Gradgrind would turn in his grave. The Bill seeks to make it easier to give someone the sack and harder for them to find out why they have been sacked or to take their case to a tribunal.

House of Commons Debates, 6th Series, 144, cc. 853–5 and 863–4.

8.11   The Employment Act 1990

The 1990 Act built on the measures of the previous decade – though by this time very few employers indeed were calling for more legislation. The Department of Employment's White Paper, *Employment for the 1990s* (Cm 540), depicted trade unions as one of the barriers obstructing the creation of jobs, with the closed shop being condemned in particular. This theme was reiterated in the Green Paper, *Removing Barriers to Employment* (Cm 655), issued in March 1989, which took up the views of some economists that closed shops resulted in higher labour costs and led to greater unemployment.

The extracts which follow provide outlines of the main features of the Act.

1(1) It is unlawful to refuse employment

(a) because he is, or is not, a member of a trade union, or

(b) because he is unwilling to accept a requirement

(i) to take steps to become or cease to be ... a member of a trade union or

(ii) to make payments or suffer deductions in the event of his not being a member of a trade union.

[4. All secondary action was made unlawful.]

[6. Trade unions were taken to have 'authorised or endorsed' unofficial strike action unless 'without delay' its senior officials repudiate the action and so inform all those involved. Without speedy repudiation of unofficial actions, the unions were liable to be sued for damages.]

9(1) In ... the Employment Protection (Consolidation) Act 1978 (unfair dismissal), after section 62 (dismissal in connection with lock-out, strike or other industrial action) insert: 62A(1) An employee has no right to complain of unfair dismissal if at the time of the dismissal he was taking part in an unofficial strike or other unofficial action.

Public General Acts of 1990, 38, pp. 1511–19.

8.12   The Trade Union Reform and Employment Rights Act 1993

Further proposals to limit trade unions were brought forward by Michael Howard, the Secretary of State for Employment, in August 1991 in the White Paper, *Industrial Relations in the 1990s*. The following extracts provide outlines of the main features of the Act.

[1 to 12 dealt with union elections and ballots, requiring counting of votes by independent persons, abolishing financial assistance and the obligation of employers to make premises available, and powers to investigate the finances of unions.]

[13. An amendment introduced by the government in the House of Lords which protects employers from legal action if they give trade union members less wages than non trade unionists.]

[14. Right of a person not to be excluded or expelled from a trade union of the person's choice, regardless of TUC membership demarcations.]

15. [Amendment to earlier legislation.] Where arrangements (subscription deduction arrangements) exist between the employer of a worker and a trade union ... the employer shall ensure ... that the authorisation is ... within the period of three years beginning with the day on which the worker signs and dates the document....

21. [Amendment to earlier legislation.] Employers must be given at least seven days' warning of industrial action, which must specify which employees will be involved, when it will begin (and the dates if it is discontinuous).

22. [Amendment to earlier legislation.] Where an individual claims that

(a) any trade union or other person has done, or is likely to do, an unlawful act to induce any person to take part ... in industrial action, and

(b) an effect, or likely effect, of the industrial action is ... to

(i) prevent or delay the supply of goods or services, or

(ii) reduce the quality of goods or services supplied to the individual making the claim, he may apply to the High Court or the Court of Session for an order [to end the industrial action].

23(1) An employee who is absent from work at any time during her maternity leave period [14 weeks] shall ... be entitled to the benefit of the terms and conditions of employment which would have been applicable to her if she had not been absent (and had not been pregnant or given birth to a child).

24(1) [Amendment to the Employment Protection (Consolidation) Act 1978.] An employee shall be treated ... as unfairly dismissed if

(a) the reason (or, if there is more than one, the principal reason) for her dismissal is that she is pregnant or any other reason connected with her pregnancy....

26. [Schedule 4.] Not later than two months after the beginning of an employee's employment with an employer, the employer shall give to the employee a written statement [of employment particulars]. [This does not apply if the employment is for less than a month or for less than eight hours weekly.]

[29. Dismissal of employees who raise statutory health and safety issues at work to be regarded as unfair.]

[35. Wages councils and the fixing of minimum wages abolished.]

[38. Extension of the jurisdiction of industrial tribunals to contracts of employment.]

43. In section 209 of the 1992 [Trade Union and Labour Relations (Consolidation)] Act (general duty of ACAS to promote improvement of industrial relations) for the words following 'industrial relations' ['and in particular to encourage the extension of collective bargaining and the development and, where necessary, reform of collective bargaining machinery'] there shall be substituted: 'in particular by exercising its functions in relation to the settlement of trade disputes ...'.

Public General Acts of 1993, 19, pp. 405–529.

9

Trade union recruitment, organisation and other concerns

While the media and critics of trade unions often focus on strikes, trade unions' day-to-day concerns are usually more mundane issues such as safety, welfare and other conditions of work matters as well as pay. The period 1945–79 saw a great growth in trade union membership. The documents in the first part of this chapter provide examples of trade unions' action (or lack of it) towards groups which in the past had been areas of less success for recruitment, notably women workers, part-time workers and homeworkers (again, predominantly women), young workers, agricultural workers and white-collar workers. Following these there are extracts concerning the role of shop stewards and case studies of industrial relations in the cotton and building industries. After selections on health, safety, welfare and sexual harassment at work, the chapter concludes with passages on the problems of gaining member participation and an up-beat comment by a leading TUC figure on trade union idealism.

9.1 Women and trade union membership

The first extract is from an Amalgamated Engineering Union pamphlet, *Three Women Speak*, circulated towards the end of the Second World War after the engineering union began recruiting women to its membership. The second is the text of a 1972 advertisement urging union members to recruit more workers, including women. The third extract concerns the marriage bar, which could be an issue even in 1974. The fourth and fifth extracts deal with the trade union movement's recognition in the late 1970s and early 1980s that campaigns for equality needed to include the trade unions themselves.

Joan Henry of Manchester, Isa Alexander of Dundee and Norah Finch of Coventry are engineering workers in the war industries.

They are also members of the Amalgamated Engineering Union [AEU] and elected shop stewards in their place of work.

Last year they, and 23 other AEU women shop stewards from all over the United Kingdom, went to Blackpool and put forward the point of view of the organised women in engineering whom they represent.

If you turn over you will see what these three girls look like and something of what they had to say. [The ensuing pages had photographs of the women accompanying the extracts from their conference speeches.]

[Joan Henry] ... The whole status of women in the industry will be decided by the wisdom with which we set about the job of organisation now. If we are content to allow ourselves to be used as cheap labour we become a threat to the men employed alongside us. If we are able to secure a decent return, based on the men's wage, we give a feeling of greater security to the men, while ensuring a proper standard of living for our women members. The modern methods have made it certain that the women necessary in industry will increase enormously over the pre-war figures. Only by trade union membership, vigilant work in the factories by the women shop stewards and the sympathetic help and understanding of the men, can we hope to attain the position to which our importance entitles us. Just as the fight for political equality was successfully taken up by the women of yesterday, so we have the task of establishing the economic rights of women in the labour market today. The opening of the AEU to women is one of the most important steps in bringing about the acceptance of the principle of equality in industry.

AEU pamphlet, *Three Women Speak*, n.d. (1944?), pp. 1–3.

Oy! Got A Card?

This little lady [picture of girl about six years old adjusting a seat on a wooden chair] may not be eligible for membership as a chairmaker, but look around and find a 'non' who should join FTAT [Furniture, Timber and Allied Trades' Union]. Pass him the *Record* and get him to fill in the application for membership form on page 2. And 'him' includes 'her'! And remember, clerical and supervisory workers too!

FTAT Record: Journal of the Furniture, Timber and Allied Trades Union,
April 1972, p. 1.

The consultative document [Equal Opportunities for Men and Women]
questions whether it would be necessary or desirable to make a marriage bar unlawful.... The General Council consider that the legislation should include a clause to make a marriage bar unlawful in any
circumstances.

D. *Lancaster* (Society of Civil Servants): ... The marriage bar is a very
emotive issue and it is astonishing in this day and age it should still be
necessary to have a paragraph of this sort in any report.

In the Civil Service there was once a rigid marriage bar. On 2 September [1939] – the day before the Second World War broke out – a
woman in the Civil Service who married was forbidden to remain in
her employment but on the following day she was forbidden to leave
her employment if she married....

... it is not for any employer to say whether or not a married woman
shall go to work, it is not for any outside body, or person, or group of
persons to make that decision. Whether or not a married woman
chooses to go out to work is a matter for herself and her husband to
decide. It is not for emotional men (and some emotional women) to
get up at rostrums to say that a woman's place is in the home.

TUC, *Report of 44th Annual Conference of Representatives of Trade
Unions Catering for Women Workers*, 1974, pp. 30–1 and 47; 13 March
1974.

The 1979 TUC Women's Conference approved a special report prepared by the Women's Advisory Committee which included a draft
Charter for trade union action to secure greater integration of women
within unions. It was intended that this Charter would complement
the long-standing Charter of Trade Union Aims for Women Workers....

The ten points in the Charter on equality for women within trade
unions include a public declaration of commitment by the national
executive committee to involving women in the activities of the union
at all levels; examination of the structure of the union and amend-

ment, where necessary, to include women in the decision making bodies either by co-option or the creation of additional seats and through special advisory committees; provision in collective agreements for meetings to be held during working hours without loss of pay; the provision of child care facilities at all meetings held outside working hours and at all union schools and conferences; special encouragement to women to attend union training courses; and careful scrutiny of journals and other union publications to ensure that the content is presented in non-sexist terms.

TUC General Council's Report, *Report of 111th Annual Trades Union Congress*, 1979, pp. 59–60.

——————

The TUC had done a great deal of work both to promote more opportunities for women in jobs and at work; and to provide a fair deal for women as members of society, and in the home, and for families also. Mr Murray [General Secretary of the TUC] stressed that the TUC believed women had the right to work either outside the home, or in the home, or a combination of the two....

Mr Murray drew particular attention to section four of the report [*Women in the Labour Market*] in which there was a tough action programme setting out two challenges to the trade union movement. The first was the need to promote equal rights within its own structure. The challenge needed to be faced vigorously because ... equality like charity began at home. The second challenge was for unions to ensure that employers recognised that women were not second class workers – and that challenge was even more difficult to face in the current economic crisis.

... Through the New Training Initiative more apprenticeships for girls could be found, because the New Training Initiative aimed at creating foundation training for all young people. It provided a major new opportunity for young people and a major challenge for the trade union movement....

Mr Murray said he did not underestimate the problems in changing men's attitudes towards this matter.

TUC, *Report of 53rd TUC Women's Conference*, 1983, pp. 7–8; 17 March 1983.

9.2 Part-time workers

The problems and advantages of part-time work are a large and interesting area. This extract provides comments on the legal disadvantages of part-time work. The extract is of a motion and the mover's speech at the TUC Women's Conference, 1973.

This Conference, recognising that the normal working hours of many women excludes them from the provisions of the Redundancy Payments Act [1965] and the Contracts of Employment Act [1963], calls upon the government to remove from those Acts the sections which discriminate against part-time workers.

R. Wollerton (National Union of Public Employees): ... I have just started working full-time again after ten years as a part-time worker.... I worked 24 hours a week for the same reason that most women work part-time – in order to bring up my family. I did not know that if I had worked 3½ hours less a week it would not have mattered how long I had worked with the firm – I have actually worked there 20 years – they could have sacked me on the spot and there was not a darned thing I could have done about it.... The Contracts of Employment Act entitles workers to a written statement setting out the terms of employment, relating to wages, hours of work, holiday pay, sick pay, pensions and so on, but not if you work less than 21 hours. The Act also entitles workers to a minimum period of notice and protects them against unfair dismissal, but not so if you work less than 21 hours a week....

Similarly the Redundancy Payments Act is also unfair to people working less than 21 hours a week.... The people in the 18 to 21 age group get half a week's pay for each year of their service, in the 22 to 40 year age group they get a week's pay for each year of service, and in the 41 to 64 years age group they get one-and-a-half weeks for each year of service. This means that a woman of 50 who has worked for the same firm for 30 years would be entitled to 45 weeks pay as redundancy money if her job folded up, but not if she worked less than 21 hours a week. She could be working alongside someone doing 22 hours a week who, after 2 years' service, would be entitled to a redundancy payment.

... Out of about eight million women at work, some 2¾ million are part-time.

TUC, *Report of 43rd Annual Conference of Representatives of Trade Unions Catering for Women Workers*, 1973, pp. 80–1; 15 March 1973.

9.3 Telehomeworking

The most recent form of outwork is telehomeworking, a notable growth area of the 1990s.

The Committee on Women's Rights recognises the potential of the information society in terms of economic growth, job creation, improved access to information and ultimately the possibilities for increased access to decision-making....

The information society could provide the setting for the creation of thousands of new jobs in Europe. Our concern is that many of those new jobs at the moment appear to be semi-skilled and often insecure, and the vast majority of these are taken by women, thus confirming the existing labour market segregation which discriminates already against women.

Telehomeworking is not yet the norm, but it is undoubtedly becoming more common. It can be advantageous both for employers and workers. A number of studies have shown that it can increase productivity, and it clearly cuts costs on office overheads. Equally, for employees, it is said to give greater autonomy, to reduce time lost in commuting to an office and to provide work for people who may otherwise have been unemployed because of the area they live in, because of their family responsibilities or because they are disabled....

The problems women in telehomeworking potentially face are a modern-day version of those experienced by women working from home in the traditional manufacturing sector: low pay; reduced job protection as employers try to move such workers on to freelance contracts; isolation from other colleagues; health and safety risks as home workplaces are less easy to control than offices; and perhaps most significantly, increased stress caused by the need to balance work and domestic responsibilities....

Alongside protection from these relatively low-skilled jobs, however, action is needed to assist women to break out of segregation in the labour market which leads them to take the jobs in the first place....

Mel Read, MEP, Opinion on 'Europe's Way to the Information Society' for the European Parliament's Committee on Women's Rights, 2 October 1995. (Mel Read was formerly a member of the National Executive Committee of the Amalgamated Union of Engineering Workers, Technical and Supervisory Section (AUEW-TASS, and an elected member of the TUC's Women's Advisory Committee.)

9.4   Racial discrimination

> The greater concern about racial discrimination is illustrated both by the Mansfield Hosiery Strike extract (see 7.6) and by this piece written for a trade union journal by an official of a major anti-racist pressure group.

Some active trade unionists have always recognised that racial discrimination, in any form, hurts the entire Labour Movement as much as it hurts those discriminated against. They know from long experience that anything which divides workers makes it more difficult for them to struggle together for the achievement of common goals. In many cases racial antagonisms have undermined solidarity during strikes and have been exploited by management as a means of weakening unions. If black workers are not fully integrated into every level of the trade union movement the danger is that they will just opt out and be used as a constant source of non-union cheap labour easily exploited by management....

There are around 80,000 black workers in this country. Many of them belong to unions but on average they are less likely than other workers to belong to unions and significantly less likely to play an active part in trade union affairs. Why is this? Mainly because they tend to work in industries where trade unionism has been traditionally weak; the service industries, the building industry and the clothing and footwear industry. Equally important is the low level of participation in trade union activity at every level. A similar observation could be made about women workers and trade unions....

Most big unions have recognised the need to make special arrangements to organise and service the needs of women workers. There is a growing acceptance in the Movement of the need to make special arrangements for young workers. It is equally important for the unions to recognise the need to make special arrangements for immigrant workers and to wage a campaign against all aspects of racism.

Now why should unions make special arrangements for immigrant workers? It is often argued that to highlight differences is divisive in itself. But in many ways immigrant workers ARE different: they do HAVE special problems. For example, many Asian workers cannot read or understand English and come from rural and non-union backgrounds. Spanish immigrant workers have similar language difficulties and come from a country where trade unions are part of the fascist state machinery. In both cases they need to be told what the aims and objectives of British trade unions are and they need to be told in their own language. These workers have problems understanding union rule books and complex national and local agreements. Unions must make special efforts to explain these through the use of translators and foreign language leaflets and publications.

Racialism in all its forms must be opposed in a principled way by the trade union movement....

Tom Sibley, Trade Union Officer, Runnymede Trust, 'Race and Trade Unions', *AUEW Journal*, 39, 12, December 1972, pp. 552–3.

9.5 Apprentices

The training of young people for industry – and then their recruitment into a union – was a major debating point at skilled unions' conferences. As well as this extract, see 9.1 (fourth and fifth extracts).

J. M. Boyd (Amalgamated Engineering Union): ... It was a terrible indictment of the engineering and shipbuilding industries that any worthwhile improvements in apprentices wages and conditions had in the main been the result of activity or strike action on the part of the apprentices. 1937, 1943, 1951, 1952 and now 1960 were all landmarks in the struggle regarding apprentices' wages....

G. H. Doughty (Association of Engineering and Shipbuilding Draughtsmen): ... Taking the relationship between the trade unions and the employers, so far as indentured apprentices were concerned, we were in a difficult position. Recently [Doughty's] union had received a document from the mother of an indentured apprentice written in strange, almost medieval jargon, stating what the apprentice should not do and grudgingly informing him that the employer would be prepared to give him training if he behaved himself. The document was reminiscent of the original indentures drawn up in the Elizabethan age when training was an act of charity on the part of the employer for whom the apprentice went to work....

These documents always made it clear that the boy could not expect to take either singular or collective action industrially no matter how aggrieved he might be....

It stemmed firstly from the historical background.... Secondly, it stemmed from the deliberate desire of the employer to keep the boy away from the trade unions as long as possible.

J. R. Longworth (Secretary of the Bedford District Committee). ... In his opinion it was not always the employers that brought about segregation. There was a tremendous prejudice in certain areas among adult workers in some unions towards organising young workers into a union until they became adults.

Confederation of Shipbuilding and Engineering Unions, *Report of Proceedings of the 25th Annual Meeting*, 1960, pp. 83 and 86–7.

9.6 Agricultural workers

> The classic problem sector for recruitment has been agricultural workers, though trade unionism expanded in this area in the major upturns of the economy in both the nineteenth and twentieth centuries.

Organising farmworkers is not easy – the majority of farms employ fewer than four workers and, especially in isolated areas, union branches will include members drawn from a considerable radius. With members scattered over a wide area, obviously the NUAAW [National Union of Agricultural and Allied Workers] does not have the kind of industrial base that gives other unions their bargaining strength. However, the problem is not insurmountable ... the NUAAW ... has maintained a considerable membership over many years, outstripping most of the agricultural unions of Western Europe.

Wages in the industry are set by the Agricultural Wages Board – a statutory body which has the power to enforce legally binding minimum rates. In the last two years alone, basic wage rates have almost doubled. During the same period, negotiations with the Wages Board have resulted in a standard 40-hour, five-day week, a statutory sick pay scheme, and a wages structure giving higher rates of pay for skilled workers....

Nowadays farming is a highly mechanised industry. The modern farmworker needs to be an engineer or mechanic, as well as being able to plough a straight furrow or milk a herd of cows.... The technical revolution that has occurred since the war has put great emphasis on the need for training, and this explains why our union was one of the first to call for an Agricultural Training Board and why we have been solidly behind it ever since....

A particular problem of ours is the industry's appalling safety record, which has caused concern over the last few years as safety measures have failed to match the massive increase in mechanisation. The number of fatalities is very high, and farming now has the dubious distinction of being at the top of the industrial accident league alongside construction and mining. We also have a continuing toll of child fatalities....

Without doubt, our main concern at present is to get rid of the tied cottage system in agriculture – the system which results in workers who have lost their jobs having to move out of house and home.

R. Bottini, General Secretary of the National Union of Agricultural and Allied Workers, 'The Problems of Others – Agriculture', *AUEW Journal*, 43, 5, May 1976, p. 25.

9.7   White- and blue-collar workers

> The first extract is from the first column written in *The Clerk* in 1951 by Helen Walker as President of the Clerical and Administrative Workers' Union. She was the first woman to be elected to that office. The second extract is from a series of reports to the Industrial Relations Committee of the Association of Supervisory Staffs, Executives and Technicians (ASSET) in 1960.

No one could occupy this position without also being keenly aware of the problems which beset us. The country will be passing through economic difficulties affecting the conditions and wages of all workers, including clerks. There will be the need to maintain living standards in relation to the cost of living. At the same time it will be necessary to pursue with greater vigour our agreed programmes for Charters and Gradings. Only by achieving these will we put interests of clerical workers upon a sound foundation. Our ability to achieve this two-fisted policy depends upon the organising strength of clerks.... Therefore, every effort must be made to increase our strength in the engineering industry and extending the membership in all other fields. I would draw the attention of ... Co-operative branches [especially] to be on their toes in recruiting new members of staff. No one should be lost to our ranks through neglect to approach him or her at the first opportunity.

In the wider field I am deeply conscious of the need to maintain the moral leadership, which has been a characteristic of our union. Too often trade unions fall into disrepute, not because they lack issues, but because candidates for office, and office holders, listen to counsels of compromise and expediency. Time and again we have seen that people will follow those who have moral convictions, and who are not afraid to utter them.

It is the obligation of trade unionism to provide a dynamic leadership upon all issues which impinge upon the interests of workers and the nation. We must be prepared to back those who by their courage and skill commend their policies to the approval of the majority. For it is only by these efforts reached through great struggles and sacrifice that the ideals of social democracy have been successfully carried through from one generation to another. In this spirit, conscious of individual limitations, but confident of the unbreakable combined strength of our union, I call upon all the members to face the coming year, and bring to bear the qualities of Realism to accept the things we cannot change; Courage to change those things we can; and Wisdom to know the difference.

Helen Walker, MBE, JP, 'The President writes ...', *The Clerk*, 40, 3, May–June 1951, p. 198.

[Large Clydeside Company]
There was a potential membership here of about 500, of which we had 120. The company had consistently refused any claims submit-

ted, and had refused to go to voluntary arbitration. They had not granted any satisfactory form of recognition, although they had agreed to meet Bro. McCusker [the Association of Supervisory Staffs, Executives and Technicians' Scottish Industrial Officer] concerning the conditions of employment of our members.

Attempts had been made without success to get the Ministry of Labour to deal with the matter under the Terms and Conditions of Employments Act. Brother McCusker had this week arranged with our members in two key departments of the factory to lodge with their management a claim for improved wages. It was their intention, if the claim was rejected, to ask the NEC [National Executive Committee] for authorisation to declare a dispute. A ban on overtime was thought to be the most effective form of dispute.

The firm was not a federated one, but the National Officer [Clive Jenkins] suggested that in view of our improved relations at the national level with the E and AENF [Engineering and Allied Employers' National Federation] he should seek to discuss the matter with them, on the basis that this very large non-federated firm in Scotland was paying very low rates....

[Foundry in Glasgow]
This firm had consistently refused recognition. Some time ago, the members decided to take industrial action in the form of a ban on overtime and a series of one day strikes. This had been endorsed by the NEC, but the company had interviewed every member, putting before him a contract of service which contains the following clause: If you desire any variations in your conditions of employment the negotiations must be conducted by you personally.

The members were informed orally that if they did not sign the contracts they could not continue in their present occupations. They therefore did so, but in discussion with Brother McCusker had indicated their regret at having done this, and their intention to remain in ASSET.

Brother McCusker had therefore lodged a complaint under the Fair Wages Clause averring that the Company was not recognising the freedom of the workpeople to be members of a trade union. He hoped to persuade some members to make a statement concerning the threats made to them during the interview before a Commissioner of Oaths. He had also lodged with the company a claim for the amendment of the above clause in the contract.

[Wireworks in Edinburgh]

Brother McCusker had recently recruited 40 odd supervisors and technicians employed by the company, which was a member of the Scottish Employers' Association of Companies engaged in the Wire Weaving Industry. The management had issued a circular letter to each staff which stated: You are reminded that dis-association from trade unionism is one condition of appointment to the staff and its benefits.

Brother McCusker had lodged a complaint under the Fair Wages Clause, but felt that this was unlikely to be sufficient. He had discussed the matter with the [trade union] Group, and a ban on overtime was suggested, plus a token stoppage for one day. Relations with the operative unions were friendly, although a ban on overtime working at a weekend would affect the operatives' earnings.

The suggestion was therefore made that it would perhaps be better to have a token stoppage on a Monday followed by a ban on overtime, which would give the rest of the week for the firm to enter into negotiations, and might result in better relations with the operatives.

ASSET, Minutes of Industrial Relations Committee, 27 May 1960; Modern Record Centre, Warwick University, MS/79/AS/1/11/4.

9.8 Shop stewards

> The first extract is the 'shop steward' part of a report prepared by shop stewards at the Austin car plant at Longbridge in 1966. The second is from the summary of a report prepared for the Donovan Commission. The third is one of the recommendations made in a 1971 Report by the Commission on Industrial Relations.

(a) [Shop stewards are the] life blood of the trade union organisation at factory level, key to effective communications and amicable industrial relations....

(b) While the 'stigma' of being a shop steward has a connotation for being a 'trouble maker' in the hands of many people outside the factory, inside the factory due to management's changed attitude to the shop stewards' movement, the position of shop stewards is seen today as a necessary and responsible one.

However, it is still as onerous a job as ever it was and calls for considerable self-sacrifice if it is done properly. In terms of 'time spent on the job' it means quite apart from being called upon by the members of his section during working hours, he should attend the Joint Shop Stewards [Committee] once per month, the shop stewards meeting of his own union, usually once a month, the quarterly shop stewards meeting of his union. He should arrange meetings of his section to report back. Added to this, he should attend his branch meetings which are usually fortnightly.

The majority of Austin shop stewards outside the activists (works committee members etc.) do not fulfil all these commitments which in terms of time and expense are considerable. Time spent away from his job, of course, means expense, but in most shops there is some form of Shop Stewards Fund to meet his expenses while he is away on business on behalf of the operators. There are of course other problems which make his functioning difficult. If he is a 'key operator' on a section it can be difficult for him to get away from his job without inconveniencing other operators....

(c) One of the most difficult problems today is to obtain and maintain a correct list of shop stewards.

The aim set back in 1945 was to establish an average position of 1 shop steward for every 30 members. It is generally felt that 30 members is sufficient for 1 shop steward to deal with and we believe that in practice this has been shown to be a correct assessment.

There will be, of course, circumstances where there will have to be a shop steward for as few as 4 or 5 members who for reasons of certain processes constitute a section.

... [Table 5] is a list of shop stewards as recorded by the management for 1962 and 1965. It is certainly not a correct list for any given moment. Neither will be the lists from the various union offices (except those with only a few shop stewards). Neither will be the lists kept by the shop stewards' organisation of the various unions; although these lists are likely to be the most accurate, where the individual union shop stewards have taken steps to constitute lists. In the case of the AEU [Amalgamated Engineering Union] they have made this the responsibility of a shop steward....

To illustrate this point we took a check of the correct number of shop stewards of two small unions, namely the two sheet metal workers unions for the date of Monday 8 August 1966. The correct figures were:

	As on list	*Now*
National Sheet Metal	9	9
Birmingham and Midland Sheet Metal	6	13

There will be much bigger discrepancies with the larger unions for the reasons outlined.

The reasons for these are ... [to do with] the large turnover of shop stewards. A further problem ... is that when a shop steward does resign he does not always notify the company, the convenor and, in many cases, not even his union officials.... However, the greatest problem is when stewards resign and do not notify anyone. In some cases they just leave the factory.

(d) *Problem of Communications.* This is probably the most important question in relation to ... industrial relations in the factory.

When you consider that the Austin Factory is equivalent to a small town with a total of 27,000 employees and try to think how a town of this size would function without adequate communication machinery, it is not difficult to see how important this question is.

In theory we suppose the shop stewards' duties are contained within the borders of the agreements reached between the employers and the unions. In reality the workpeople expect the shop stewards to be the caretakers of all their problems, including mental sickness, welfare, disciplinary problems, labour pay etc., and the reality is that it is very necessary for the shop stewards to pay attention to these matters.

[Table 5] Number of shop stewards at Longbridge, 1962 and 1965

Union	1962	1965
Amalgamated Engineering Union	191	236
Transport & General Workers Union	122	172
National Union of Vehicle Builders	92	142
National Union of Sheet Metal Workers	11	9
B'ham & Midland Sheet Metal Workers Society	15	6
National Society of Metal Mechanics	9	9
Amalgamated Union of Foundry Workers	7	8
United Patternmakers Association	1	1
Electrical Trades Union	9	17
Heating & Domestic Engineers Union	4	7
Union of Building Trade Workers	1	1
Society of Woodworking Machinists	1	1
United Society of Boilermakers	1	2
Total Stewards	464	611
Total Check Employees	18,900	22,100
Ratio – shop steward : employee	1 : 40.7	1 : 36.2

(e) Inside the factory the normal channel for dealing with questions between the unions is through the Works Committee. It would lead to suspicion and bad feelings if it was done in any other way.

This does not preclude the leading shop stewards of various unions discussing matters that might be their business only, but this is a rare occurrence because most issues concern the factory as a whole.

Problems [arise] from receiving instructions from one particular union in a factory where members of various unions are working together. The usual attitude of the workshop organisation is that we work together and if any action is to be taken, then the Works Committee should be informed.

(f) The relations between the shop stewards and [trade union] officials on an individual union basis are quite good. The general attitude seems to be so long as the shop stewards are able to handle the situation, then it is OK and the officials are ready to come in as soon as they are requested to do so.

Austin Shop Stewards, *Report on 'Restrictive Practices'* (roneod report, 1966; copy in editor's possession), pp. 39, 49, 44–6, 33, 35 and 37.

Constitutional and Procedural Provisions
Union rule books and formal procedure agreements are not accurate guides to the role played by shop stewards as workplace representatives. Many important aspects of the job are not regulated by rule and many stewards enjoy *de facto* privileges in the workplace that are not embodied in procedure agreements....

Methods and Effects of Shop Steward Bargaining
The most common arguments used by shop stewards to justify their demands are appeals to precedent and comparisons with other individuals and groups. Studies show how they often back these demands with various types of collective sanctions, of which the 'unconstitutional strike' is only the most immediate and apparent. Employers have at their disposal a similar range of sanctions, and it appears there has developed a form of workplace bargaining in which sanctions are a normal feature....

Workplace settlements are rarely embodied in any formal agreement and formal procedures for dealing with disputes are usually supplemented by informal customs and practices that add to the steward's privileges. Any move towards formalisation might be resisted by stewards or management because it would affect their power position in relation to each other.

As the influence of shop stewards grows in a firm, the lower levels of supervision tend to be left out of the industrial relations process. This is partly because shop stewards demand unrestricted access to top management, to get speedy and satisfactory settlements, and partly because management is forced to systematise and centralise industrial relations decisions.

Another result of the rise of shop stewards is the decline and transformation of joint consultative committees. This is largely because stewards regard joint consultation as an ineffective and unfair substitute for collective bargaining.

Shop Stewards and their Unions
Shop stewards are usually elected by members of their union in the shop. Unions depend on them to collect the bulk of subscriptions, to maintain communication with the membership, and to provide the disputes machinery with grievances and claims. The great majority of members, who do not attend branch meetings, must obtain their facts and opinions from shop stewards.

There are marked variations in the frequency of contacts between shop stewards and full time officials in different unions, and there is evidence that in the engineering industry, where appointment of full time officials has not kept pace with the growth of shop stewards, existing officials are working under increasing pressure....

Shop stewards play a crucial part in governing and administering unions at branch level. A substantial number of them act as branch secretaries and serve on union committees. It seems that about a third of them would like to become full time union officers.

Factors Affecting the Behaviour and Influence of Shop Stewards
... It seems plausible to assume that to some extent the continued growth of shop steward influence is the result of the continuance of a relatively tight labour market, although it is difficult to explain all the variations in behaviour and influence by this factor alone.

What is termed the socio-technical system of the plant probably has some effect on differences in behaviour between industries, and even within the same industry variations in the way work is organised may help to explain the existence of so-called 'militant' groups.

Institutional factors, such as the degree of centralisation in a firm or industry, the form of its collective agreements, and the nature of its wage structure, may also be important influences which help to explain differences in shop steward behaviour and power.

Finally, the attitudes of managers, full time officials and the workers themselves cannot be left out of account, although there is very little reliable evidence concerning these matters. On the basis of existing evidence it looks as though British managers have contributed to the present growth in shop steward influence, in that they seem to prefer to deal with stewards rather than full time officials, and like to keep disputes within the confines of the firm.

W. E. J. McCarthy, *The Role of Shop Stewards in British Industrial Relations: A Survey of Existing Information and Research* (Research Paper 1, Royal Commission on Trade Unions and Employers' Associations), 1966, pp. 2–3.

Agreements at industry level should cover as far as possible the main functions of the steward together with the broad principles which relate to the provision of facilities. The main functions to be covered will normally be those which arise out of the industry's grievance procedure, the steward's responsibility to his union and to the establishment. The broad principles of facility provision to be covered will normally be leave from the job, payment, elections and credentials. Industry agreements should also cover the prior conditions for the steward's job, that is recognition of the union and the steward and some assurance for the individual steward against discrimination. Finally, general guidelines should be produced at this level which can then form the basis of more detailed agreements at company or establishment level.

Commission on Industrial Relations, *Report No. 17: Facilities Afforded to Shop Stewards* (Cmnd 4668), 1971, p. 45.

9.9 Negotiating a three-shift system in the cotton industry

This extract is an example of the pattern of collective bargaining in a sector with well-established trade unions and joint negotiating machinery.

The necessity for running a night shift in a three-shift system had been agitating the minds of the employers, and in May 1955, the Cotton Spinners and Manufacturers' Association sent a letter requesting a joint meeting with the Central Board [of the Northern Counties Textile Trades Federation] to consider the matter.... The employers said they realised that such a system would not be adopted on a wide scale, but there were individual firms where it could be inaugurated with advantage. The employers considered it desirable that the principle should be jointly recognised on a permissive basis. The employers argued that in present conditions determined steps should be taken to establish the most effective and economic methods of working, if the industry was to survive. Whilst three-shift working was not the only means to that end, it would be one of the most important in view of the economies that would be directly achieved....

The Central Board made a recommendation to the Federation Annual Meeting held in October 1955 and the following resolution was passed:

> That the action of the Central Board be confirmed in recommending to the respective affiliated amalgamations that, having regard to the economic state of our industry, they should agree to permit three-shift working in such cases where they are satisfied that the circumstances at any mill making application are such as economically justify three-shift working, and where the employer is willing to provide wages, working conditions, and welfare facilities acceptable to the workers and the trade unions.

... [The Central Board's consideration of the details] was influenced by favourable terms which had been proposed by an individual firm in the Wigan area, where excellent conditions and wages were already being experienced on the double-day shift system. The Central Board felt that night-shift working should only be permitted at the most up-to-date mills, and the following qualifications were agreed upon as basic essentials:

1. Only weaving sheds at present operating a double-day shift system on automatic looms, or other highly expensive looms, will receive consideration.

2. That a premium of 20 per cent on double-day shift earnings be paid to night-shift workers.

3. A five-day week to operate, the last shift to end at 6am on Satur-

day morning.

4. That no male workers at present working at firms making application shall be compelled to work night-shifts. [Only men were under consideration for these shifts.]

5. That all night-shift workers shall be members of the appropriate trade union.

... After lengthy arguments agreement was reached on four of the main points of our original five-point plan, but on the question of compulsory trade union membership, the employers remained adamant in their refusal to agree, and the negotiations broke down without any agreement being reached.

The situation, therefore, was that whilst the central employers' association would not bring themselves to meet all our safeguarding proposals, a number of individual firms were willing to do so.... Up to the present three-shift running has been instituted, by permission of the operatives' organisations, at 13 firms.

Amalgamated Weavers' Association, *72nd Report: For the Year Ending 31 March 1956*, 1956, pp. 9–12.

9.10 'The lump'

These extracts deal with an industrial relations problem which has much worried the trade unions in the building industry, and reflects their weak position in at least a sizeable part of the industry.

It is now clear that the government and the construction industry will have to tackle 'the lump'. The unions are determined to end the practice before the industry disintegrates. Local authorities are disturbed on various counts and the London Boroughs Association has called on the Department of the Environment to convene a meeting to consider the problem. Even the private building firms admit that they have a 'serious industrial relations problem' on their hands.

... the position today is quite clear. Clause 3 of the Memorandum of Agreement of the Building NJC [National Joint Committee] lays down:

All building trades operatives shall be in the employment of a builder, contractor or sub-contractor; and be employed at the rates of wages and under the terms and conditions of employment laid down by the National Joint Council.

Labour-only subcontracting on these terms – the provision by a subcontractor of workers who are paid wages – is permitted, and is almost non-existent. The lump means self-employment, and not the type which has long been known in the industry – the small man engaged in repair and decoration of private houses. The lump takes two main forms; supply of self-employed workers by agencies … and gangs of self-employed workers who organise themselves and move around from site to site.

Self-employment in construction has been growing fast. The Phelps Brown Committee [*Committee of Enquiry into Certain Matters Concerning Labour in Building and Civil Engineering* (Cmnd 3714), 1968] reported that in 1961 there were 1.4 million employees in the industry and 168,000 self-employed, in 1966 1.7 million and 213,000 self-employed. Today employment is down to 1.2 million and there are probably at least 400,000 self-employed – over 25 per cent of the whole labour force and some say 30 per cent.

Part of the attraction of the lump, both to contractors and workers, has been the possibility of escaping various payments – SET [Selective Employment Tax], the training levy, income tax and national insurance among others. The Labour Government [1964–70] introduced a Bill (the Construction Industry Contracts Bill) which would have made all building contractors register or pay a levy to cover everything they ought to have paid under SET, training levy, national insurance, redundancy fund and holiday pay. The conditions for registration were that the contractor must be an employer and have a satisfactory record on insurance and tax information. The Bill had not been passed by the [1970] general election. The Labour government also proposed in the next Finance Act to provide a separate levy to cover income tax liability....

Very high payments to lump workers have been quoted – £70 and even £100 a week. But as the Yorkshire region of the NFBTE [National Federation of Building Trade Employers] recently reported:

labour-only rates are not as attractive as they appear. A rate of £75 quoted from Halifax proved to be for a job outside the town, not easily accessible, with no transport offered, no travelling time, no wet time, no holiday pay and no sick pay.

Labour Research Department, 'The Lump', reprinted in *FTAT Record*, June 1973, p. 12.

Increasing activity by private firms, or 'cowboys' as they are known in the Flat Glass Industry, is causing serious concern to those of us who are constantly striving to maintain and improve working conditions.

Safety is only one of the big factors when handling glass…. Workers who allow themselves to be lured into the 'lump' take a shortsighted view. They never know when they may be in need of Legal Assistance or representation of any kind.

B. Rubner, Trade Organiser, General Membership, 'The "lump" in glass', *FTAT Record*, June 1973, p. 12.

9.11 Health and safety at work

> After the publication of a *Report on Safety and Health at Work* by the Robens Committee, Vic Feather, the General Secretary of the TUC, wrote on the subject in the Amalgamated Union of Engineering Workers' journal. The first extract is from this article. The TUC held a national and then regional conferences to discuss trade unions' contributions to accident prevention. The second extract is from a report that followed the publication of the Health and Safety Executive's guide book, *Safety Representatives and Safety Committees* (HMSO, 1976).

In the ten years from 1961 to 1971 more than 12,000 workers were killed, and over 5½ million injured. I have not included deaths from industrial diseases – that would put the figure up to over 20,000 deaths – nor have I included the estimates of unreported accidents or the number of claims for industrial injury benefits. If we use the number of successful claims for benefit, the number of injuries is getting on for 10 million. The cost of accidents, to the employer, to the state, and to the community at large, is estimated at £200 million a year….

The disregard for safety and health at work is not only practised by the media but can be seen right at the very centre of our social system. The amount of time that Parliament spends on industrial relations, for example, far outstrips that spent on safety and health.

For the year 1970–71, the government spent £10,948,000 on safety and health, including the salaries and expenses of the inspectorates and supporting staff. This amount, compared with the estimated cost of accidents, is ludicrously small, but compared to the number of establishments it is expected to cover, the amount is bordering on farce.

The various inspectorates are responsible for nearly 1¼ million establishments – that is £10 a year of government money on safety and health in each establishment.

The number of central inspectors appointed to cope with the 1¼ million establishments reached a total in 1971 of 1,014. That is about 1,000 establishments for each inspector. It is little wonder that the average rate of inspection of factories alone is only once every four years, whereas the ILO [International Labour Organisation] recommends once every year.

Of course the trade union movement must look to its own contribution in the accident prevention field. In many industries but particularly coal mining, the contribution is extensive.

Large numbers of shop stewards and other trade unionists sit on joint safety committees and encourage their workmates to be safety conscious and to work safely....

The TUC Centenary Institute of Occupational Health, in which trade unions have invested considerable resources, has already begun to have a major impact.... We must devote more resources to accident prevention.

Victor Feather, 'Two Challenges', *AUEW Journal*, 39, 9, September 1972, p. 396.

––––––––––––

Don't let safety stewards get cut off from the mainstream of shop steward work. That's the message the TGWU [Transport and General Workers' Union] has sent out to factories and offices advising how to make the best of the forthcoming safety committee laws.

The TGWU takes the view that ordinary shop stewards should also be the safety stewards for their departments, unless of course there are active members with specialised knowledge in the safety field.

The union feels very strongly about keeping safety work and ordinary steward's work tied together. The opposite way would be to develop specialist stewards, but the union has learned from industry's own experience that specialisation on the side of the main business of management can easily result in isolation from the real pressures and issues that crop up in the process of production.

'Shop Stewards Should Be Safety Stewards Too', *TGWU Record*, December 1976, p. 15.

9.12 Welfare

The building trade was still notorious for lack of basic welfare facilities for its workforce. The following extracts are from the 1963 building workers' conference. The first is a motion passed at the conference.

This Conference expresses its disgust and concern at the appalling general level of welfare arrangements provided for building workers on sites. It declares that a revision of the Code of Welfare conditions is urgently required to sweep away primitive conditions such as trench and bucket type of sanitary conveniences.

In addition to such a revision, Conference asserts that the EC [Executive Committee] should institute a militant campaign, using every available method of propaganda and publicity, in an endeavour to bring about welfare facilities on sites more in accordance with present day conditions....

L. C. Kemp: ... I feel that to abolish slums is a laudable and worthy objective of this industry, and that to abolish the slums which are prevalent on building sites at the present moment is a laudable and worthy objective of the Federation.

... We ask for some very simple things for our members. First of all, canteens. We feel that it is not too much to ask that hot meals are provided in clean and adequate surroundings. Drying rooms are not too much to ask for with heat laid on, and we do not think it is too much to ask that there shall be changing facilities provided, so that the building trade worker can come to the site and leave it at the end of the day as clean as his next door neighbour. Surely, wash basins with hot water ... and ... soap and towels.

A. E. Lloyd: ... It is part of my job as an Organiser to tackle the apprentices. We issue literature to them to show what a wonderful trade the building trade is…. Then, having got these lads to come into the building trade … we show them the bucket type of lavatory, and that is a damnable thing….

As recently as a fortnight ago I went on what was [an] … over-a-million-pounds job which had been going on for eighteen months…. When the painters came on it, employed by a sub-contractor, there was a complaint straightaway about the lavatory accommodation. I took that up with the site agent and inside three days it was put right…. I feel that if we do not press, especially for lavatory accommodation and washing facilities with hot water, we are letting down the coming generation of the building trade.

National Federation of Building Trades Operatives, *Proceedings at the 46th Annual Conference*, 1963, pp. 74–6; 12 June 1963.

Vic Feather (Assistant General Secretary of the TUC): … I have thought for a long, long time that building trade workers … are kinds of Dr Jekyl and Mr Hyde in excelsis. They come from decent homes and expect a high standard in their living conditions … and then, when they come to their places of work, the standards they accept are so miserably low that if you expected people to live in these conditions they would say that you were compelling them to go back to medieval times. To be talking about buckets and trenches in 1963 is really terrible, and for you people who … put in the perfect sanitation, who put in the best arrangements for eating, who put in the best arrangements for washing … to be satisfied with the standards you accept on building sites is … going back to the middle ages.

National Federation of Building Trades Operatives, *Proceedings at the 46th Annual Conference*, 1963, p. 72; 12 June 1963.

9.13   Sexual harassment

[Susan Knights, machinist.]
Joint action by management and unions is needed if sexual harassment in factories is to be abolished…. Insisting that it was no joke but a real threat to working women she won the complete support of

delegates for a survey to be carried out by the NEC [National Executive Committee] as to the existence and extent of sexual harassment at work within the industry....

She quoted a United States survey by a New York women's institute which found that 70 per cent of 155 working women polled had suffered some form of sexual harassment. In Canada results from surveys were even higher – a staggering 82 per cent.

'In this country we seem very slow off the mark', she said. 'Only one union I know has issued any sort of guidelines.'

[She] said sexual harassment not only affected a person's promotion prospects but also affected their health and led to emotional stress, nervousness and fear. It affected their job performance and they had nowhere to turn for help as management and unions did not take the matter seriously.

'The victim has to carry on knowing it will continue, or resign, giving some other reason for leaving because they feel ashamed, frightened or even guilty. Management should develop training programmes for their staff, must protect their employees, and offer strong support. Unions can help push management to set up procedures and make recommendations for guidelines', she urged.

She added that men too were finding themselves on the receiving end of this type of harassment and maybe felt alone and embarrassed but they must also come forward and take action.

The time for crying in the toilets and keeping quiet was over.

'Sexual Harassment – No Joke' (Report of June 1982 annual conference), *National Union of Hosiery and Knitwear Workers Journal*, August 1982, p. 6.

9.14 Training

> This extract is part of a motion, which was passed, and the mover's speech at the 1962 TUC Women Workers' Conference.

This Conference, conscious that women now provide one-third of the country's labour force, calls the attention of the TUC and affiliated unions to the need for providing adequate training facilities for girls and women....

A. Davis (Amalgamated Engineering Union) stated that too often, due to the emphasis placed upon the training of the young male, the training needs of women and girls had been overlooked. The times of constant high level unemployment coupled with Victorian views on women's place had gone.... While traditional attitudes remained, women would continue to perform the menial tasks. In 1955 her union had attempted to negotiate an apprentice scheme for girls with the employers, but they had been rather ahead of their time and met with no success. In many factories women were efficiently doing the same work as men, but for lower wages and there would be even less excuse for that if apprenticeships and adequate training were fully open to women. One of the reasons for this traditional attitude towards women was, of course, the advantage of cheap labour, but it was most unfair and mitigated against the national interest.

TUC, *Report of 32nd Conference of Representatives Catering for Women Workers*, 1962, p. 22; 27 April 1962.

9.15   Member apathy or participation and non unionism

A major problem of trade unions as democratic bodies has been to stimulate member participation. The first extract is an account of stagnation in 1951, the second is a 1959 complaint of non-unionism in the building trade, and the third is from the boom years of the 1970s.

We still have to complain of the apathy of the membership; branch meetings are not as well attended as they should be, in fact even the interest in voting for Conference delegates is so lacking that we have made comment in the *Journeyman Baker* of the number of branches not bothering to cast their votes; as we have often said, it may be that the membership is prepared to accept things as they are obtained for them in very many instances.

During 1951 some 7,226 new members were placed upon the books of the union, but the number of members on the books at the end of 1951 shows a reduction of 777....

Amalgamated Union of Operative Bakers, Confectioners and Allied Workers, *Annual Report 1951*, 1952, p. 9.

We are all aware that large numbers of men are outside any union and most unions ... are losing members. The reasons for this are sometimes a little hard to find. One wonders if the opposition of television programmes is one of the things that keep men outside of the union, because rather than attend a branch meeting they will watch television.... One wonders if the Welfare State has provided such conditions that men are inclined to say that they no longer need the union to look after all those little things which we used to have to do for them. Often political action rather than industrial action has been taken to take care of many of these things.

One wonders if what George Woodcock [General Secretary of the TUC] said the other day was right, that trade unionism no longer belongs in the branches but on the jobs.... Perhaps if and when we get one union for the building industry, it might be more suitable to try to devise a form of organisation centred around the jobs rather than the branches.

... We find our members in all trades working alongside apprentices, training them, but failing to bring them into their unions....

... It is an extremely difficult problem to eradicate piecework, but I think we have got to eradicate piecework before we can go very much further in recruiting men who are only concerned with what they can get, who just have a greed for money and are not much concerned with principles....

J. W. Higgs, a full-time trade union official, when moving a motion expressing concern at large numbers in the building trade not in a trade union, in National Federation of Building Trades Operatives, *Proceedings at the 42nd Annual Conference*, 1959, pp. 150–1; 19 June 1959.

The union, with membership figures now at record levels, has developed a new dynamism in recruitment. We have overcome the difficulties encountered by the decline of some of our traditional centres of membership, like gas, electricity and heavy engineering.

By improving our recruitment drives, our back-up facilities, the number of our officers, our financial and administrative arrangements (particularly the growth of check-off) and by the general public image of the union, we have not only attracted thousands of new members, we have also retained a far higher proportion than in the past.

Two of the main reasons for this must be the clear stand taken by the union on industrial and political issues on the one hand. On the other there is the increased democracy within the union demonstrated by the development of industrial conferences and the increased level of participation of ordinary members of the union at the shop floor, as shop stewards, collectors and local activists.

At the end of the day, the effectiveness, the image, the success of the union depend not so much on its national leadership as on the attitude, energy and direction of its members in the branches and on the shop floor.

Harold Hickling, Chairman of the General and Municipal Workers' Union, 'Union's new dynamism' (opening address at GMWU 1977 Congress), *GMWU Herald*, winter 1977–78, Congress Special, p. 8.

9.16 Ideals

... we believe that the trade union movement in this country, like industry, has got to modernise itself to meet the present-day circumstances and present-day conditions....

... the real object of the trade union movement is not only to improve the standard of living, not only to get better wages and, as a consequence, improve purchasing power, or shorter hours so that more leisure can be enjoyed, or better conditions at work so that there can be more safety and better welfare. The trade union movement may be concerned with wages, hours and conditions: but people who have dedicated their lives to this trade union movement have not been doing this merely to put extra pounds in the pay packet so that workers can buy two lollipops for their children instead of one, but for the purpose of raising the level of human dignity, of establishing peace and prosperity and of establishing social justice.

Vic Feather, General Secretary of the TUC 1969–73, speaking in 1963 when Assistant Secretary at the building trade workers' conference, in National Federation of Building Trades Operatives, *Proceedings at the 46th Annual Conference*, 1963, p. 73; 12 June 1963.

Guide to further reading

General

The best general accounts are Robert Taylor, *The Trade Union Question in British Politics* (Oxford, 1993) and Ben Pimlott and Chris Cook (eds), *Trade Unions in British Politics* (London, 1991 edn). For long-run overviews see Henry Pelling, *A History of British Trade Unions* (London, 1992 edn) and Keith Laybourn, *A History of British Trade Unionism, c. 1770–1990* (Stroud, 1992). For the period up to 1979 there is also Chris Wrigley (ed.), *A History of British Industrial Relations 1939–79* (Cheltenham, 1996).

The best account of labour law for the whole period is Paul Davies and Mark Freedland, *Labour Legislation and Public Policy* (Oxford, 1993). Other important accounts include W. Wedderburn, *The Worker and the Law* (Harmsworth, 1986 edn), Otto Kahn-Freud, *Labour Relations: Heritage and Adjustment* (London, 1979), W. Wedderburn, R. Lewis and J. Clark, *Labour Law and Industrial Relations* (Oxford, 1983) as well as the essays in W. McCarthy (ed.), *Legal Intervention in Industrial Relations* (Oxford, 1992).

On strikes, there is a useful historical long-term survey by J. E. Cronin, *Industrial Conflict in Modern Britain* (London, 1979), reviews of strike patterns and theories in M. P. Jackson, *Strikes: Industrial Conflict in Britain, USA and Australia* (Brighton, 1987) and Richard Hyman, *Strikes* (London, 1989 edn), maps of some major disputes in Andrew Charlesworth *et al.*, *An Atlas of Industrial Protest in Britain 1750-1990* (London, 1996), as well as a shrewd survey by David Gilbert in Wrigley (ed.), *A History of British Industrial Relations*. An important monograph on the subject is W. Durcan, W. E. J. McCarthy and G. P. Redman, *Strikes in Post-War Britain: A Study of Stoppages of Work due to Industrial Disputes, 1946-73* (London, 1983).

Among the best surveys of British industrial relations are Alan Fox, *History and Heritage: The Social Origins of the British Industrial*

Relations System (London, 1985), Henry Phelps Brown, *The Origins of Trade Union Power* (Oxford, 1983), Paul Edwards (ed.), *Industrial Relations: Theory and Practice in Britain* (Oxford, 1995), Sid Kessler and Fred Bayliss, *Contemporary British Industrial Relations* (London, 1995 edn) and Howard Gospel and Gill Palmer, *British Industrial Relations* (London, 1993 edn). There are also useful essays in T. Gourvish and A. O'Day, *Britain Since 1945* (London, 1991) and the two volumes edited by A. Ferner and R. Hyman, *Industrial Relations in the New Europe* (Oxford, 1992) and *New Frontiers in European Industrial Relations* (Oxford, 1994). See also J. West (ed.), *Work, Women and the Labour Market* (London, 1982) and T. Rees, *Women and the Labour Market* (London, 1992).

For detailed studies of the role of the state see Keith Middlemas's three volumes *Power, Competition and the State* (London, 1986, 1990 and 1991). For trade unions and the Labour Party see Martin Harrison, *The Trade Unions and the Labour Party Since 1945* (London, 1960), A. Taylor, *The Trade Unions and the Labour Party* (London, 1987) and Lewis Minkin, *The Contentious Alliance* (Edinburgh, 1991). For the Conservatives and the trade unions see Peter Dorey, *The Conservative Party and the Trade Unions* (London, 1995) and A. Taylor's essay in A. Selsdon and S. Ball (eds), *Conservative Century* (Oxford, 1994).

For the employers generally see Howard Gospel, *Markets, Firms and the Management of Labour in Modern Britain* (Cambridge, 1992). For the FBI see Stephen Blank, *Industry and Government in Britain: The Federation of British Industries in Politics, 1945–65* (Farnborough, 1973) and Sir Norman Kipping, *Summing Up* (London, 1972). For the CBI see W. Grant and D. Marsh, *The Confederation of British Industries* (London, 1977).

For trade union statistics see G. S. Bain and R. Price, *Profiles of Union Growth: A Comparative Statistical Portrait of Eight Countries* (Oxford, 1980), which can be supplemented by updates and reviews of the figures by Jeremy Waddington and others in the *British Journal of Industrial Relations*. More generally, there is Department of Employment, *British Labour Statistics: Historical Abstract 1886–1968* (London, 1971) and B. R. Mitchell, *British Historical Statistics* (Cambridge, 1988). For important attempts at assessing the economic impact of the trade unions see essays by David Metcalf and others in the *British Journal of Industrial Relations* (including 1989 and 1990).

1945–1955

There is substantial detail in H. A. Clegg, *A History of British Trade Unionism Since 1889, Vol. 3: 1934–51* (Oxford, 1994). The role of the government is explored in Justin Davis Smith's *The Attlee and Churchill Administrations and Industrial Unrest 1945–55* (London, 1990) and essays by Richard Hyman in Jim Fyrth (ed.), *Labour's High Tide* (London, 1992) and Jim Tomlinson in N. Tiratsoo (ed.), *The Attlee Years* (London, 1991). V. L. Allen's *Trade Unions and Government* (London, 1960) is still valuable, as is his *Trade Union Leadership: Based on a Study of Arthur Deakin* (London, 1957). For the issue of productivity see James Hinton, *Shop Floor Citizens* (Cheltenham, 1994) and N. Tiratsoo and J. Tomlinson, *Industrial Efficiency and State Intervention: Labour 1939–51* (London, 1993).

For Attlee's government generally see K. O. Morgan's *Labour in Power 1945–1951* (Oxford, 1987). For Churchill and his last government see Paul Addison, *Churchill on the Home Front* (London, 1992), John Ramsden, *The Age of Churchill and Eden, 1940–1957* (London, 1995) and Anthony Seldon's *Churchill's Indian Summer* (London, 1981).

The Conservatives and the trade unions 1955–1964

For the Conservatives see John Ramsden, *The Winds of Change: Macmillan and Heath, 1957–75* (London, 1996). For important studies of aspects of these years see H. A. Clegg and R. Adams, *The Employers' Challenge: A Study of the National Shipbuilding and Engineering Dispute of 1957* (Oxford, 1957), Alan Flanders, *The Fawley Productivity Agreement* (London, 1964) and the later study of that plant, B. Ahlstrand, *The Quest for Productivity: A Study of Fawley after Flanders* (Cambridge, 1991).

For a biography of one of the most important trade union leaders of the period see Geoffrey Goodman's *The Awkward Warrior: Frank Cousins, His Life and Times* (London, 1979). The most useful memoirs are Harold Macmillan's *Riding the Storm 1956–59* (London, 1971), *Pointing the Way* (London, 1972) and *At the End of the Day* (London, 1973).

The Donovan Commission and trade union legislation 1971–1976

The Donovan Report and the TUC's evidence to the Commission are readable: *The Royal Commission on Trade Unions and Employers' Associations 1965–1968* (Cmnd 3623, London, 1969) and TUC, *Trade Unionism* (London, 1966). There is an important analysis of strikes between 1966 and 1973: C. T. B. Smith, Richard Clifton, Peter Makeham, S. W. Creagh and R. V. Burn, *Strikes in Britain* (Department of Employment Manpower Paper 15, London, 1978).

On the Labour Party's internal conflict over industrial relations legislation see Peter Jenkins, *The Battle of Downing Street* (London, 1970). More generally there is Dennis Barnes and Eileen Reid, *Governments and Trade Unions: The British Experience 1964–1979* (London, 1980). On the 1971 Industrial Relations Act, see Michael Moran, *The Politics of Industrial Relations* (London, 1977) and B. Weekes *et al.* (eds), *Industrial Relations and the Limits of Law* (Oxford, 1975).

The most useful biographies and autobiographies are Eric Silver, *Vic Feather, TUC* (London, 1983), Jack Jones, *Union Man* (London, 1986), Clive Jenkins, *All Against the Collar: Struggles of a White Collar Leader* (London, 1990), Harold Wilson, *The Labour Government 1964–70* (London, 1971) and *Final Term* (London, 1979), John Campbell, *Edward Heath* (London, 1993), Denis Healey, *The Time of My Life* (London, 1989) and James Callaghan, *Time and Chance* (London, 1987). In addition, there are the published diaries of Tony Benn, *Out of the Wilderness, 1963–1967* (London, 1987) and *Office Without Power* (London, 1988), Richard Crossman, *The Diaries of a Cabinet Minister*, 3 vols (London, 1975–77) and Barbara Castle, *The Castle Diaries 1964–70* (London, 1984) and *The Castle Diaries 1974–76* (London, 1980).

The incomes policies of the 1960s and 1970s

As well as the books by Keith Middlemas (above), there are studies of incomes policies by R. J. Flanagan, D. W. Soskice and L. Ulman, *Unionism, Economic Stability and Incomes Policy* (Washington, DC, 1983), Leo Panitch, *Social Democracy and Industrial Militancy* (Cambridge, 1976), Gerald Dorfman, *Government versus Trade Unionism in British Politics Since 1968* (Stanford, 1979), Warren Fishbein, *Wage Restraint By Consensus* (London, 1984), and R. Jones, *Wages and Employment Policy 1936–1985* (London, 1987).

The Thatcher and Major governments and the trade unions

For legislation see John McIlroy, *The Permanent Revolution? Conservative Law and the Trade Unions* (Nottingham, 1991) and Simon Auerbach, *Legislating for Conflict* (Oxford, 1990). For the Radical Right case against the trade unions see Charles Hanson, *Taming the Trade Unions* (London, 1991). More generally, see P. Bassett, *Strike Free* (London, 1986), John McInnes, *Thatcherism at Work* (Milton Keynes, 1987), David Marsh, *The New Politics of British Trade Unionism* (Cornell, 1992), R. Taylor, *The Future of the Trade* Unions (London, 1994) and D. Gallie, R. Penn and M. Rose (eds), *Trade Unionism in Recession* (Oxford, 1996). For economic analyses of the impact of strikes, see D. Metcalf and S. Milner (eds), *New Perspectives on Industrial Disputes* (London, 1993).

On the 1984–85 miners' strike, see P. Wilsher and D. McIntyre, *Strike: Thatcher, Scargill and the Miners* (London, 1985), G. Goodman, *The Miners' Strike* (London, 1985), M. Adeney and J. Lloyd, *The Miners' Strike 1984–5: Loss Without Limit* (London, 1986), Vicky Seddon (ed.), *The Cutting Edge: Women and the Pit Strike* (London, 1986), D. Howell, *The Politics of the NUM* (Manchester, 1989) and J. and R. Winterton, *Coal, Crisis and Conflict* (Manchester, 1989). On the suppression of trade unionism at GCHQ, see H. Lanning and R. Norton-Taylor, *A Conflict of Loyalties: GCHQ 1984–1991* (Cheltenham, 1991).

The most useful biographies and autobiographies include Margaret Thatcher, *The Downing Street Years* (London, 1993), Hugo Young, *One of Us* (London, 1991 edn), Jim Prior, *A Balance of Power* (London, 1986), Norman Tebbit, *Upwardly Mobile* (London, 1988) and Nigel Lawson, *Inside Number 11* (London, 1992). Also of value are Ian Gilmour, *Dancing With Dogma: Britain Under Thatcherism* (London, 1992), Peter Riddell, *The Thatcher Era and its Legacy* (Oxford, 1991) and Dennis Kavanagh and Anthony Seldon's edited volumes, *The Thatcher Effect* (Oxford, 1988) and *The Major Effect* (London, 1994).

Trade union organisation and development

In addition to essays in Wrigley (ed.), *A History of British Industrial Relations* and Edwards (ed.), *Industrial Relations*, see Joseph Goldstein, *The Government of British Trade Unions* (London, 1952), H. A. Clegg, A. J. Killick and R. Adams, *Trade Union Officers* (Oxford, 1961), R. Undy, V. Ellis, W. E. J. McCarthy and A. M. Halmos, *Change in Trade Unions: The Development of UK Unions Since the 1960s* (London, 1981), D. Watson, *Managers of Discontent* (London, 1988), P. Willman, T. Morris and B. Aston, *Union Business: Trade Union Organisation and Financial Reform in the Thatcher Years* (Cambridge, 1993), J. Kelly and E. Heery, *Working for the Union: British Trade Union Officers* (Cambridge, 1994) and, more generally, Jeremy Waddington, *The Politics of Bargaining: The Merger Process and British Trade Union Structural Development 1892–1987* (London, 1995). There are also two useful collections of documents: N. Robertson and K. I. Sams (eds), *British Trade Unionism: Select Documents*, 2 vols (Oxford, 1972) and John Hughes and Harold Pollins (eds), *Trade Unions in Great Britain* (Newton Abbot, 1973).

Index

216